The Science of
Learning Disabilities

The Science of Learning Disabilities

Kenneth A. Kavale, Ph.D.
University of California, Riverside

Steven R. Forness, Ed.D
University of California, Los Angeles

A College-Hill Publication
Little, Brown and Company
Boston/Toronto/San Diego

College-Hill Press
A division of
Little, Brown and Company (Inc.)
34 Beacon Street
Boston, Massachusetts 02108

Library of Congress Cataloging in Publication Data

Kavale, Kenneth A., 1946–
    The science of learning disabilities.

    Bibliography: p. 145
    Includes index.
    1. Learning disabilities. I. Forness, Steven R.
II. Title.
LC4704.K39   1984   371.9   84-17008
ISBN 0-316-48372-9

Printed in The United States of America

Dedication

"For love exacts what is possible
rather than what is due:
what is due is sometimes impossible,
as, for instance, in the case of the honor due parents;
for no one could ever pay all his debt to them."
Aristotle
Nicomachean Ethics

To my mother and father with love and gratitude
(K.A.K.)

To Rejeana and Larry
(S.R.F.)

TABLE OF CONTENTS

PREFACE

As no other phenomenon in the history of special education, learning disabilities has expanded remarkably and has captured the interest of a variety of professionals. Because of its rapid growth, the field of learning disabilities has experienced many "growing pains" in the form of disagreement and dispute over almost all issues regarding theory and practice. Over the past several years, we have attempted to look for resolution of some fundamental issues and to understand the basic nature of learning disabilities. These attempts, however, became increasingly more troublesome and more confusing. We then began to wonder why it was so difficult to apprehend the phenomenon of learning disabilities and why, when we believed we understood, that such understanding proved so ephemeral. After all, research efforts in learning disabilities have produced a voluminous data base and surely the answers can be found among the available data if . . . . The complexities surrounding the "if" make the field of learning disabilities so problematic. After reflecting upon our conceptual quandary, we realized that our professional training, which was, for the most part, within the empiricist tradition, provided an unsatisfactory approach for the fundamental task of comprehending the basic nature of learning disabilities. In subsequent study which transcended the circumscribed confines of empiricist methodology, we became convinced that the means to resolve controversy in the learning disabilities field were to be found in an analysis of its epistemological foundation. Such an analysis must acknowledge not only empirical techniques but also the influence of history and philosophy.

It is a critical analysis of these latter influences on theory in learning disabilities that forms the basis of this volume.

Alice asks "What is a Caucus-Race?" and the Dodo replies, "The best way to explain it is to do it." Thus, instead of a thinly anticipatory, yet laborious, recitation about our subject and how we are going to present it, we believe that is is much more satisfying when, like the Dodo, we simply do it.

ACKNOWLEDGMENTS

We would like to acknowledge the influence of our friends and colleagues who have both inspired and supported us over the years: Dick Eyman, Gene Glass, Frank Hewett, Barbara Keogh, Don MacMillan, Rob McKeown, Bob Schreiner, and Jim Simmons. Although they should not be held accountable for the ideas expressed herein, we do owe them a debt of gratitude for our being in a position to express them.

To Ted Logan and the staff at College-Hill, our sincere appreciation for their support and guidance in bringing this volume to fruition.

A special thank you to Betty Medved, Linda Faulkner, and Trisha Mettam for their skill, speed, cooperation, and good humor in typing (and retyping) the manuscript.

A note of love and appreciation to Linda and Chris Kavale who graciously resigned themselves to a regimen of a sullen husband and father when the book was going poorly, and an absent one when it was going well.

Finally, in the best sense, this was a collaborative effort and represents our aggregate thinking about learning disabilities.

Kenneth A. Kavale
Steven R. Forness

PROLOGUE

The first condition to be fulfilled by men of science, applying themselves to the investigation of natural phenomena, is to maintain absolute freedom of mind, based on philosophical doubt. Yet we must not be in the least skeptical; we must believe in science; we must believe in a complete and necessary relation between things, among the phenomena proper to living things as well as in others; but at the same time we must be thoroughly convinced that we know this relation only in a more or less approximate way, and that the theories we hold are far from embodying changeless truths. When we propound a general theory in our sciences we are sure only that, literally speaking, all such theories are false. They are only partial and provisional truths which are necessary to us, as steps on which we rest, so as to go on with investigation; they embody only the present state of our knowledge, and consequently they must change with the growth of science, and all the more often when sciences are less advanced in their evolution.

C. Bernard
An Introduction to the Study of Experimental Medicine, 1865

1

Introduction: Learning Disabilities and Science

Bertrand Russell's definition of mathematics as "the subject in which we never know what we are talking about, nor whether what we are saying is true" is perhaps even more applicable and appropriate to the field of learning disabilities (LD). The contention and controversy that has been an integral part of LD since its inception now places the field at a critical juncture historically. A diagnostic entity that emerged not much over two decades ago has now become the category containing by far the most children receiving special education. More than two in five handicapped children are considered LD, according to latest figures from the U.S. Department of Education. This is more than four percent of all school-aged children. The number of LD children has increased more than 100 percent in the past five years since federal legislation mandating special education first took effect. This rapid growth has alarmed those in government who see LD as the diagnostic category most open to vague interpretation and thus most likely to contain children who were never intended to receive special education funds. This is witnessed by the fact that initial drafts of federal legislation on the handicapped contained a provision, later eliminated, that no more than two percent of all school children could be considered eligible for these funds under the LD category.

At the same time, professionals in the LD field have tended to factionalize into groups that represent polar opposites with respect to substantive, methodological, and ideological issues. This polarization was most clearly articulated in the recent reorganization of the principal LD professional organizations. The Council for Learning Disabilities (CLD) recently seceded from its parent special education association, the Council for Exceptional Children (CEC) and was reformed as an entirely separate professional organization. It was subsequently replaced by a new Division of Learning Disabilities (DLD) within CEC.

While several matters were at issue, at heart was a bitter struggle between two factions whose disagreement on the very nature of LD had rapidly led them down quite separate paths of scientific inquiry and adherence to radically different remedial techniques. Indeed, the two major journals in the field, *Journal of Learning Disabilities* and *Learning Disability Quarterly*, have, to some observers, become the separate voices of each faction, a dangerous editorial development in a field that desperately needs scientific rigor.

The state of scientific knowledge in the LD field has always been subject to extraordinary dispute and misinterpretation. It is our belief that the reason for this state of affairs rests in the domain of epistemology; the fundamental perspective on knowledge brought to the field, which in turn determines the topics studied, the methodological procedures employed, and therefore the character of the results obtained. A primary issue is the question of what constitutes scientific inquiry. Debate abounds as to whether or not a given inquiry can be pursued scientifically and involves not only empirical questions but also competing notions of "scientific." An even more fundamental issue regarding inquiry is whether subject matter or method should be primary. Advocates for the primacy of subject matter believe that research agenda are set either by theoretical developments within science or by value premises outside of science.

The proponents of method maintain there is *one* scientific method (although many different techniques can be used in that method). Research topics are chosen on the basis of whether they can be handled by the method. The advocates of method suggest that if subject matter is primary, then research becomes too philosophic, and the need for scientific rigor is not well understood. Conversely, subject matter proponents deplore the consequences of preoccupation with method (techniques, instruments) rather than problems. It is claimed that undue emphasis on method has contributed to excessive stress on polish and elegance, and neglect of significance and creativity; the fitting of problems to techniques rather than evolving techniques suited to new and important problems, and the establishment of scientific orthodoxy that tends to inhibit new methods, excludes major problems, and makes science conservative by focusing on trivial problems.

The consequences of the present epistemological base of LD, when compared to that found in the physical sciences, is the very different nature of the theories constructed in LD as compared to theories in the physical sciences. The physical sciences build dual-faced theories with one face pointing toward empirical justifications while the other face maintains linkages with the primary constructs in its theoretical hierarchy. Theories in LD, on the other hand, tend to be relatively insular, pointing out neither the requisites for empirical justification nor the broader conceptual roots which serve as the theories' context-dependent rationale. In short, theories in the progressive, concatenative physical sciences are explicitly articulated both with the conceptual predicates of the field *and* with the emergent empirical data base that will serve either to validate or to invalidate them. By the nature of their construction, LD theories tend to live a life apart, and as such tend to become ephemerals of emotive significance rather than connectives of universal significance.

This manner of theory construction insures that there will also be a lack of articulation between theory and practice. The pragmatic implications are not rationally induced from theoretical statement, but rather assume their own character without rhyme or reason. The debate continues, however, in the many competitive theories which purport to explain the behavior of the same phenomenon (i.e., LD). The many available LD theories turn LD professionals into evangelists for one or another of these conflicting theories, but too often without troubling to examine the validity (or lack thereof) of the premises or predicates of the theories. To this extent, LD professionals often become more interested in changing LD practices than in understanding them. Moreover, there is a tendency to attenuate this parallelism rather than resolve it; consequently, there are several LDs with fundamentally different premises. Sadly then, the most fundamental ontological platforms within LD illustrate the lack of success in forcing convergences between a priori polarized positions regarding the fundamental nature of LD.

The state of scientific inquiry in LD has convinced us not only that certain practices in the field need to be reexamined, but more importantly, that certain core assumptions in and about the science of LD need to be thoroughly altered. The temptation was indeed great to put quotations marks around the word science in the title of this work, connoting that LD research has indeed not been scientific in the strict sense of this term. But we consider LD to be a science, though a not yet fully developed science. The lack of development is not just quantitative: lack of development in a quantitative sense simply requires doing more of the same–multiplying experiments, obtaining new findings, formulating new insights, and the like. We believe, rather, that LD as a science is qualitatively different from the advanced natural sciences in lacking certain characteristics the latter sciences display. Instead, we hope to keep the quotation marks away from this term by suggesting how the LD field may have strayed from its scientific course and how it may regain its scientific status by proposing alternative conceptualizations from theory and practice. These alternative conceptualizations will be based upon the critical analysis of scientific knowledge offered by the history and philosophy of science. We believe both the history and philosophy of science are required to reconceptualize fully the scientific status of the LD field since, to paraphrase Kant's famous dictum, "Philosophy of science without history is empty; history of science without philosophy is blind."

To accomplish our goals, in chapter 2, the problems in LD research are reviewed and its problematic nature examined. A case is presented to show the pseudoscientific nature of LD because of its basis in empiricism. Chapter 3 addresses the history question wherein speculations are offered as to why LD research has failed to influence clinical and educational practice, at least as compared with the same phenomenon in a related field (i.e., mental retardation). This analysis is based upon Kuhn's concept of paradigm, and a reanalysis of the original data of Alfred Strauss and Heinz Werner, whose research is considered the very origin of the LD field. In chapter 4, the philosophy question is addressed with respect to methods of theory validation. A case is presented to show that the tradition of statistical significance in validating LD theory is inadequate and needs to be reformulated on the basis of Karl Popper's methodological approach to theory validation. In addition, an epistemological framework is presented that allows for a more scientific stance in the LD field. Finally, in chapter 5, we present a meta-theoretical framework for viewing LD. It incorporates much of what is understood about normal learning and learning disability in an effort to conclude on a positive note that points to a new science of LD.

In writing this work, we realize that it is of interest primarily to LD researchers and those interested in LD research (including graduate and advanced undergraduate students). We also hope that a larger audience of LD professionals may find some value in understanding the scientific status of the field in which they practice. We thus hope that this work will help advance both theory and practice in LD since the articulation of these strands is required to establish a true (i.e., no quotation marks) science of learning disabilities.

2

Learning Disability: A Pseudoscience

"Recently, I have used the term 'learning disabilities' to describe a group of children who have disorders in the development of language, speech, reading, and associated communication skills needed for social interaction." With this statement delivered, on April 6, 1963, at the Fund for Perceptually Handicapped Children conference, by Samuel A. Kirk, a new entity was established that was the result of the convergence of a variety of forces. These forces were conceptualized within a two-dimensional model by Weiderholt (1974). One dimension consisted of three separate disorders overlapping in time, each leading to the present classification of LD: (1) disorders of spoken language, (2) disorders of written language, and (3) disorders of perceptual–motor processes. The other dimension viewed development along a chronological continuum. It was divided into three phases: (1) the Foundation Phase (ca. 1800–1940), comprised primarily of neurologists (e.g., Broca, Orton, Goldstein, Strauss) and ophthalmologists (e.g., Hinshelwood), (2) the Transition Phase (ca. 1940–1963), culminating in Kirk's address and the subsequent formation of the Association for Children with Learning Disabilities (ACLD), and (3) the Integration Phase (1963–present). These latter two phases present multidisciplinary perspectives including optometry (e.g., Getman), speech pathology (e.g., Eisenson, Myklebust), reading disability (e.g., Monroe, Fernald), psychology (e.g., Kirk, Cruickshank, Kephart), and special education (e.g., Lehtinen, Frostig). Thus, the Foundation Phase focused upon the study of adults with acquired brain injuries who demonstrated loss of previously acquired skill. The Transition Phase attempted to translate the basic theoretical assumptions of the initial stage (i.e., brain insult results in perceptual, learning, and behavioral deficits) into formulations about such disabilities in children. The Integration Phase placed these diverse emphases under the rubric of learning disabilities and was marked by a surge of organizational growth, federal and state legislation, and educational programs specifically for the learning disabled.

As the Integration Phase continues, there has been increased investigation and debate over the validity of many fundamental assumptions, tests administered, and intervention approaches. These investigations have taken on a more empirical posture that is both an asset and a liability. It is an asset because the accumulated data have increased our knowledge of the parameters of LD but a liability since the accumulated data has not propelled the LD field towards a more scientific stance. This is evident in the LD field's inability to answer its most basic questions and thus prevent resolution of fundamental issues.

The Problematic Nature of LD

To illustrate the disparity between the quantity of data and scientific knowledge, consider the case of the efficacy of psycholinguistic training and the difficulties in marking a scientific decision based upon "what the research says." The literature reveals that the *Illinois Test of Psycholinguistic Abilities* (ITPA) has served as the clinical model for a variety of remedial and developmental language programs. These programs are based upon the assumption that language is comprised of discrete components and that these components can be trained. It is this last assumption that has precipitated debate over the efficacy of psycholinguistic training. Further examination of the literature would identify reviews summarizing available primary research. At this point, however, scientific knowledge becomes obscured because of different interpretations of this literature. To illustrate, Hammill and Larsen (1974a) constructed a table of " + " and "0" which paralleled statistical significance (.05 level) or nonsignificance and summarized the findings from 39 studies for either total ITPA score, ITPA subtests, or both. Two other aggregations, for subject groups and psycholinguistic constructs, were based upon the percentage of positive analyses. Commentary on specific studies was also provided which followed the usual course of narrative reviews. Hammill and Larsen (1974a) concluded that "researchers have been unsuccessful in developing those skills which would enable their subjects to do well on the ITPA . . . [and] . . . the idea that psycholinguistic constructs, as measured by the ITPA, can be trained by existing techniques remains nonvalidated" (pp. 10–11).

Minskoff (1975) offered a critique of Hammill and Larsen's (1974a) review which suggested that, "Because of Hammill and Larsen's oversimplified approach, 39 studies with noncomparable subjects and treatments were grouped together. Moreover, for the most part, they reviewed methodologically inadequate studies in which there was short-term training using general approaches to treatment primarily with mentally retarded or disadvantaged subjects having no diagnosed learning disabilities" (p. 137). In effect, Minskoff (1975) suggested that Hammill and Larsen had compared "apples and oranges." Ten specific methodological errors were described which limited conclusions drawn from the studies. Minskoff (1975) then provided guidelines for research on psycholinguistic training; specifically, 15 criteria were established for evaluating psycholinguistic remediation. It was suggested that psycholinguistic disabilities can be trained, and a major criterion for evaluating effectiveness should be its relationship to various academic and social demands made upon a child at a particular age. Minskoff (1975) concluded by decrying the skepticism surrounding psycholinguistic training since, "it can be dangerous if it leads to the abolition of training methods that may be beneficial to some children with psycholinguistic disabilities" (p. 143).

Immediately following was a response by Newcomer, Larsen, and Hammill (1975) which contested the major points made by Minskoff (1975). Suffice it to say that the rhetoric became increasingly confusing and enmeshed in trivial controversy. Nevertheless, Newcomer et al. (1975) contended that, "the reported literature raises doubts regarding the efficacy of presently available Kirk-Osgood psycholinguistic training programs" (p. 147).

The debate lay dormant for some three years when Lund, Foster, and McCall-Perez (1978) offered a reevaluation of the 39 studies reviewed by Hammill and Larsen (1974a). The studies were reexamined individually to determine the validity of negative conclusions regarding the effectiveness of psycholinguistic training. Six of the 24 studies clearly showed positive results for psycholinguistic training and "contraindicate the conclusions that such training is nonvalidated" (p. 317). Of 10 studies showing negative results, only two were reported accurately. The remaining eight were either equivocal or showed positive results. Specifically, four of the 10 studies were inaccurately reported since the original data showed positive results; two of the 10 studies compared groups under different training programs, thus making the negative results reported inaccurate since both groups made substantial progress; and two of the 10 studies contained insufficient data on which to base judgments. The eight studies that showed some positive results (less than six subtests) actually included: three studies that attempted to improve abilities only in one or more specific areas, one study that compared treatment groups instead of trained versus nontrained subjects, and four studies that had only varying degrees of relevance to the primary question. Lund et al. (1978) reached conclusions markedly at variance with the statement that psycholinguistic training is nonvalidated:

> our analysis indicates that some studies show significant positive results as measured by the ITPA, some studies show positive results in the areas remediated, and some do not show results from which any conclusions can be drawn. It is, therefore, not logical to conclude either that all studies in psycholinguistic training are effective or that all studies on psycholinguistic training are not effective (p. 317).

The LD community did not wait long for the debate to continue. Hammill and Larsen (1978) reaffirmed their original position. The point-by-point rebuttal of the Lund et al. (1978) reevaluation was presumed to show that, in fact, their original report did not either inaccurately report, inappropriately categorize, or misinterpret any of the original 39 studies. The rebuttal concluded with the statement that

> the cumulative results of the pertinent research have failed to demonstrate that psycholinguistic training has value, at least with the ITPA as the criterion for successful training. It is important to note that, regardless of the reevaluations by pro-psycholinguistic educators, the current state of the research strongly questions the efficacy of psycholinguistic training and suggests that programs designed to improve psycholinguistic functioning need to be viewed cautiously and monitored with great care (Hammill & Larsen, 1978, p. 413).

Learning Disability as a Pseudoscience

Thus, after some five years of feckless debate, polemics abounded but a nagging question remained: What is really known about the efficacy of psycholinguistic training? (A partial answer is found later in this chapter.) Increasingly, the principal issue had become entangled in a maze of extraneous detail only tangentially related to the major question. This is not the stuff of scientific debate nor the foundation for scientific knowledge. Science should be more than semantic arguments and statistical nitpicking but, unfortunately, most issues in LD resist scientific resolution because efforts to design a single study to extend and to improve existing basic research generally fail. This is due partially to the difficulties in controlling the many sources of variability that impinge upon research in LD. Many of these main sources of variation are noted in Table 2-1.

The example provided by psycholinguistic training demonstrates the fragility of many findings in LD. Too often, findings from individual studies have proved to be conflicting, variable, and sometimes paradoxical. Although a dozen studies may resolve a matter in the physical sciences, a dozen studies investigating something like the efficacy of psycholinguistic training yield inconsistent findings. Such

TABLE 2-1   Sources of Variability in Learning Disabilities Research

- Differences in the theoretical frameworks (paradigms) underlying research in special education (e.g., behavioral, biophysical, cognitive, process, psychodynamic, psychoeducational).
- Differences in research design (e.g., subject sampling, subject assignment, data collection, measurement scale, experimental control).
- Differences in data analysis methods (e.g., unit of analysis).
- Differences in procedural rigor (i.e., degree of imprecision in the experimental protocol).
- Differences in LD samples (i.e., heterogeneity resulting from the lack of precise identification criteria).
- Differences in similarly labeled treatments or programs (i.e., important and subtle diversity among, for example, psycholinguistic or perceptual-motor models).
- Differences in setting-by-treatment interactions (i.e., program effectiveness as a function of who participates, where they participate, and other situational factors).
- Differences in outcome assessments (e.g., reliability, validity, norm interpretation, reactivity).
- Differences in scope of LD research (i.e., alternative theoretical foundations and research designs favored by psychology, medicine, sociology, and child development).

conditions led Andreski (1972) to argue that what passes as scientific study of human behavior (e.g., learning disabilities) is little more than sorcery. Consequently, an analogy for LD may be drawn from Frazer's (1963) account of early man's development from magic to science. The comparison may seem otiose but consider the following: because of an inability to explain phenomenon in terms of natural and predictable laws, early man reverted to a primitive cause and effect termed *sympathetic magic* wherein events may exert influence on other events, though separated by distance, time, or relevance. Sympathetic magic may be further divided into homeopathic magic based upon the principle of similarity ("like produces like") and contagious magic based upon the principle of contiguity ("once in contact, two things influence each other, even when separated").

These principles formed the basic approach to reality but were applied in the wrong places to the wrong events. Thus, magical thinking possessed the irreparable flaw of unreliability (the magic neither produced nor explained the phenomenon). Unfortunately, some current conceptions in LD evidence such magical thinking. For example, the assertion that perceptual–motor training improves academic functioning represents a form of homeopathic magic while conceptions about "minimal brain dysfunction" and its influences are akin to contagious magic. These types of magical thinking have led LD professionals to neglect fundamental principles of logic and scientific method in favor of mystical notions that ignore reason, disregard rationale, and assume "truth" can be discovered without disciplined inquiry. Under these circumstances, the science of LD is likely to be irrational, illogical, and without scientific merit.

Within such a pseudoscientific context, the LD professional functions much like astrologers in the Middle Ages, whose chief business was prediction. They predicted and advised but it was customary for their predictions to be hedged with "ifs" and "buts" or other caveats, or to be phrased ambiguously so that if things went wrong, the astrologers' reputation was not impaired. But in evaluating the claims of astrology and of its practitioners, Frazer (1963) tells us, "Nothing did more to make [it] seductive than the ambitious scale of its intellectual pretensions. It offered a systematic scheme of explanation for all the vagaries of human and natural behavior, and there was in principle no question which it could not answer" (p. 224). The parallel with LD is not unexact; it may be argued that the LD field has dispatched just that mixture of mystification and superstition peddled by the astrologers.

Learning Disability as Empiricism

The field of LD has been committed since its inception to a particular methodological approach—"empiricism" that is often defined as an emphasis upon data collection and analysis. But there is no necessary connection between an empiricist's viewpoint and a concentration in "empirical" research. It is possible to be an empiricist without ever touching data, or to be committed to empirical research without having an empiricist's viewpoint (as in the physical sciences). The manifestations of empiricism in LD research can be seen since the time of Alfred Strauss and Heinz Werner. From an empiricist's point of view, it is better if a researcher has more facts at his disposal (which translates into larger samples), allowing for a wider range of measures. With data collection complete, attention is directed at data analysis, wherein a variety of inferential techniques are used to make comparisons that might reveal all sorts of associations and tendencies in the data. Finally, conclusions are drawn that relate the findings to theory. But such theory is not scientific; it is empiricist and thus suggests that no scientific laws have been established in LD since the rise of its empiricist foundation.

Scientific theory is concerned with concepts, terms not defined by reference to observations, which consequently enter into exact theoretical relations with one another (often expressed mathematically).

The theoretical empiricism found in LD is characterized by the use of observationally defined empirical categories that cannot be related by any theoretical means (even mathematical connectives). Empiricist theorizing in LD has thus been general rather than abstract and therefore vague rather than exact. The purpose of theory in science is to explain, predict, and guide new research. But the empirical character of LD theorizing consists of nothing more than generalizing, a process which simply summarizes what has been observed. Such a summary of past observations, however, cannot be used to explain and predict because its inherent vagueness limits accuracy.

For the physical sciences, theories and techniques have resulted in explanation and prediction through scientific laws. Because the basis of knowledge is well established in the physical sciences, there is little concern with the logical foundation of methodology, since it is directed by the scientific laws. But, after some 50 years of investigation, LD phenomena still cannot be explained and predicted, since the LD field does not possess an effective and established system of knowledge. This lack of knowledge is reflected in the considerable energy directed at the codification of scientific methodology for LD. But such codification is not evidence of greater methodological sophistication, but rather, the lack of success in constructing a workable science.

The primary methodology found in LD only aims at improving observation, but not on techniques of anchoring these observations at a theoretical level through rational and abstract thought. Because the connections are only at the level of observation, empirical thought represents an integrated set of perceptions of the phenomenon under study. Because they lack relationships at the theoretical level, however, these perceptions do not meet the requirements for the development of scientific concepts or ideas. This system of empirical connection is the basic approach found in empiricism. Such empiricism underlies Frazer's (1963) analysis of magical thinking, in which the only connection is between observable to observable. Consider the example of the relationship between minimal brain dysfunction (MBD) and learning disability (LD). It might be noted that an observation (MBD-type behavior such as hyperactivity, distractibility, perceptual–motor problems and the like) is followed by another observation (learning problems in school). Philosophers of the empiricist school like Hume would suggest that MBD may be said to have caused LD. Such instances concerned only with the connection of observable terms are, in actuality, cases of magical belief. Although many empirical connections in the LD field are not accepted, labeled "magic," and described as false or spurious, the basic methodology (empiricism) utilized by the LD field ensures that all its conjectures are based on such empirical connections. Consequently, schools of thought in the LD field simply represent a situation in which we believe our empirical thought connections but disbelieve the tenets of the other schools. This empiricism is logically identical to magic but improved measurement and control simply means that our empiricism is more effective. Thus, the differentiation of magic from other forms of empiricism is no more than ethnocentrism; our ideas are sensible, but theirs are not. The consequences are found in a distinct separatism found in LD that is characterized by an emphasis on intertheory competition. The competition among theories results in a disorganized body of knowledge since there are no rules for correlating findings (and showing commonality) that characterize the unification found in organized sciences. The separatism in LD is based on differences in experimental method that represent broad conceptual oppositions (e.g., holistic vs. atomistic, subjective vs. objective, idiographic vs. nomothetic, biological vs. environmental). Science is, thus, not simply the generation of data, but the generation of data that provides a body of organized knowledge. Although LD possesses the accoutrements of science in abundance, this abundance can be a problem, if it results in complexity, confusion, competition, and chaos — when the need is for simplification and organization.

Science differs in logical form from empiricism. Although including empirical connections linking observables as well as rational connections linking concepts at a theoretical level (e.g., mathematics), science is defined through the abstractive connection of theoretical concepts with observations in order to achieve empirical meaning. Scientific knowledge, thus, does not consist of either empirical or rational connection alone but, rather, rational connections which correspond to observational connections. This is the isomorphism of concepts and observations, a structural similarity between theoretical and observational levels that imparts power to a scientific system.

The power of science allows its laws and theories to possess a broad scope, as opposed to the particular case found in the empirical associations found in the observations obtained under empiricism. The problem with empiricism, then, is that it attempts to do what it cannot do — generate empirical knowledge of broad scope. To cover a broad scope, knowledge must not be particular but, rather, must be generalized through the abstractive connections found in science. If, however, the empirical connections become more dissimilar and are not anchored at a theoretical level, then the more vague they become and the less useful.

Empiricism lacks a complete system of knowledge because its elements, although systematically obtained through observation, cannot be rationally connected, and thus form independent lists of knowledge. For example, we may observe that LD is associated with academic deficits, academic deficits with poor reading, poor reading with perceptual problems, perceptual problems with poor memory, poor memory with poor abstract thinking, and so on. Although each function is concerned with LD, each forms an independent association and is otherwise unrelated to the other functions.

Science forms a system of knowledge because it consistently uses a combination of empirical, rational, and abstractive connections to integrate its explanatory statements into a conceptual whole. This interconnection of components means that science is developmental and that its scope may be extended beyond its empirical associations. This increased scope may lead to more refined theoretical statement capable of more precise or more inclusive explanation through either more elegant statements or better isomorphism with empirical phenomena. In contrast, empiricism develops only in the quantity of facts gathered, and the improvement of techniques for gathering them. The knowledge gained, however, forms a vast, unconnected mass which the methods of empiricism are unable to rationalize into a conceptual whole involving a theoretical level.

The empiricism of LD has produced an expanded data base that presents a multifarious and variegated picture. Without a science of LD, it is not possible to place these empirical data into a comprehensive context. Yet, the LD field needs to extract information and to unravel the variation likely to be found in primary research. If it is assumed that knowledge should be cumulative (Ayer, 1956), then the proliferation of primary research that simply adds new samples, new measures, new designs, and new analyses can only corroborate or contradict previous findings. This dichotomy means that each study remains as an isolated data point and is not incorporated into a larger theoretical context. Instead, the empiricist tradition allows only for the combining of results in which the desired outcomes are consistent and generalizable empirical associations across studies. Because these generalizations are not based on scientific laws, it is likely that complex and contingent patterns will emerge leading to premature explanation and faulty understanding. With no conceptual structure to guide interpretation, the reasoning process involved in conjoining empirical associations is not based on rational processes and is subject to many false notions as described in Bacon's (1960) Idols. These Idols (illusions) include:

1. Idols of the tribe: an error founded in the tendency to be anthropomorphic, that is, to interpret things in terms of personal feelings and attitudes.

2. Idols of the cave: an error that results from a misperception or peculiar quirk of an individual personality that perceives reality in an idiosyncratic way.

3. Idols of the marketplace: imprecise and misleading language or

the vague and equivocal use of terms which prevent specificity.

4. Idols of the theatre: principles or explanations that by tradition, belief, and negligence have been accepted and may act like a set of conceptual blinders to prevent new interpretation.

Thus, Bacon's Idols possess relevance by suggesting the restrictions and limitations imposed by empiricism in the reasoning process.

Quantitative Research Synthesis and the Unification of Empiricism

The recent emphasis upon quantitative research synthesis in LD (Kavale, 1983; Kavale & Glass, 1981, 1982), while not a panacea for LD's empiricism, allows for an explicit, unambiguous, and well-defined methodology to distillate empirical associations into generalizable forms. By improving upon the traditional techniques for integrating data across studies, quantitative methods which have come to be called meta-analysis hold promise for the systematic summarization of study findings useful for LD policy and practice, if not the formulation of scientific laws (Kavale, 1984). As opposed to other more traditional forms of research synthesis, meta-analysis allows for the unification of empirical findings that possesses pragmatic value by providing practical knowledge of what is and what was. But this practical knowledge should not be confused with science, since its foundation is rooted in empiricism. Meta-analysis may be of value for unifying findings, but it cannot remove the constraints of empiricism since conclusions still state that what is, is and must be. Science, on the other hand, ignores what is and what was, in order to generate new theoretical postulates.

Meta-analysis represents an inductive method of research synthesis — inductive because it proceeds from particular observations to a general inclusive statement wherein an inference may be applied from a sample to an individual out of it, a "singular predictive inference" (Carnap, 1950); and a method because of its applicability across disciplines rather than a technique which is a discipline-specific procedure for inquiry (Kaplan, 1964). The aim is to provide insights of understanding in the sense that Kuhn (1970) termed the "decoding of reality." The understanding provided by meta-analysis may be conceptualized as consisting of four components: (1) clarifying the parameters of the phenomenon under consideration by summarizing data, (2) making explicit what is only implicit, (3) reducing inessential parameters by providing a logical whole, and (4) placing a phenomenon into an appropriate context (Brodbeck, 1963; Nagel, 1961; Toulmin, 1961).

Meta-analysis (see Glass, McGaw, & Smith, 1981) is based upon a statistic that represents the magnitude of experimental effect or relationship. The basic "effect size" (*ES*) statistic for experimental treatments or programs is

$$ES = (\overline{X}_e - \overline{X}_c) / SD_c$$

where X_e = average score for the experimental group on the outcome measure, X_c = average score for the control group on the outcome measure, and SD_c = standard deviation of the control group. In the case of correlational research, where the magnitude of the relationship between two variables is investigated, the basic *ES* is

$$ES = r_{xy}$$

where r_{xy} = Pearson product-moment correlation coefficient.

An *ES* may be interpreted as a z-score and translated into notions of overlapping distributions of groups and comparable percentiles. An *ES* of +1.00 indicates that a subject at the 50th percentile of the control group would be expected to rise to the 84th percentile of the control group at the end of treatment. The average subject receiving treatment would be better off than 84% of the control group while only 16% of the control group would be improved after treatment. Similar interpretations are appropriate for a negative *ES*.

The interpretation of an *ES* may be further clarified by comparisons (1) to other known interventions (e.g., *ES* for one year's instruction in elementary school achievement = +1.00), (2) within a meta-analysis (e.g., teaching methods *X* and *Y* produce mean *ES*s of +1.00 and .50, respectively, thus *X* is half again more beneficial than *Y*), or (3) to the aggregated findings of other meta-analyses (e.g., treatment A [mean *ES* = .60] is approximately five times as effective as treatment B [mean *ES* = .12] for treating hyperdystonia). But *ES* interpretation cannot and should not be made in a vacuum; it requires a context to provide meaning. An *ES* of 2.5 or .25 possesses no inherent value when dissociated from a context of decision and comparative value found in the total milieu of the *ES* which is likely to vary from setting to setting.

Meta-analysis seeks general conclusions that neither confirm nor reject hypotheses in the classical statistical sense but, rather, establish facts. These facts represent generalizations which have been empirically confirmed and, as such, meta-analysis clarifies the parameters of the phenomenon under study by summarizing a multitude of empirical associations into a logical whole. This logical whole represents the integrated findings encompassing a structure spanning global to discrete aggregations. By providing *ES*s for aggregated subsets of data, the findings from meta-analysis yield a form of expectation for the phenomenon under study based upon "explanation by inductive subsumption under statistical laws" (Hempel, 1955). The *ES* may be conceptualized as a "calculus of probability" (Kaplan, 1964) that provides a probabilistic boundary rather than a deterministic uniformity. Because meta-analysis is a nomothetic rather than an idiographic procedure, the expectation is appropriate only across many LD children rather than any particular LD child. Brodbeck (1958) termed this "explanatory emergence," the fact that group conjectures cannot be reduced to conjectures about individual behavior; this suggests that the *ES* (and the associated standard deviation) represents a range rather than a particular point in an outcome scale.

Meta-Analysis and LD

To provide a context for viewing problems in LD, the findings of several meta-analyses will be summarized. Although such findings are not the basis for developing scientific laws in a theoretical sense, they do elucidate the problems encountered because of the empiricism of LD and the rather embarrassing position of LD professionals of knowing less than has been proven.

1. Process Training

The issue of process training is likely either to vex or to mollify LD practitioners. Strong conviction exists on both sides, but the question remains: How efficacious is process training?

a. Psycholinguistic Training. Kavale (1981a) performed a meta-analysis on 34 studies investigating its effectiveness. The studies yielded 240 *ES*s that produced an overall $\overline{ES}$ of .39. This finding was based on data representing approximately 1,850 subjects who averaged 7.5 years of age with a mean IQ of 82 and who received an average of 50 hours of psycholinguistic training. Thus, the average subject receiving psycholinguistic training stands at approximately the 65th percentile of subjects receiving no special psycholinguistic training, who remain at the 50th percentile.

Table 2-2 presents $\overline{ES}$s classified by Illinois Test of Psycholinguistic Abilities (ITPA) subtest. These *ES*s are modest by most standards. If subtests for which the data are thin (i.e., five or fewer *ES*s) are eliminated, five of the nine subtests show small, albeit positive, effects. The case is different, however, for four abilities: auditory and visual association, verbal and manual expression. Thus, the average-trained subject would be better off than approximately 65% to 73% of untrained subjects on associative or expressive abilities.

Subtests of ITPA were patterned upon psycholinguistic construct derived from Osgood's (1957) model of communication. Table 2-3 shows the effects of training upon theoretical dimensions underlying the ITPA.

The findings regarding responsiveness to intervention of the expressive constructs, particularly Verbal Expression, and the Representational Level subtests are most encouraging since they embody the "language" aspects of the ITPA and, ultimately, productive

TABLE 2-2   Average Effect Sizes for ITPA Subtests

ITPA subtest	Mean effect size	No. of effect sizes
Auditory reception	.21	20
Visual reception	.21	20
Auditory association	.44	24
Visual association	.39	21
Verbal expression	.63	24
Manual expression	.54	23
Grammatic closure	.30	21
Visual closure	.48	5
Auditory sequential memory	.32	21
Visual sequential memory	.27	21
Auditory closure	−.05	3
Sound blending	.38	3

TABLE 2-3   Average Effect Size for ITPA Psycholinguistic Constructs

Dimension	Construct	Mean effect size
Level	Representational	.40
	Automatic	.21
Processes	Reception	.21
	Organization	.32
	Expression	.59
Modalities	Auditory–Verbal	.32
	Visual–Motor	.38

language behavior. For a basic area like language, the average elementary school pupil gains about one standard deviation (ES = + 1.00) over the school year and exceeds about 84% of the pupils' scores made on a language achievement measure at the beginning of the school year. The approximately 60% success rate for training Verbal Expression is thus substantial. In fact, roughly 50 hours of psycholinguistic training produce benefits on the Verbal Expression subtest ($\overline{ES}$ = .63), exceeding that which would be expected from one-half year of schooling in language achievement (ES = .50).

b. Perceptual–Motor Training. Perceptual–motor training represents a wide assortment of techniques aimed at improving abilities deemed necessary for both perceptual–motor functioning and academic achievement. Its popularity is based both on historical influences (since the days of Itard and Seguin) and the wide dissemination of clinical programs acknowledging the efficacy of perceptual–motor training.

Kavale and Mattson (1983) found 180 experiments assessing the efficacy of perceptual–motor training. A total of 637 ES measurements was obtained, representing about 13,000 subjects who averaged 8 years of age with an average IQ of 89 and who received an average of 65 hours of perceptual–motor training. The $\overline{ES}$ across 637 ES measurements was .082 which, in relative terms, indicates that a child who is no better off than average (i.e., at the 50th percentile) rises to the 53rd percentile as a result of perceptual–motor interventions. Additionally, of 637 ESs, 48% were negative, suggesting that the probability of obtaining a positive response to training is only slightly better than chance.

The overall effect of perceptual–motor training is thus negligible. Perhaps a single index may mask an important subset in which perceptual–motor training is more effective. Consequently, ES data were aggregated into increasingly differentiated groupings of outcome measures. The findings are shown in Tables 2-4 and 2-5. These findings

TABLE 2-4   Average Effect Size for Perceptual–Motor Outcome Classes

Outcome class	Mean effect size	No. of effect sizes
Perceptual / Sensory Motor	.166	233
Academic Achievement	.013	283
Cognitive / Aptitude	.028	95
Adaptive Behavior	.267	26

TABLE 2-5   Average Effect Sizes for Perceptual–Motor General Outcome Categories

General outcome categories	Mean effect size	No. of effect sizes
Perceptual/Sensory Motor		
Gross motor	.214	44
Fine motor	.178	28
Visual perception	.149	145
Auditory perception	.122	16
Academic achievement		
Readiness	.076	69
Reading	−.039	142
Arithmetic	.095	26
Language	.031	18
Spelling	.021	16
Handwriting	.053	12
Cognitive/Aptitude		
Verbal IQ	−.007	53
Performance IQ	.068	34

speak for themselves. Regardless of how global or discrete the aggregation, the effects of perceptual–motor training present an unbroken vista of disappointment. There are no positive effects and nothing indicative of an effective intervention.

Table 2-6 provides aggregated *ES* data for diagnostic category. The interpretation is clear: essentially zero effects are seen in all groups. In no instance were perceptual–motor interventions effective. In fact, among the lowest $\overline{ES}$s were those found for learning/reading disabled children for whom perceptual–motor training is a favored treatment approach.

Perceptual–motor training programs have taken a variety of forms, and the names associated with these programs read like the roster from the learning disabilities Hall of Fame. The $\overline{ES}$s for the various training methods are shown in Table 2-7. Again, the findings offer a bleak picture; nothing even hints at positive effects.

TABLE 2-6   Average Effect Size for Subject Groups

Subject	Mean effect size	No. of effect sizes
Normal	.054	58
Educable mentally retarded (IQ 50–75)	.132	143
Trainable mentally retarded (IQ 25–50)	.147	66
Slow learner (IQ 75–90)	.098	14
Culturally disadvantaged	.045	85
Learning disabled	.018	77
Reading disabled	–.007	74
Motor disabled	.121	118

TABLE 2-7   Average Effect Sizes for Perceptual–Motor Training Programs

Training program	Mean effect size	No. of effect sizes
Barsch	.157	18
Cratty	.113	27
Delacato	.161	79
Frostig	.096	173
Getman	.124	48
Kephart	.064	132
Combination	.057	78
Other	–.021	82

2. Special Versus Regular Class Placement — "The Efficacy Question"

Passage of Public Law 94–142 mandated placement in the "least restrictive environment" which, for many exceptional children, meant placement in the regular class. Justification was found in efficacy studies suggesting that the special class may be inappropriate for the education of exceptional children. The research literature, however, has been criticized for a number of methodological flaws that confound interpretation. Consequently, research has provided little convincing evidence that either supports or rejects the efficacy of special or regular class placement for exceptional children.

Carlberg and Kavale (1980) performed a meta-analysis on 50 studies examining the "efficacy" question. The studies included experiments comparing special class students with those who might otherwise have been placed in special classes, but for experimental purposes, were placed in regular classes. It was, thus, not a comparison of exceptional versus average pupils. In this case, the special class was treated as the experimental group, which mean a positive *ES* favors the special class while a negative *ES* favors the regular class.

The 50 studies produced 322 *ES* measurements and, at the highest level of aggregation, yielded an $\overline{ES}$ of −.12. These data represented approximately 27,000 students, who averaged 11 years of age, with a mean IQ of 74, and who remained in the special class for a little under two years. Approximately 58% of the *ES*s were negative; in more than half the cases, special classes were less effective. Since the average comparison regular class subject would be at the 50th percentile, the effects of approximately two years of special class placement were to reduce the relative standing of the average special class pupil by 5 percentile ranks.

Efficacy studies generally measured two outcomes: achievement and social-personality variables, which revealed $\overline{ES}$s of −.15 and −.11, respectively. Thus, special class placement was inferior to regular class placement, regardless of outcome measure.

These findings lend support for a significant, albeit small, negative effect for special class placement. The critics were apparently correct; special class placement produced no tangible benefits. The *ES* measurements were classified and averaged in a number of different ways. They were correlated with important study features, but the primary finding was not challenged. Regardless of age, IQ, length of special class placement, and the like, the fact remained: the special class was an inferior placement option.

This meta-analysis brought to light, however, a surprising finding related to diagnosis of pupils. The findings are shown in Table 2-8. Special class placement was most disadvantageous for exceptional children whose primary problem was lowered IQ levels. The average learning disabled (LD) or behaviorally/emotionally disturbed (BD/ED) pupil in a *special class* was better off than 61% of those placed in a regular class. Thus, unconditional judgments about mainstreaming must be tempered lest the special education field find itself in a morass similar to that created by the nature–nurture debate over intelligence.

TABLE 2-8   Average Effect Size by Special Education Diagnosis

Diagnosis	Average effect of special vs. regular placement	No. of effect sizes
Educable mentally retarded (EMR) (IQ 50–75)	–.14	249
Slow learner (SL) (IQ 75–90)	–.34	38
Learning disabled and Behaviorally Disordered Emotionally Disturbed (LD & BD / ED)	.29	35

3. Assessment

a. Auditory and Visual Perception. Auditory and visual perceptual skills have been assumed to be related to reading ability and have often been used in assessments to predict reading achievement. But the research investigating the nature of the relationships has produced mixed results that have been interpreted both positively and negatively.

Kavale (1981b, 1982b) performed meta-analyses on 267 studies investigating the relationship between auditory (n = 106) and visual (n = 161) perception and reading ability. A total of 2294 correlation coefficients (*ES*) were collected with 1509 descriptive of the relationship of auditory (n = 447) and visual (n = 1062) perception to reading achievement. The remainder (785) were descriptive of the relationships among perceptual skills and intelligence, intelligence and reading, and reading skills. These data represented approximately 50,000 subjects whose average age was 7.87 years, in grade 3.3, and average IQ was 104.55.

For auditory perception and reading, the average correlation ($\overline{ES}$) was .369 while the average correlation was .387 for visual perception and reading. Because the usual method for interpreting the importance of a correlation in terms of a coefficient of determination (r^2) that reflects the percent of variance explained was found to underestimate the importance of relationships, Rosenthal and Rubin (1982) suggested an alternative in the binomial effect size display (BESD) that indicates the change in predictive accuracy attributable to a certain assessment variable and is computed by $.50 \pm r/2$. Suppose a particular relationship reveals an r of .32; it is said to account for "only 10% of the variance," but the BESD shows that this proportion of variance accounted for is equivalent to increasing the predictive accuracy from 34% to 66%, which would mean reducing the number of incorrect predictions from 66% to 34%. With a BESD interpretation, auditory perception increases predictive accuracy from 32% to 68%, while visual perception produces an increase from 31% to 69%.

The findings for the relationship between five auditory perceptual skills and eight visual perceptual skills to reading ability are displayed in Table 2-9. On average, each auditory and each visual perceptual skill increased the accuracy of predicting reading ability by 40%. Little variability emerged among auditory perceptual skills, while visual perceptual skills exhibited greater divergence which was accounted for primarily by the small increase (26%) for figure ground discrimination (FG), compared to the large increase in predictive accuracy for VMem (48%). Although, on average, prediction of reading ability was approximately equal to that of auditory perceptual skills (68%), VMem emerged as the best predictor with successful predictions increased from 28% to 76%.

The perceptual skill data were next aggregated across individual reading skills as shown in Table 2-10. For general reading (GR), auditory perceptual skills increased predictive accuracy by 38%, on average, which was almost the same as the average 39% increase in predictive accuracy for visual perceptual skill. Word recognition (WR) found the auditory skills of auditory discrimination (AD), auditory blending (AB), and auditory memory (AM) increasing predictive accuracy to 69% while

TABLE 2-9 Relationship of Auditory and Visual Perceptual Skills To Reading Achievement

Skill	N	M	Predictive accuracy increased From	To	Difference in predictive accuracy
Auditory					
Auditory discrimination (AD)	183	.371	31%	69%	37%
Auditory blending (AB)	67	.377	33%	71%	38%
Auditory memory (AM)	99	.383	29%	67%	38%
Auditory comprehension (AC)	26	.402	30%	70%	40%
Auditory – Visual integration (A-V)	72	.324	34%	66%	32%
Visual					
Visual discrimination (VD)	291	.385	33%	71%	38%
Visual memory (VMem)	139	.472	28%	76%	48%
Visual motor integration (VMot)	305	.361	28%	64%	36%
Visual closure (VC)	77	.427	24%	66%	42%
Visual spatial (VS)	64	.326	34%	66%	32%
Visual association (VA)	95	.377	31%	69%	38%
Figure ground discrimination (FG)	46	.251	39%	65%	26%
Visual – Auditory integration (V-A)	45	.338	33%	67%	34%

TABLE 2-10 Relationship of Auditory and Visual Perceptual Skills to Reading Skills

Skill	General reading ability (GR)				Word recognition (WR)				Reading comprehension (RC)				Vocabulary (VO)			
			PAI				PAI				PAI				PAI	
	N	M	From	To	N	M	From	To	N	M	From	To	N	M	From	To
Auditory																
AD	59	.382	31%	69%	46	.342	35%	69%	32	.361	32%	68%	19	.399	30%	70%
AB	22	.413	31%	73%	12	.307	39%	69%	14	.336	33%	67%	5	.242	35%	59%
AM	33	.368	32%	68%	24	.418	27%	69%	23	.404	30%	70%	9	.603	22%	82%
AC	11	.394	28%	68%	5	.277	34%	62%	6	.381	31%	69%	4	.267	39%	65%
A-V	24	.318	34%	66%	27	.332	33%	63%	15	.355	34%	70%	5	.161	42%	58%
Visual																
VD	143	.418	29%	71%	18	.477	26%	74%	25	.372	31%	69%	14	.315	34%	66%
VMem	52	.472	29%	77%	45	.463	27%	73%	49	.463	31%	77%	21	.488	28%	76%
VMot	164	.409	28%	68%	16	.398	28%	68%	13	.361	30%	66%	14	.342	31%	65%
VC	23	.376	29%	67%	18	.272	36%	64%	16	.363	32%	68%	9	.297	33%	63%
VS	11	.367	32%	68%	23	.348	31%	65%	20	.345	31%	65%	17	.401	28%	68%
VA	17	.410	29%	71%	24	.356	32%	68%	26	.301	35%	65%	20	.355	30%	66%
FG	18	.262	37%	63%	6	.266	37%	63%	9	.244	38%	62%	8	.225	37%	59%
V-A	15	.416	29%	71%	8	.441	28%	72%	5	.273	39%	61%	6	.199	40%	60%

PAI = Predictive accuracy increased.

the visual skills, visual spatial (VS), visual memory (VMem), and visual association (V-A) increased predictive accuracy to approximately 73%. Measures of reading comprehension (RC) found approximately equal percentage increases (to about 69%) for all auditory perceptual skills. Greater variability was found among visual skills ranging from 22% for V-A to 46% for VMem. For vocabulary (VO) measures, AM was by far the best predictor and increased predictive accuracy by 60% (from 22% to 82%). The only visual skill approaching AM was VMem, where the predictive success increased from 28% to 76% for a predictive improvement of 48%.

Several popular tests of auditory and visual perceptual functioning were used frequently enough to allow for meaningful integration with the results shown in Table 2-11. The AD (Wepman, Murphy–Durrell) and VMot (Bender) measures were less effective, by an average 4%, in increasing predictive accuracy when compared to the averages across all AD (.371) and VMot (.361) measures. The two most popular AM instruments (WISC–Digit Span, ITPA–ASM) increased predictive accuracy to levels greater than the average 67% across all AM measures. The most often used AB measures (Roswell–Chall, ITPA–SB) were also more effective than the average percentage increase (38%) for all AB measures. The Frostig test was significantly less effective in increasing predictive accuracy than the average coefficient for visual perception measures (.387). The ITPA subtests increase predictive accuracy by percentages ranging from 34% to 60%, with an average increase of 41%. The best predictor is sound blending (SB), which increases successful prediction of reading achievement from 22% to 82%.

To complete the description of the relationship between auditory and visual perceptual skills and reading, the role of intelligence (IQ) was assessed through calculating partial correlations with IQ constant. When IQ was partialed out, the magnitude of the relationships decreased. Auditory perceptual skills declined in predictive accuracy by an average 13% while visual perceptual skills revealed an average 23% decline in predictive accuracy. The greatest suppression in predictive accuracy was found for the memory skills (AM and VMem) while the discrimination abilities (AD and VD) exhibited the most independence from IQ. With respect to reading skills, the accuracy of predicting WR was least effected while the predictive accuracy for RC and VO was most attenuated with IQ constant.

A step-wise multiple regression analysis was used to determine the extent and significance as well as the best combination of variables for predicting reading achievement, and is shown in Table 2-12 (with and without IQ entered as a variable). With IQ entered, it was the first variable for three reading skills (GR, RC, VO), while only a minimal

TABLE 2-11 Relationship of Auditory and Visual Perceptual Measures to Reading Ability

Measure	N	M	Predictive accuracy increased		Difference in predictive accuracy
			From	To	
Bender[1]	81	.318	34%	66%	32%
Wepman[2]	59	.352	32%	68%	36%
Roswell–Chall[3]	29	.465	27%	73%	46%
Murphy–Durrell[4]	35	.313	32%	64%	32%
WISC–Digit span[5]	34	.329	36%	68%	32%
Frostig[6]					
Eye motor	31	.237	36%	60%	24%
Figure ground	32	.226	39%	61%	22%
Form constancy	31	.292	33%	63%	30%
Position in space	37	.268	37%	63%	26%
Spatial relations	37	.274	36%	64%	28%
Total	36	.253	36%	62%	26%
ITPA[7]					
Visual reception	24	.337	33%	67%	34%
Auditory association	15	.389	31%	69%	38%
Visual association	19	.347	33%	67%	34%
Auditory sequential memory	27	.388	33%	71%	38%
Visual sequential memory	57	.412	29%	71%	42%
Visual closure	17	.375	29%	67%	38%
Sound blending	16	.597	22%	82%	60%

[1]Bender visual motor gestalt
[2]Wepman auditory discrimination test
[3]Roswell–Chall auditory blending test
[4]Murphy–Durrell diagnostic reading readiness test
[5]Wechsler intelligence scale for children
[6]Marianne Frostig developmental test of visual perception
[7]Illinois Test of Psycholinguistic Abilities

factor for WR. For GR, the next three steps were visual skills while, for RC and VO, AC was the second step. The remaining steps added only slightly to the predicted variance. The initial variable (VMem) for WR accounted for less than one-half the variance when compared to the cases with IQ as the initial variable. When IQ was not entered, VMem was the initial variable while the second step in each case was an auditory variable. Again, the remaining variables did not add significantly to the proportion of predicted variance.

The magnitude and nature of the relationship of auditory and visual perception to reading indicated that they successfully increased the

TABLE 2-12 **Step-Wise Multiple Regression of Auditory Perceptual Skills and Visual Perceptual Skills in Predicting Reading Abilities With and Without Intelligence as a Variable**

			READING SKILL				
GR		WR		RC		VO	
Variable	R^2	Variable	R^2	Variable	R^2	Variable	R^2
IQ	.580	VMem	.212	IQ	.578	IQ	.449
VD	.612	AM	.314	AC	.657	AC	.508
VC	.634	VD	.365	VD	.693	AD	.558
VMem	.646	VC	.398	AD	.707	VMem	.586
AB	.658	AC	.427	A-V	.715	A-V	.616
VMot	.666	AB	.461	VC	.717	VMot	.634
AD	.670	Vmot	.483	VA	.720	VA	.648
AC	.675	AD	.497	AM	.722	AM	.661
VA	.676	A-V	.502	VMot	.723	AB	.661
AM	.676	IQ	.504	AB	.724	VD	.662
A-V	.676	VA	.504	VMem	.724	VC	.662
VMem	.203	VMem	.212	VMem	.212	VMem	.240
AB	.317	AM	.314	AM	.314	AM	.360
VC	.373	VD	.365	VD	.351	AD	.396
VD	.400	VC	.399	AB	.373	A-V	.447
VMot	.419	AB	.427	AC	.395	VMot	.493
AD	.431	AB	.461	VC	.420	VA	.520
AM	.434	VMot	.483	AD	.437	AC	.539
AC	.437	AD	.497	VMot	.446	AB	.547
VA	.439	A-V	.502	A-V	.451	VC	.547
A-V	.440	VA	Not Entered	VA	.452	VD	.548

accuracy of predicting reading skills. The magnitude of that increase, however, was either amplified or attenuated by the particular subset of perceptual and reading variables considered.

b. Wechsler Profiles. The *Wechsler Intelligence Scales* (WISC, WISC-R, and WPPSI), with their separate Verbal and Performance Scales composed of 10 (or 12) subtests, have made them particularly attractive for attempting to identify a set of characteristics that might be useful for differential diagnosis. Research has suggested that LD children may differ from normal children with respect to verbal-performance discrepancies and patterns of subtest scatter evidenced in recategorizations and profiles based on factor scores or theoretical models of cognitive abilities.

Kavale and Forness (1984b) performed a meta-analysis on 94 studies investigating WISC differences between normal and LD children. The average study included subjects in grade 6.2 whose average age was 11.47 years, and was published in 1973 with a sample size of 105 (total N = 9372) which was 63% male. The obtained $\overline{ES}$s for Full Scale (−.199), Verbal Scale (−.391), and Performance Scale (−.160) suggest that approximately 58%, 65%, and 54%, respectively, of normal children would possible score above the LD group and indicates considerable overlap between the distributions of normal and LD populations. When translated into IQ scores, the LD group revealed FSIQ, VSIQ, and PSIQ scores of 97, 94, and 98, respectively, that fall within the average classification. Traditional thinking has suggested that LD children are characterized by VSIQ and PSIQ (V–P) differences. The V–P discrepancy (PSIQ > VSIQ) exhibited an $\overline{ES}$ of .231 that translates into a 3.46 IQ point difference that fails to meet the 11 IQ point difference required for significance (.05).

The findings for WISC Verbal and Performance subtests are presented in Table 2-13. The Verbal subtests revealed greater suppression than the Performance subtests. The Verbal ES data indicate that anywhere from 48% (C) to 73% (DS) of the general population may exhibit higher scores than the LD group in Verbal subtests. When translated into scaled score equivalents, the average value for the five regular tests (M = 9.41) was only about one-half point below the mean

TABLE 2–13 Average Effect Size for WISC Verbal and Performance Subtests

	Number of effect sizes	Mean effect size	Scaled score equivalent	Percentile rank
Verbal subtests				
Information (I)	62	−.377	8.87	37
Similarities (S)	62	−.001	10.00	50
Arithmetic (A)	63	−.436	8.69	37
Vocabulary (V)	63	−.210	9.37	37
Comprehension (C)	61	+.044	10.13	50
Digit span (DS)	43	−.610	8.17	25
Performance Subtests				
Picture completion (PC)	60	+.234	10.70	63
Picture arrangement (PA)	60	+.105	10.32	50
Block design (BD)	60	+.038	10.11	50
Object assembly (OA)	58	+.092	10.28	50
Coding (CO)	57	−.410	8.77	37
Mazes (M)	6	−.355	8.93	37

(10), with all percentile rankings within the average classification. The Performance subtests revealed four instances when the LD group performed better than the normal comparison group. The findings suggest that anywhere from 41% (PC) to 66% (CO) of the total population would be expected to score at a higher level than LD subjects, which again reveals considerable overlap between the populations. The five Performance subtests produced an average value (10.04) practically equal to the mean-scaled score (10).

Differentiation between normal and LD groups has been suggested on the basis of intersubtest variability or scatter. Although several approaches to scatter have been suggested, each approach revealed the same finding: the LD group actually exhibits less variability than the normal group, which results in little uniqueness or diagnostic value in WISC subtest scatter and a relatively flat profile.

The WISC subtests have also been recategorized into groupings based upon hypotheses about cognitive abilities and these more popular WISC recategorizations are displayed in Table 2-14. Although $\overline{ES}$ data indicated some pattern of strength and weakness, translation into scaled score equivalents found the LD group only about a half point above the mean (10) in the areas of strength while only depressed by approximately a point and one-half in the weaker areas. When compared to the required deviation (± 3) for significance, none of the recategorized scores revealed any area to be a significant strength or weakness for the LD group, and all scaled scores place the LD group within the average range. Similar findings were found for WISC profiles (either a specification of subtests as low versus high, or only an indication of subtests where the LD group scores low), WISC factor scores (based upon factor analytic studies assessing construct validity), and WISC patterns (based upon descriptions of cognitive abilities and operations). Thus, in each instance, the regroupings failed to demonstrate distinctive ability clusterings that might be useful for clinical differentiation of LD and normal children.

The differential diagnosis of LD with the WISC, although intuitively appealing, appears unwarranted. Although the structure of the WISC leads to the assumption that there ought to be subtest patterns, and established clinical practice operates as if these patterns were fact, this meta-analysis found no distinctive characteristics that would be useful for LD diagnosis. Regardless of the manner in which WISC subtests were grouped and regrouped, no recategorization, profile, pattern, or factor cluster emerged as a clinically significant indicator of LD. In fact, the average WISC profile for LD does not reveal anything extraordinary and appears not unlike that found for the average normal child illustrated by a composite rendering of findings as shown in Figure 2-1.

4. Medically Based Interventions

From its inception, special education has always shown a fascination for medicine. Conversely, at times, medicine has sometimes experienced a fascination with schools. The interface of this relationship has resulted in medically oriented interventions being an integral part of the special education repertoire of remedial techniques.

TABLE 2–14 Average Effect Sizes for WISC Recategorized Scores

Recategorization	Subtests	Number of effect sizes	Mean effect size	Scaled score equiva- lent
Bannatyne I				
Spatial	PC, BD, OA	178	+.122	10.37
Conceptual	S, V, C	186	−.057	9.83
Sequential	DS, PA, CO	160	−.271	9.19
Bannatyne II				
Spatial	PC, BD, OA	178	+.122	10.37
Conceptual	S, V, C	186	−.057	9.83
Sequential	A, DS, CO	163	−.473	8.58
Acquired knowledge	I, A, V	188	−.341	8.98
Keogh & Hall				
Verbal comprehension	I, V, C	186	−.182	9.45
Attention – Concentration	A, DS, CO	163	−.473	8.58
Analytical field approach	PC, BD, OA	178	+.122	10.37
Bush & Waugh				
Spatial	PC, BD, OA	178	+.122	10.37
Conceptual	S, V, C	186	−.057	9.83
Perceptual organization	BD, OA	118	−.065	9.81
Verbal comprehension	I, S, V, C	248	−.137	9.59
Concentration	DS, A, CO	163	−.473	8.58
Vance & Singer				
Spatial	PC, BD, OA	178	+.122	10.37
Conceptual	S, V, C	186	−.057	9.83
Sequential	A, DS, CO	163	−.473	8.58
Acquired knowledge	I, A, V	188	−.341	8.98
Distractibility	A, DS, CO, M	169	−.469	8.59

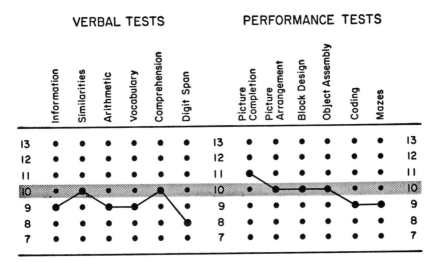

FIGURE 2-1 The WISC Scaled Score Profile of the Average Learning Disabled Child

a. Stimulant Drugs and Hyperactivity. The practice of treating hyperactive children with stimulant drugs is among the most controversial and emotionally loaded issues in special education. The medical community considers stimulant drugs to be the most efficacious treatment for hyperactivity. This conclusion has been challenged, first in the form of critical reviews suggesting that no positive interpretation could be drawn from extant literature because of numerous methodological flaws, and second in the form of ideological, political, and moral attacks upon stimulant drug treatment. Thus, empirical findings have proven less manifest than ethical positions, and the question of the efficacy of stimulant drug treatment remains.

Kavale (1982a) found 135 studies assessing the effectiveness of stimulant drug treatment for hyperactivity. The studies sampled represented approximately 5,300 subjects averaging 8.75 years of age with an average IQ of 102 who received medication for an average of 10 weeks. The $\overline{ES}$ across 984 ES measurements was .578, which suggests that an average drug-treated child would be expected to be better off than 72% of untreated control children.

The diverse assortment of outcomes measured in drug research makes it difficult to fully interpret a single index of drug efficacy. Three major outcome classes were identified (behavioral, cognitive, and physiological), and the findings are illustrated in Figure 2-2 in the form of normal distributions comparing hypothetical drug-treated and control populations. This more refined analysis revealed substantial positive effects on behavioral and cognitive outcomes. The negative effect for physiological outcomes indicated that drug intervention produced some negative consequences. (The physiological findings are generally difficult to interpret and are outside the scope of this chapter.)

Further refinement of the data in each outcome class is presented in Table 2-15. Note (with the exception of anxiety) the impressive gains on behavioral outcomes. Substantial benefits were found in ratings of behavioral functioning, lowered activity levels, and improved attending skills. Although not of the same magnitude as behavioral improvements, cognitive functioning also exhibited improvement.

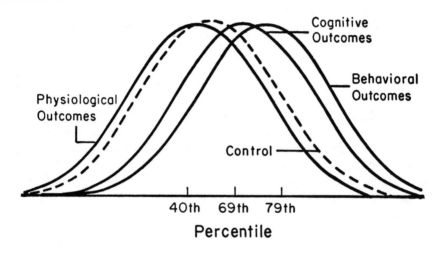

Behavioral ES = 0.804
Cognitive ES = 0.491
Physiological ES = 0.246

FIGURE 2-2 Effect of Stimulant Drug Therapy on Behavioral, Cognitive, and Physiological Outcome Classes

The overall $\overline{ES}$ of .578 for stimulant drugs was obtained from six major drugs as shown in Table 2-16. All major drugs, with the exception of caffeine, appear to be effective in the treatment of hyperactivity. These findings provide support for stimulants being the most popular treatment for hyperactivity.

b. Diet Treatment of Hyperactivity. Dr. Benjamin Feingold offered the hypothesis that ingestion of artificial (synthetic) food additives (colors and flavors) results in hyperactivity in children. The suggested treatment was based upon the Feingold Kaiser–Permanente (K–P) diet designed to eliminate from the diet all foods containing artificial food additives. Empirical support has been equivocal and raises the question: Are the major dietary changes required by the Feingold K–P diet justified in terms of reduced hyperactivity?

Kavale and Forness (1983) examined 23 studies assessing the efficacy of the Feingold K–P diet in treating hyperactivity. The 23 studies produced 125 ES measurements and yielded an $\overline{ES}$ of .118. The average subject was 8.3 years of age, had an IQ of 99, and remained on the

TABLE 2-15 Average Effect Sizes for Outcome Categories.

	Mean effect size	No. of effect sizes
Behavioral		
Global improvement ratings	.886	192
Rating scales & checklists	.837	113
Activity level	.846	127
Attention & concentration	.782	119
Behavior (social & classroom)	.634	92
Anxiety	.118	12
Cognitive		
Intelligence	.391	54
Achievement	.383	47
Drawing & copying	.467	38
Perceptual, memory, & motor	.412	91
Learning characteristics	.367	41
Physiological		
Biochemical	.558	7
Psychophysiological	–.275	51

Feingold K-P diet for 39 weeks. In relative terms, the .118 $\overline{ES}$ indicates that a child no better off than average (i.e., at the 50th percentile) would rise to the 55th percentile as a result of the Feingold K-P diet. When compared to the 22 percentile ranks gain for stimulant drug treatment, the 5 percentile rank improvement for diet intervention is less than one-fourth as large. Although the average ages and IQs were similar for drug-treated and diet-treated subjects, the average duration of treatment differed: 39 versus 10 weeks. In relation to ES (.118 vs. .587), these comparisons suggest that drug treatment is approximately five times as effective in about one-fourth the time when compared to Feingold K-P diet treatment.

The ES data were next aggregated into descriptive outcome categories. The findings are shown in Table 2-17. The only obvious effect of diet treatment is upon overt behavior—specifically, a reduction in hyperactivity—with little influence upon more cognitive aspects of behavior. This conclusion, however, must be tempered. Global ratings of improvement possess two major problems: objectively defining improvement, and psychometric deficiencies (reliability and validity). These problems influence the "reactivity" or subjectivity of outcome measures. The correlation of ES and ratings of reactivity was significant ($r = .181$), suggesting that larger treatment effects were slightly associated with more reactive measures. Additionally, aggregations of reactive versus non-reactive measures found $\overline{ES}$s of .179 and .001, respectively, suggesting that, in instances in which instruments paralleled the valued outcomes of observers, there was a tendency to view more improvement as revealed in larger treatment effects.

Of the 23 studies, six were uncontrolled clinical trials that yielded an $\overline{ES}$ of .337 compared to the $\overline{ES}$ of .089 for the 17 controlled studies. There was, however, a significant relationship ($r = .193$) between ES

TABLE 2-16 Average Effect Sizes for Stimulant Drugs

Drug	Mean effect size	No. of effect sizes
Methylphenidate (Ritalin)	.634	540
Dextroamphetamine (Dexedrine)	.585	276
Magnesium Pemoline (Cylert)	.540	61
Levoamphetamine	.447	29
Amphetamine (Benzedrine)	.438	33
Caffeine	.111	45

and ratings of design quality. Larger *ES*s were associated with studies rated low on internal validity, which makes it difficult to attribute improvement to the treatment rather than to artifacts of the study conditions.

The controlled studies used two primary experimental designs. The diet crossover studies (N = 7) exhibited an $\overline{ES}$ of .196, while challenge studies (N = 10) revealed an $\overline{ES}$ of .045. Diet crossover studies (ones in which the control group is placed on a disguised Feingold K–P diet), though an improvement over uncontrolled clinical studies, still possess methodological difficulties. Challenge studies (ones in which the experimental group is "challenged" with a food containing eliminated substances) offer a methodology that permits attribution of behavioral change to the substances eliminated in the Feingold K–P diet. Challenge studies can thus be considered the "best" studies, but the weight of this evidence is decidedly negative ($\overline{ES}$ = .045).

Empiricism, Meta-Analysis, and LD

Meta-analysis provides unification for the many empirical associations found in LD research in the form of facts that are empirically confirmed generalizations. As such, these facts are "logically equivalent truths" (Scheffler, 1963) that meet the standards of objectivity, verifiability, replicability, and clarity. The facts of meta-analysis thus contribute to pragmatic knowledge by extending its boundaries but, without a theoretical and scientific foundation, they never reach complete closure. This means that the explanations and

TABLE 2-17 Average Effect Size for Outcome Categories

Category	Mean effect size	No. of effect sizes
Conners Scale-parents	.156	26
Conners Scale-teachers	.268	9
Global improvement	.128	23
Hyperkinesis rating	.293	15
Attention	.015	36
Disruptive behavior	.052	6
Impulsivity	.153	5
Learning ability	–.055	10

predictions based on these facts are partial, conditional, approximate, indeterminate, inconclusive, uncertain, and intermediate (Kaplan, 1964).

Because there is no science of LD, its facts (as obtained from a procedure like meta-analysis) are limited since they apply *in* (not *to*) particular situations. This makes the question of external validity (Bracht & Glass, 1968) problematic, since the extent to which these facts may be generalized to "real" situations is unknown without the theoretical connections that characterize elements in the physical sciences. Consequently, within an LD system, there exists an intricate (and bewildering) set of intervening variables that only serve to complicate judgments about LD knowledge. Without specification of the associations among intervening variables that is provided by scientific theory, judgments about LD may be right or wrong for right or wrong reasons.

The linking of elements into a theoretical whole that describes the relationship among variables limits the focus to provide more precision in explanation and prediction. This is why LD models reveal enormous variability; they are not intimately joined in any theoretically based scientific system. Therefore, any LD phenomenon will demonstrate wide variability that is the result of the combination of variables in the specific circumstance. Recall that the findings from meta-analysis represent a form of expectation (mean *ES* and the associated standard deviation) for the phenomenon under study. But the LD phenomenon reviewed previously revealed the disconcerting fact that they demonstrate variability that is nearly equal to or greater than its average effect. Consider: psycholinguistic training ($\overline{ES}$ = .39; SD = .54), perceptual–motor training ($\overline{ES}$ = .08; SD = .27), regular versus special class placement ($\overline{ES}$ = –.12; SD = .65), auditory perception ($\overline{ES}$ = .36; SD = .17), visual perception ($\overline{ES}$ = .38; SD = .14), Wechsler profiles ($\overline{ES}$ = –.20; SD = .57), stimulant drug treatment ($\overline{ES}$ = .58; SD = .61), and diet intervention ($\overline{ES}$ = .12; SD = .42). With the exception of the correlational analyses (where a standard deviation approximately half as great as the magnitude of association is considerable), in each other instance, the phenomenon exhibited greater variability than effect; on average, the effect size was consistently one-half as large as the standard deviation of effect size. This means that from one situation to the next, the effect of any phenomenon can vary from negative to zero to positive over a wide range. This variability means that LD lacks the precision to make it scientific.

The variability makes the LD phenomenon essentially unpredictable. In an effort to harness, at least, some of the variability, meta-analysis techniques attempt to determine if some study feature might correlate significantly with effect size. If a particular characteristic (e.g., age, sex, IQ level, diagnosis, treatment duration, *SES* level, setting, or the like) could be discovered that correlated substantially with *ES*, then it would be possible to predict (albeit somewhat inaccurately) a more circumscribed expectation for some LD phenomenon. Unfortunately, none of the LD phenomena studied yielded correlations of a magnitude that would permit useful prediction even in this limited sense. The reason is that the intervening variables that set the boundaries of the system remain as "intervening" in the sense that they defy description within a theoretical context (Rudner, 1966).

The variability and unpredictability of LD phenomena suggest that it is not "perfect" knowledge (Bergmann, 1957; Brodbeck, 1962) which is characterized by complete and closed scientific laws wherein the value of any one phenomenon at any one time can be calculated by means of these laws. The empiricism of LD that builds a foundation on empirical associations not embedded within a theoretical structure suggests that LD is "imperfect" knowledge with its understandings neither complete nor closed. The field of LD possesses no scientific laws; it is essentially indeterminate. The consequences for LD are found in an inability to operate on the bases of scientific prescription, that is, a course of action based on particular circumstances. Phenomena in LD simply cannot be reduced to a simple set of input–output relationships (e.g., do *A* in circumstances *X* and *Y*, and do *B* in circumstance *Z*).

The LD field, thus, needs to be treated as an enterprise that is unlawful, unpredictable, and unknowable in the complete and closed sense in which scientists speak. Because its empirical associations are derived from a sample only representative of the phenomenon, the explanations provided by LDs empiricism are inconclusive and introduce a degree of uncertainty. This uncertainty introduces "risk" (Kaplan, 1964) into the process, as represented by the random elements found in the system. Although it is possible to provide an expectation (as in meta-analysis findings, for example), the "risk" inherent in the system makes any action uncertain, particularly in cases of individuals as opposed to groups.

The uncertainty in LD precludes rational action in the scientific sense. Although LD has learned to cope with its uncertainty (Glass, 1979), its empiricism suggests that research findings (i.e., empirical associations) not anchored in a theoretical system do not automatically apply in the real world. Phillips (1980) termed this distinction the *is/ought* dichotomy: research findings take an *is* form (i.e., *X* is *Y*) while pragmatic implications, because of the uncertainty, take an *ought* form (i.e., *A* ought to do *B* to *C*). Simon (1969) made a similar distinction between state and process descriptions; the former characterizes knowledge while the latter characterizes the knowledge acted upon. Difficulties arise, however, because there is no necessary process description from a state description, or, in relation to the earlier distinction, no *ought* from an *is*.

Simon (1969) suggested that actions should be based on information that reduces the distinction between an existing state and a desired state. Within a complete and closed scientific system, this is achieved through means–ends analysis that permits precise and accurate actions. But without the theoretical connections found in the physical sciences, the LD field must use means–ends analyses that are based on a "minimax" criterion, that is, acting so as to minimize the maximum loss which might be incurred. This criterion represents a pessimistic attitude that is unlike the "minimim" criterion (Scriven, 1958) of the physical sciences that emphasizes a strategy to minimize the minimum risk. Because of its variability and unpredictability (and the realization of this), LD cannot adopt the minimim criterion that results in optimization methods for explanation and prediction. Instead, the LD field is left with "satisficing" (Simon, 1969) methods that provide sufficient but not necessary conditions for actions. Until the LD field moves away from its empiricism and demands a more scientific stance that incorporates a fully developed theoretical system, it will not be able to specify the necessary as well as the sufficient conditions which are the essence of science.

Conclusion

Although a relatively new entry into the special education community, LD has produced a voluminous data base. But the quantity of data has not resulted in scientific knowledge; instead, LD has resulted in empiricism that has made it a pseudoscience. Its research findings have produced only empirical associations that are not rationally connected to concepts at a theoretical level. Consequently, LD has not integrated its empirical knowledge into a conceptual whole that would permit the explication of laws useful for explanation and prediction. Even the quantitative synthesis of research findings cannot completely unify the LD field because the lack of a theoretical system introduces a measure of variability and unpredictability that has been difficult to harness in any precise manner. Thus, any pragmatic action is uncertain because a measure of certainty is only possible within the boundaries of a complete and closed scientific system. The empiricism of LD must be replaced by a more scientific posture if we are to remove the pseudo-modifier from the present science of LD.

3
Learning Disability: A Victim of Its Own History

The history of the field of LD has been influenced by a variety of events contributing to its development. The differing perspectives of the individuals involved led to varied interpretations of how LD should be defined. A group of children had been identified as having LD but the parameters delineating the conditions remained in dispute. Consequently, the LD field still had a fundamental problem of finding an acceptable definition (Cruickshank, 1972). This problem is reflected in the lack of compliance with federal definitions by federally funded projects (Mann, Davis, Boyer, Metz, & Wolford, 1983), with diversity found in state definitions of LD (Gillespie, Miller, & Fielder, 1975; Mercer, Forgnone, & Wolking, 1976), and with disparate professional opinions about the scope of definitional statements (McDonald, 1968; Vaughan & Hodges, 1973; Tucker, Stevens & Ysseldyke, 1983). The lack of definitional consensus impedes scientific progress because it is possible for economic and administrative functions to operate without precise definition but not research functions related to theory development (Senf, 1977). This is because no standard identification criteria emerge without consensus about definition, which prevents the target population (i.e., LD) from being clearly identified. The problems in specifying who is being studied makes it difficult to integrate research findings because the basic requirements for scientific progress—replication and generalization—are not met (Morrison, MacMillan & Kavale, in press).

Lovitt and Jenkins (1979) found a lack of uniform reporting in defining the selected LD populations. There was a lack of consistency with respect to information concerning situational, demographic, instructional, and motivational variables, making it difficult to replicate and implement study findings. Similar conclusions were reached in other reviews (Harber, 1981; Olson & Mealor, 1981; Torgesen & Dice, 1980) finding serious problems in sampling which were compounded by a failure to adequately describe the obtained LD samples. For example, Kavale and Nye (1981), in a survey of 307 LD research studies, found that 50% of the studies defined their LD samples on the basis of previous classification or diagnosis. In most cases, neither the criteria nor the extent to which a subject met the criteria was reported. With the difficulties found in federal, state, and professional definitions of LD, selection presumably based upon these definitions would appear to be less than satisfactory. Yet, about 20% of LD research studies used an intact or established definition based upon federal or state criteria for LD. Analysis of the intact or established definitions found that a majority (68%) was taken from state definitions while 32% were based upon federal definitions. The most popular federal definition was an approximation of the *National Advisory Committee on Handicapped Children* (NACHC) (1968) definition (74%) while the remaining definitions were related to PL 94–142 (*Education for All Handicapped Children Act*) (1975). These findings led to the conclusion that

> The LD research literature surveyed presented a divergent perspective of learning disabilities as illustrated by the identification criteria employed in LD research studies. This marked variability prevented any narrowing of the focus of LD identification criteria resulting in heterogeneous samples of children labeled LD (Kavale & Nye, 1981, p. 387).

The failure to integrate research findings suggests that the expansive LD literature (Black, 1974b) has not moved the field closer to resolution of the definitional problem. The consequences of not providing an acceptable definition is a split among theory and practice that makes the LD category over-inclusive because of "the well-intentioned tendency to accept under the LD rubric all persons who have any potential claim of possessing this disabling condition" (Senf, 1977, p. 538).

Definitions of LD: An Overview

The LD field has not provided a definition acceptable to a broad constituency but has implicitly acknowledged the problem by proposing different definitions. Over the past 40 years, definitions of LD have reflected the different conceptions in vogue at the time. To provide perspective, the development of LD definitions will be traced to the present.

a. Brain Injury Stage

The initial emphasis grew out of the work of Strauss and Werner who defined the characteristics of the brain injured child and the consequent disturbances in learning ability. Strauss and Lehtinen (1947) defined a brain-injured child as

the child who before, during or after birth has received an injury to or suffered an infection of the brain. As a result of such organic impairment, defects of the neuromotor system may be present or absent; however, such a child may show disturbances in perception, thinking, and emotional behavior, either separately or in combination. This disturbance can be demonstrated by specific tests. These disturbances prevent or impede a normal learning process (p. 4).

With this definition, Strauss and Lehtinen (1947) also established biological and behavioral criteria for delineating brain injury. Strauss (Strauss & Kephart, 1955) later suggested that brain injury could be diagnosed solely on the basis of behavioral criteria (i.e., perceptual difficulties, conceptual difficulties, and behavioral disorders) without reference to biological criteria (i.e., neurological signs, history indicating neurological injury, and no mental retardation). The Strauss and Lehtinen definition was widely accepted because it related the problems manifested by a group of children with learning problems to known or supposed brain damage and described a recognizable combination of symptoms displayed by children with demonstrable brain damage.

Despite the wide acceptance of the Strauss and Lehtinen definition, objection was raised to their terminology. The definition of brain injury was not a narrowly defined category but, rather, a broad and elastic categorization spanning a continuum from children with gross brain injury easily documented to children with slight brain injury not easily documented but assumed to be present because of the presence of behavioral criteria. Because of the wide spectrum of conditions associated with brain injury, Sarason (1949) suggested that the Strauss and Lehtinen definition results in tautological reasoning since "The logically minded may of course object to a reasoning which appears to go like this: Some individuals with known brain damage have certain behavioral characteristics, therefore individuals with these same behavioral characteristics must be presumed to be brain damaged" (p. 415).

Stevens and Birch (1957) raised four objections to the use of the term brain injured:

1. The term is an etiological concept and does not appropriately describe the symptom complex.

2. The term is associated with other conditions, some of which have no relation to the symptom complex commonly referred to as "brain injury."

3. The term does not help in the development of sound therapeutic approaches.

4. The term is not descriptive since it is a generic expression, the use of which results in oversimplification.

Wortis (1957) suggested that the concept of "brain injury" was faulty and misleading; this idea was echoed by Birch (1964), who differentiated the *fact* of brain damage, any anatomic or physiological alteration of the brain, from the *concept* of brain damage, a pattern of behavioral disturbance not necessarily applicable to all children who are, in fact, brain damaged.

The difficulties surrounding the term "brain damage" led Stevens and Birch (1957) to suggest the term "Strauss syndrome" to describe the symptom complex associated with presumed brain damage. The syndrome may be defined by any or most of the following observable characteristics:

1. erratic and inappropriate behavior on mild provocation
2. poor organization of behavior
3. increased motor activity disproportionate to the stimulus
4. distractibility of more than ordinary degree under ordinary conditions
5. persistent faulty perceptions
6. persistent hyperactivity
7. awkwardness and consistently poor motor performance

The delineation of the "Strauss syndrome" (brain damage behavior syndrome) shifted the focus away from brain damage as an etiological concept to those behavioral characteristics defining the child with "brain damage." Thus the negative connotation and irreversibility of the brain damage condition were de-emphasized. Although the original description of the brain damage condition pertained to moderate and severe levels of neurologic disorder, the shift extended the brain damage concept to relatively borderline disturbances only suggestive of brain damage. Strauss and Lehtinen (1947) also recognized this possibility by referring to "minor brain damage" and "minimal brain injury" whereby, "behavior and learning . . . may be affected by minimal brain injuries without apparent lowering of the intelligence level" (p. 128). The exogenous group was subsequently enlarged "to include the clinical syndrome of the brain-injured child who is not mentally defective, but who in spite of 'normalcy in IQ' as tested is still 'defective' " (Strauss & Kephart, 1955, p. ix) in the sense of school learning problems related to uneven development of cognitive skills and behavior problems presumed to be due to brain injury.

b. The Minimal Brain Injury Stage

The clinical psychiatric literature had long recognized a condition of minor brain impairment which affected academic and behavioral functioning (Strother, 1973). The precursor was found in Gessell's concept of "minimal cerebral injury" (Gessell & Amatruda, 1941) which was suggested to explain atypical development because of clinically subtle, but behaviorally significant damage to the brain. The concept of minimal brain damage was subsequently elaborated by Pasamanick and Knobloch (1959), who defined it as "minor but clearly defined deviations from the normal neurological and behavioral developmental patterns, usually with more or less complete compensation by 15 to 18 months of age, as determined by the standard neurological examination" (p. 1384).

The minor nature of brain damage was emphasized by the addition of "minimal" as a modifying adjective (Paine, 1962). A problem remained, however, because "Regardless of any adjectives, we have the overriding obligation to demonstrate, in terms of replicable, valid, and clearly defined criteria, that the multiplicity of aberrant behaviors we now attribute to 'minimal brain damage' are, in fact, the result of damage to the brain" (Birch, 1964, p. 5). This could not be accomplished and, consequently, the same objections to the term "brain damage" were equally applicable to "minimal brain damage." The modifier "minimal" did little to alter the perception that the inherent difficulties are the result of injury to the CNS, even though it is not possible to specify the nature of that injury.

Since brain injury was difficult to infer from behavioral signs alone, there was a suggestion that "damage" should be replaced by "dysfunction" (Bax & MacKeith, 1963), which indicates that brain injury may be present even with "as yet unnamed subtle deviations of brain function" (Clements & Peters, 1962). The additional modification to "dysfunction" carried the implication that there could be no structural change in the brain but, rather, only deviation of function. Thus, the original "brain damage" idea evolved into "minimal brain dysfunction" (MBD), suggesting a subclinical impairment of brain functioning without the negative connotations associated with the term "brain damage."

The term MBD presumably referred to symptomatology involving specific areas of the brain but in a mild or subclinical form not affecting overall intellectual functioning. The term, however, described a variety of conditions grouped under the general rubric "MBD" when damage was not severe enough to warrant inclusion in an established category suggesting brain damage. In an attempt to bring order to the confusion surrounding terminology and symptomatology, a task force was launched to interpret the nomenclature. The results were reported by Clements (1966), who defined minimal brain dysfunction (MBD) as a state descriptive of

> children of near average, average, or above average general intelligence with certain learning or behavioral disabilities ranging from mild to severe, which are associated with deviations of functions of the central nervous system.
> These deviations may manifest themselves by various combinations of impair-

ment in perception, conceptualization, language, memory, and control of attention, impulse, or motor function. The aberrations may arise from genetic variation, biochemical irregularities, perinatal brain insults, or other illnesses or injuries sustained during the years which are critical for the development and maturation of CNS or from unknown causes . . . . During the school years, a variety of learning disabilities is the most prominent manifestation of the condition which can be designated by this term (pp. 9–10).

In reviewing the symptomatology associated with MBD, Clements (1966) listed the 10 most frequently cited characteristics, in order of frequency:
1. hyperactivity
2. perceptual–motor impairments
3. emotional lability
4. general coordination deficits
5. disorder of attention (short attention span, distractibility, perseveration)
6. impulsivity
7. disorders of memory and thinking
8. specific learning disabilities:
    a. reading
    b. arithmetic
    c. writing
    d. spelling
9. disorders of speech and hearing
10. equivocal neurological signs and EEG irregularities

With the publication of Clements' (1966) report, MBD achieved wide currency and became synonymous with the learning difficulties experienced by some children in school. Although imprecise, the MBD concept left little doubt that the etiology of the associated learning and behavioral problems was some sub-clinical aberration in the CNS which emphasized the role of organicity in the problems manifested.

Controversy over the MBD concept continued but it regained popularity with the publication of Wender's (1971) report which further elaborated the MBD syndrome by delineating six primary areas of dysfunction:

1. Motor behavior characterized by high activity level (hyperactivity) and impaired coordination (dyspraxia).

2. Attentional and perceptual–cognitive function characterized by a short attention span and poor concentration (distractibility).

3. Learning difficulties, particularly in learning to read, write, and spell even with normal intelligence.

4. Impulse control characterized by a decreased ability to inhibit; marked by low frustration tolerance and antisocial behavior.

5. Interpersonal relations characterized by increased resistance to social demands.

6. Emotionality characterized by increased lability, altered reactivity (responses normal in kind but abnormal in degree), increased aggressiveness, increased irritability, depression, and low self-esteem.

Through the efforts of Clements (1966) and Wender (1971) in the medical community, the learning problems manifested by children in school were now linked to the MBD condition. Within the educational domain, the MBD concept was incorporated by Myklebust (1968) in the definition of "psychoneurological learning disability," a condition wherein the difficulty in learning is the "result of a dysfunction in the brain and the problem is one of altered processes, not of a generalized incapacity to learn."

The MBD concept, however, was subject to criticism in the educational community because it reflected a medical–etiological perspective rather than an educational focus concerned with assessment and remedial techniques for learning problems. Therefore, concomitant with efforts in the medical community to define and delineate MBD were efforts in the educational community to provide an educational focus to the problem. As early as 1962, Kirk (1962) introduced the term "learning disability."

The Educational Discrepancy Stage

The educational focus was most clearly seen in definitions of LD which emphasized difficulties in academic achievement. Bateman (1965) emphasized a discrepancy dimension, a difference between estimated capacity and actual achievement, in the definition of *learning disorders.*

> Children who have learning disorders are those who manifest an educationally significant discrepancy between their estimated intellectual potential and actual level of performance related to basic disorders in the learning process, which may or may not be accompanied by demonstrable central nervous system dysfunction, and which are not secondary to generalized mental retardation, educational or cultural deprivation, severe emotional disturbance, or sensory loss (p. 220).

The emphasis on academic difficulties was echoed by Kirk (1968) in a definition that focused on behavioral manifestations by defining LD as a "specific retardation or disorder in one or more of the processes of speech, language, perception, behavior, reading, spelling, or arithmetic" (pp. 1–2). The *Association for Children with Learning Disabilities* (ACLD) (1967) adopted the following definition, omitting reference to etiology and emphasizing the learning problems, "A child with learning disabilities is one with adequate mental ability, sensory processes, and emotional stability who has specific deficits in perceptual, integrative, or expressive processes which severely impair learning efficiency."

An *Institute for Advanced Study* (Kass & Myklebust, 1969) was convened to evolve a definition that would be behavioral in nature and advantageous for special education personnel. The following definition was developed:

> Learning disability refers to one or more significant deficits in essential learning processes requiring special education techniques for remediation. Children with learning disability generally demonstrate a discrepancy between expected and actual achievement in one or more areas, such as spoken, read, or written language, mathematics, and spatial orientation. The learning disability referred to is not primarily the result of sensory, motor, intellectual, or emotional handicap, or lack of opportunity to learn (pp. 378–379).

Thus, the education community shifted LD definitions away from an etiological focus to a behavioral focus emphasizing the primary difficulty—reduced learning performance manifested in academic achievement deficits. In an effort to broaden an LD definition, Gallagher (1966) suggested that the emphasis should not be on specific abilities but rather on ability patterns. The definition proposed was for children with *developmental imbalances*, "who reveal a developmental disparity in psychological processes related to education of such a degree (often four years or more) as to require the instructional programming of developmental tasks appropriate to the nature and level of the deviant developmental process" (p. 28). Because of a perceived overgeneralization of LD characteristics which tends to weaken both the quality and quantity of LD characteristics, Kass (1977) proposed the term *dyssymbolia* as a professional label and definition for LD. The term is defined as follows:

> The handicap of dyssymbolia is characterized by extreme deviance in the acquisition and use of symbols in reading, writing, computing, listening, or talking; such deviance is due to an interaction between significant deficits in developmental functions and environmental conditions which make the individual vulnerable to those dysfunctions (p. 426).

d. The Legislative Stage

The two strands of professionals, medical and educational, attempting to provide a definition of LD, produced a variety of definitions differing in form and content. The need for a single definition was recognized when the *Bureau of Education for Handicapped* (BEH) was made responsible for funding services for LD children. The search for an acceptable definition became the responsibility of the NACHC, headed by Samuel A. Kirk. The definition formulated by this group was incorporated into Public Law 91–230 *Children with Specific Learning Disabilities Act* (1969). This definition stated:

> Children with special (specific) learning disabilities exhibit a disorder in one or more of the basic psychological processes involved in understanding or using

spoken or written language. These may be manifested in disorders of listening, thinking, talking, reading, writing, spelling, or arithmetic. They include conditions which have been referred to as perceptual handicaps, brain injury, minimal brain dysfunction, dyslexia, developmental aphasia, etc. They do not include learning problems which are due primarily to visual, hearing, or motor handicaps, to mental retardation, emotional disturbance or to environmental disadvantage (NACHC, 1968, p. 34).

The NACHC definition established the LD field as a category of special education and served the purpose of providing a framework for establishing LD programs. Although these administrative concerns were important, the NACHC definition failed to provide a clear delineation of LD parameters which was functional for educational classification and intervention. McIntosh and Dunn (1973) found six inherent problems in the NACHC definition.

1. The definition specifies no level of severity for the disability.

2. Bateman's (1965) discrepancy idea was not incorporated.

3. The inclusion of the phrase "one or more" in describing process disturbances is at variance with the modifier "specific."

4. The variety of children and conditions included precludes the establishment of an LD syndrome, a group of common characteristics.

5. The conditions associated with LD are not specified; the definition provides only examples.

6. The definition relies upon exclusion to define the LD population, even though children classified in other traditional handicapping conditions may also have a specific learning disability.

Hammill (1974) argued that the NACHC definition was too general and ambiguous. Myers and Hammill (1976) analyzed the definition and when several vague and superfluous phrases were deleted, the resulting definition would be, "Children with special learning disabilities exhibit problems in listening, thinking, reading, writing, spelling and/or arithmetic" (p. 10). Such a definition is not acceptable since it defines "exceptional children" in general rather than LD in particular and might include a majority of students in some school systems. Thus, the definitional problem had not been solved with the NACHC definition but it did aid the administrative considerations of funding, program development, and keeping areas of exceptionality mutually exclusive.

Because of the vagueness of the NACHC definition, it remained difficult to define a learning disability because the category became a "catch-all" for children excluded previously from the other traditional categories of exceptionality.

More Proposed Definitions

The lack of consensus regarding LD definitions led to a variety of proposed definitions attempting to remedy the perceived deficiencies in existing LD definitions. In an effort to narrow the focus of existing open-ended definitions and provide a more functional basis for LD, McIntosh and Dunn (1973) offered the following definition.

> Children with major specific learning disabilities (MSLDs) are those 1.0 to 2.0 percent of the school population (1) who display one primary severe or moderately severe discrepancy between capacity and performance in a specific basic learning process involving perception, conception, or expression associated with the areas of oral and written language or mathematics; (2) yet whose MSLDs are neither mental retardation nor any of the other traditional handicapping conditions; (3) but who may have one or more additional, secondary traditional or specific learning disabilities to a milder degree; (4) none of whom have MSLDs that can be adequately treated in the regular school program even when special education consultant-helping teacher services are extensively provided; (5) half or more of whom, therefore, will require more intensive special education instruction under such administrative plans as the resource room, the combined resource room and special class, the special class, and the special day and boarding school; and (6) yet any of whom may also require other remedial and special education services to deal with their secondary tertiary or specific learning disabilities (p. 542).

Kirk and Gallagher (1983) suggested that three criteria must exist before a child can be classified as having a *specific learning disability*. The three criteria are (1) discrepancy, (2) exclusion, and (3) special education, all of which were incorporated into the following definition:

> A specific learning disability is a psychological or neurological impediment to spoken or written language, or perceptual, cognitive, or motor behavior. The impediment (1) is manifested by discrepancies among specific behaviors and achievement or between evidenced ability and academic achievement, (2) is of such nature and extent that the child does not learn by the instructional methods and materials appropriate for the majority of children and requires specialized procedures for development, and (3) is not primarily due to severe mental retardation, sensory handicaps, emotional problems, or lack of opportunity to learn (p. 285).

A different approach to defining LD attempted to focus on teaching rather than characteristics of children. The rationale is based upon the view that the most significant variable surrounds instruction, that is, how a child is taught. Information gained from intellectual, neurological, perceptual, and personality testing is useful for delineating characteristics but is not functional for teaching (Hewett & Forness, 1983). Reynolds and Birch (1977) suggested that formula-based definitions of LD are too rigid since they remove professional insight and judgment. Consequently, the focus should be upon the child and the practical matter of teaching that child. These ideas were incorporated into the suggestion (Hallahan & Kauffman, 1976) that the term "learning disabilities" be used as a concept rather than as a specific category of special education. Hallahan and Kauffman (1976) suggested

> Literally, learning disabilities is a term indicating *learning problems in one or more areas of development of ability*, and this definition is common to ED, LD, and EMR alike. Because children placed in each of these categories all have learning problems, "learning disabilities" can provide a much needed unifying theme whose emphasis is upon specific behavior, abilities, and disabilities of the child (p. 41).

Although none of these proposed definitions or modifications were widely accepted, discussion over the term "learning disability" is useful because it directs attention to a particular problem (Ross, 1976). Such attention is necessary to prevent professionals in different disciplines from viewing the problem from their own perspectives. Consequently, the search for a definition continued, with more emphasis placed on attempts to operationalize the parameters of LD.

e. The Operational Definition Stage

Operational definitions were assumed to possess the advantage of converting theoretical concepts into specific quantified terms meaningful for special education practitioners. Kerlinger (1973) suggested that an operational definition assigns meaning to a construct or a variable by specifying the activities or "operations" necessary to measure it. "An operational definition is a sort of manual of instructions to the investigator. It says, in effect, 'Do such-and-such in so-and-so a manner' " (p. 31).

Chalfant and King (1976) analyzed LD definitions and found five common components including: task failure, exclusion factors, physiological correlates, discrepancy, and psychological correlates. For each component, operational criteria were presented. The most difficult component to operationalize was psychological process, which Chalfant and King (1974) conceptualized within an information processing model encompassing sensory input, response output, and psychological processes. The psychological processes included attention, discrimination (auditory, visual, haptic), memory, sensory integration, concept formation, and problem solving.

Brenton and Gilmore (1976) provided an operational definition of discrepancy between intellectual capacity and academic performance to assist in the identification of LD. The discrepancy was based upon a comparison of adjusted Mental Age (MA), based upon the Wechsler Intelligence Scale for Children–Full Scale IQ corrected to the lower limit of the standard error of measurement at the 95% level of confidence, and subtest scores from the *Peabody Individual Achievement Test* (Mathematics, Reading Recognition, Reading Comprehension, and Spelling).

Schere, Richardson, and Bialer (1980) provided an operational definition of LD which attempted to relate LD to educational processes, specifically day-to-day learning and management issues. They argued that this is best accomplished by not excluding children whose learning problems are compounded only by mild levels of mental retardation, emotional disturbance, or physical handicaps and by not over-emphasizing etiology. The proposed operational definition included four of the components discussed by Chalfant and King (1974) but excluded physiology since LD was viewed as having multiple causes. Schere et al. (1980) proposed the following operational definition:

> Learning disability refers to an academic deficit accompanied by a disorder in one or more of the basic psychological processes involved in understanding or in using language — spoken or written — in a child whose intellectual, emotional, and/or physical status allows participation in a traditional academic curriculum (p. 9).

Although operational definitions hold promise, they possess difficulties which hinder their usefulness. Among the pragmatic difficulties are (1) the lack of reliable and valid tests to assess psychological processes, (2) the problems associated with measuring intellectual ability (MA) for determining discrepancy, (3) the problem of setting criteria for severity levels of academic and process functioning at different grade levels, and (4) the problems of setting criteria for academic discrepancy at the primary levels. Additionally, the operational approach has been criticized on theoretical grounds (Deese, 1972) because the insistence on making concrete concepts out of those that were abstract substitutes the appearance of rigor for explicit theoretical verification. Given an operational approach, Deese (1972) concluded that, "At best what our example may have accomplished is a low grade of psychometric engineering and at worst a systematic fraud" (p. 10).

More Legislative Definitions

The influential *Project on the Classification of Exceptional Children* (Hobbs, 1975) attempted to synthesize the knowledge regarding the classification and labeling of handicapped children. A number of distinguished panels were convened to discuss the issues in the classification of exceptional children. The committee studying LD proposed the following definition:

> Specific learning disability refers to those children of any age who demonstrate a substantial deficiency in a particular aspect of academic achievement because of perceptual or perceptual-motor handicaps, regardless of etiology or other contributing factors (Wepman, Cruickshank, Deutsch, Morency & Strother, 1975, p. 306).

The Wepman et al. (1975) definition attempted to eliminate many of the difficulties found in previous definitions. The focus of the LD problem was centered upon perception, that is, difficulties in organizing and interpreting sensory information. Additionally, there is no inherent etiological explanation for the LD condition; there exists a variety of possible causes but no one is primary. Finally, the definition includes no exclusion clause which broadens the LD parameters to include other handicapping conditions.

Neither the operational definition nor the Hobbs' task force definition ever gained wide popularity, which left the NACHC definition as the standard. The next major LD definition was proposed in Public Law 94-142 *The Education for All Handicapped Children Act* (1975). This law defined LD as follows:

> Specific learning disability means a disorder in one or more of the basic psychological processes involved in understanding or in using language, spoken or written, which may manifest itself in an imperfect ability to listen, think, speak, read, write, spell, or to do mathematical calculations. The term includes such conditions as perceptual handicaps, brain injury, minimal brain dysfunction, dyslexia, and developmental aphasia. The term does not include children who have learning problems which are primarily the result of visual, hearing, or motor handicaps, of mental retardation, of emotional disturbance, or of environmental, cultural, or economic disadvantage (Section 5B-4).

Comparison with the NACHC (1968) definition finds no substantive differences in the PL 94-142 definition. The primary reason for this was found in the conflicting nature of the reported LD research. In the Congressional testimony, a Congressman indicated that since there are 53 basic learning disabilities and 99 minimal brain dysfunctions, "No one really knows what a learning disability is" (Congressional Record, 1975). Consequently, until research establishes more definitive parameters, it was recommended that no major legislative changes be made in LD definitions. Thus, only minor modifications in the NACHC (1968) definition were introduced in the new standard definition of LD.

Although the "new" LD definition did not offer any real substantive changes, the USOE attempted to clarify the law and to provide procedural guidelines for interpretation. The major dimension considered to define LD was a "major discrepancy between expected achievement and ability which is not the result of other known and generally accepted handicapping conditions or circumstances" (U.S. Office of Education, 1976, 52404). A discrepancy was presumed to exist when a child was achieving at or below the expected achievement level which was based upon a formula for determining a severe discrepancy level (SDL).

Sulzbacher and Kenowitz (1977) believed that the new rules reflected "the most eclectic and flexible approach that the U.S. Office of Education could take and still have a workable definition" (p. 67). A different view was taken by Lloyd, Sabatino, Miller, and Miller (1977) who raised several questions regarding the federal guidelines. A primary problem was perceived to be the consequence of the procedures being based upon numerous value decisions. These negative evaluations of the formula-based procedure led the USOE to drop the formula from consideration with the revised federal rules suggesting that LD classification be based upon the vague notion of an already existing severe discrepancy between capacity and achievement:

(1) the child does not achieve commensurate with his or her age and ability when provided with appropriate educational experiences, and (2) the child has a severe discrepancy between achievement and intellectual ability in one or more of seven areas relating to communication skills and mathematics abilities (USOE, 1977, 65083).

Evaluation procedures must be conducted by an interdisciplinary team which includes (1) the child's regular teacher (or a qualified substitute), and (2) at least one individual qualified to conduct an individual diagnostic examination. The child must be evaluated in the following areas:

(1) oral expression, (2) listening comprehension, (3) written expression, (4) basic reading skill, (5) reading comprehension, (6) mathematical calculation, or (7) mathematical reasoning (USOE, 1977, 65083).

A child may not be identified as LD if the team determines that the discrepancy is *primarily* the result of: (1) a visual, hearing, or motor handicap; (2) mental retardation; (3) emotional disturbance; or (4) environmental, cultural, or economic disadvantage (USOE, 1977, 65083).

Thus, after several years of modification intended to improve the definition of LD, the final regulations endorsed a definition which left the NACHC's (1968) definition essentially intact. After almost 10 years, the LD definition remained formally unchanged.

The most recent attempt at formulating an LD definition was attempted by the *National Joint Committee for Learning Disabilities (NJCLD)*, comprised of individuals from six major organizations concerned with LD. The *NJCLD* believed that the PL 94–142 LD definition possessed inherent weaknesses which limited its usefulness for the LD field. Hammill, Leigh, McNutt, and Larsen (1981) outlined the perceived difficulties in the NACHC and PL 94–142 definitions:

1. The use of the term *children* is unnecessarily restrictive with respect to age since the LD field has recently expanded to include adolescent and adult levels.

2. The phrase *basic psychological processes* has generated considerable debate and should be eliminated in favor of a statement worded to indicate that the cause of LD is intrinsic to the affected person. This phrasing would probably result in less polarization and be more acceptable regardless of theoretical positions concerning the status of *basic psychological processing*.

3. Since the U.S. Office of Education (1977) eliminated "spelling" as a specific manifestation because it was subsumed under other areas of functioning (written expression), its inclusion in a definition would be redundant.

4. Because LD definitions have included reference to related

"conditions" (e.g., perceptual handicap, dyslexia, minimal brain dysfunction) which have caused controversy and confusion, the *NJCLD* believed misinterpretation could be avoided by removing these labels from any definition of LD.

5. The "exclusion" clause has been misinterpreted as suggesting that LD cannot occur in conjunction with other handicapping or adverse environmental conditions. In fact, while LD cannot be the primary or direct result of such conditions, it is possible for LD to be either secondary or combined with other conditions. Thus, the ambiguity found in PL 94-142 required clarification.

The definition issued by the *NJCLD* was basically a theoretical statement specifying the characteristics delineating the LD condition. The *NJCLD* (1981) definition is as follows:

> Learning disabilities is a generic term that refers to a heterogeneous group of disorders manifested by significant difficulties in the acquisition and use of listening, speaking, reading, writing, reasoning, or mathematical abilities. These disorders are intrinsic to the individual and presumed to be due to central nervous system dysfunction. Even though a learning disability may occur concomitantly with other handicapping conditions (e.g., sensory impairment, mental retardation, social and emotional disturbance) or environmental influences (e.g., cultural differences, insufficient/inappropriate instruction, psychological factors), it is not the direct result of those conditions or influences.

The influence of the *NJCLD* definition on policy is unclear; its purpose was to establish LD theoretically but there remains the practical task of specifying operational identification criteria. The real test will be whether abstract notions can be implemented in administrative rules and regulations acceptable to a broad constituency.

A Perspective on the Problem of LD Definitions

Although the lack of a standard LD definition has negative implications, the LD field appears to have reached a *status quo*: definitional modifications have appeared, but no major changes have occurred. Without a standard definition, a child experiencing academic problems is often described as being *like* an LD child. With no consensual basis for comparison, it becomes fact that the child *is* LD, and, consequently, the simile becomes the metaphor (Smith & Polloway, 1979). The problems surrounding definitions of LD lead to the question: Why has the LD field experienced so much difficulty in providing a definition acceptable to a broad constituency?

We believe that possible answers can be found in the history of the LD field. Weiderholt (1974) traced the development of the LD field and described the major influences in its formation. Although marked by a variety of early theories, the most important were provided by the seminal work of Alfred Strauss, Heinz Werner, and their colleagues at the Wayne County Training School (Strauss & Kephart, 1955; Strauss & Lehtinen, 1947). From their foundation work with the brain-injured, mentally retarded child, there was an evolution to the present-day LD field that incorporated Strauss and Werner's concepts into formulations about the nature of LD. It is by examining the theoretical ideas of Strauss and Werner that insights can be gleaned suggesting why the definitional problem remains at the core of the LD field's difficulties.

The Exogenous Versus Endogenous Distinction

From their program of basic research into the effects of brain injury, Strauss and Werner laid the cornerstone for the entire LD field. In a summary volume (Strauss & Lehtinen, (1947), findings related to the nature and characteristics of exogenous (brain injured) versus endogenous (familiar-cultural) mentally retarded (MR) children were described as well as implications for educational programming. In a subsequent volume (Strauss & Kephart, 1955), the concepts related to exogenous MR children were extended to children with normal levels of intelligence. Here, the brain damage behavior syndrome was described in terms of disturbed perception, disordered conceptual processes, language disabilities, thinking disorders, attention deficits, and behavioral problems that were similar to the fundamental pathological characteristics found in the brain-injured adult (Strauss & Werner, 1943). This syndrome became accepted as the prototype of brain injury and was slowly transformed into concepts describing what is now termed LD.

Although controversy centered upon the efficacy of the exogenous and endogenous classifications (Sarason, 1949), the behavioral differences between these groups were generally accepted. The studies reported by Strauss and Werner, however, did not typically involve rigorous statistical analysis but rather, reported data descriptively (most usually as mean or percentage differences). As a result, it is unclear the extent to which these groups differed along the behavioral dimensions investigated. To clarify this situation, we decided to synthesize quantitatively the research of Strauss and Werner investigating the magnitude of the behavioral differences between exogenous and endogenous children and, consequently, the validity of their generalizations regarding the consequences of brain injury.

The methods of meta-analysis (Glass, 1976, 1977: Glass, McGaw & Smith, 1981) were used to integrate statistically the research studies of Strauss and Werner into a comprehensive summary. Meta-analysis is based on the "effect size" (*ES*) statistic defined by $ES = \bar{X}en - \bar{X}ex/SDen$ where $\bar{X}en$ = average score of the endogenous group, $\bar{X}ex$ = average score of the exogenous group, and SDen = standard deviation of the endogenous group. The calculated *ES* statistic thus describes group differences with a common metric (standard deviation units) and makes comparisons based upon different outcome variables feasible. In the absence of fundamental descriptive statistics, Glass et al. (1981) provided statistical procedures for reconstructing *ES*s from other summary data.

An *ES* may be interpreted as a z-score and its meaning translated into notions of overlapping distributions and comparable percentages. For example, suppose that a comparison between groups *X* and *Y* finds group *X* superior with an *ES* of + 1.00. This would indicate that the average subject in group *X* would be at the 84th percentile of the comparison group *Y* who are at the 50th percentile. The obtained *ES* of + 1.00 indicates a superiority of one standard deviation for group *X* where the average child is superior to 84% of the comparison group *Y*, while only 16% of group *Y* reveal performance levels superior to the average child in group *X*.

a. Exogenous Versus Endogenous Across Studies

The data for this meta-analysis was found in 26 studies conducted by Strauss, Werner, and colleagues that compared exogenous and endogenous children and contained data appropriate for calculating the *ES* statistic. Because Strauss and Werner sampled from the same population at the Wayne County Training School, it was difficult to determine the total number of subjects from which the samples were drawn, but the 26 studies typically included samples ranging from 30 to 50 subjects. The exogenous and endogenous groups with mean IQs of 67.42 and 68.45, respectively, and mean ages of 13.39 and 13.35, respectively, did not differ significantly for either IQ (t(25) = .660, *p* < .30) or age (t(10) = .054, *p* > .50). A correlational analysis between *ES* and both age (r = .083) and IQ (r = .117) revealed nonsignificant correlations. These findings suggest that neither IQ nor age were factors related to any obtained group differences between exogenous and endogenous groups.

The 24 studies yielded 241 *ES* measurements with an $\overline{ES}$ (mean *ES*) of .104 with a standard deviation of .112 and standard error of .007.

The $\overline{ES}$ of .104 indicates that the exogenous group differs from only 54% of the endogenous group while 46% of the endogenous group differs from the exogenous group. This 4 percentile rank difference represents a level only slightly above that which might be expected by chance (50th percentile). If two separate distributions are drawn for exogenous and endogenous samples, the distributions will be separated by .104 standard deviations at their means, as shown in Figure 3-1.

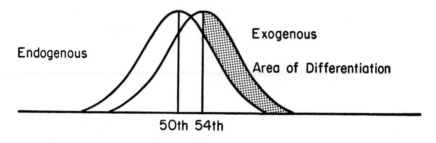

FIGURE 3-1 Magnitude of Exogenous Versus Endogenous Differences

At this highest level of aggregation, the exogenous and endogenous groups did not exhibit a large difference. In only 4% of the comparisons would there be differences that differentiate unequivocally exogenous and endogenous subjects. This finding must temper any generalization related to the particular functioning of exogenous children in comparison to endogenous children.

b. Exogenous Versus Endogenous Across Outcome Variables

The 26 studies investigated a variety of areas of functioning and it is possible that a single *ES* summarizing data across all studies could mask group differences related to more discrete ability areas. Therefore, it was necessary to attain a coarser level of analysis where *ES* data could be grouped into more discrete composites. The summary volumes (Strauss & Kephart, 1955; Strauss & Lehtinen, 1947) aided this process by providing chapter headings that subsumed each of the 26 studies. Five areas were identified and included perceptual-motor, cognition, language, behavior, and intelligence. The data for these aggregations are presented in Table 3-1.

TABLE 3-1 Exogenous Versus Endogenous Comparisons for Outcome Areas

Area	n	M	SE	Percent of exogenous different from endogenous
Perceptual-Motor	59	.106	.035	54%
Cognition	66	.138	.024	56%
Language	30	.097	.041	54%
Behavior	66	.089	.022	54%
Intelligence	20	.045	.036	52%

The greatest difference between the exogenous and endogenous groups were found in the area of cognition ($\overline{ES}$ = .138). Yet, this difference indicates that only 56% of the exogenous group scored at a level clearly differentiating them from the endogenous group while 44% did not. The remaining comparisons revealed even less differentiation between groups suggesting that the obtained differences were only slightly above chance differences. With the remaining difference levels ranging from 2% to 4%, it can be concluded that considerable overlap existed between the performance of exogenous and endogenous samples. The obtained $\overline{ES}$s revealed no significant differences ($F(4,236) = 1.02$, $p > .50$), suggesting no outcome area to be a useful indicator of exogenous versus endogenous distinctions.

In conclusion, this meta-analytic synthesis offered little empirical support for the alleged behavioral differences between exogenous (brain injured) and endogenous (non-brain injured) mentally retarded children. The evidence, when integrated statistically, indicated that exogenous versus endogenous comparisons produced group differences that, on average, approximated only one-tenth standard deviation. This difference suggests that in experimental comparisons between exogenous and endogenous groups, only 54% of the exogenous groups would reveal inferior performance. When compared to the level expected by chance (50%), the present findings mean that in only 4% of the cases would there be unequivocal performance differences. Thus, the considerable overlap among exogenous and endogenous samples makes it difficult to differentiate clear behavioral characteristics that might indicate functional distinctions between exogenous and endogenous groups.

The refinement of *ES* measurements into more discrete groupings found no distinguishing characteristics in either general areas of functioning or individual experimental tasks and assessment. The lack of clear differentiation between groups suggests that the perceptual-motor, cognitive, linguistic, behavioral, and intellectual characteristics of exogenous and endogenous groups were far more similar than different. There was nothing in any experimental comparisons of exogenous and endogenous children's abilities made by Strauss and Werner that reveals anything more than minimal differences and thus cast considerable doubt on the statement, "brain-injured children reveal characteristic disorders in perception, concept formation, and behavior," and the implication that, "Such markedly different mental organization should require educational methods which would specifically aim to correct or modify the deficiencies" (Strauss & Lehtinen, 1947, p. 118).

The significance of these findings is found in the fact that the present-day LD field owes much of its theoretical orientation to the presumed differences found by Strauss and Werner in their study of exogenous and endogenous children. On the basis of their findings, Strauss and Werner concluded that the effects of brain injury were manifested in a definite set of behavioral characteristics across a broad range of functioning. From these assumptions and a series of modifications (e.g., the equivalent characteristics in children with brain injury but normal intelligence and the specification of the parameters of the Strauss syndrome), the concepts surrounding exogenous mental retardation evolved into the present conceptualization of LD. But the present findings call into question Strauss and Werner's notions regarding the supposed behavioral consequences of brain injury because of the failure to uncover useful distinctions between exogenous and endogenous groups. The comparisons failed to produce differences of the magnitude that unequivocally separated exogenous and endogenous functioning that might provide a prototype for LD.

Consequently, it appears that the foundation of the present-day LD field was based on overgeneralized assumptions regarding the nature of brain injury. The presuppositions found in the Strauss and Werner paradigm were not anchored in exogenous and exogenous behavioral differences that were of sufficient magnitude for presumptive inference about the consequences of brain damage. When coupled with debate over validity of their diagnoses, the present findings suggest that the LD field must not continue to provide fallacious arguments for continuing to believe what it as been accustomed to accepting as true.

The Validity of the Strauss and Werner Paradigm

Kuhn (1970), the philosopher of science, discussed development and progress in science by explicating the nature of paradigms (theories). During the "pre-paradigm" period, multiple explanations are provided wherein ranges of phenomena are interpreted differently. This diversity disappears when a single interpretation achieves a synthesis of existing explanations. For example, in astronomy there is the Copernican (heliocentric) paradigm that differed markedly from and which gradually replaced the Ptolemaic (geocentric) paradigm. The singular theoretical orientation (paradigm) provides a conceptual framework and a body of assumptions, beliefs, and methods for research. In this way, paradigms set boundaries for "normal science" which now proceeds in a relatively conservative manner wherein exceptions to paradigm-based expectations (anomalies) are either ignored or rejected in favor of problems having a predictable solution in terms of the established normal science paradigm. A paradigm thus provides an implicit framework for researchers; the assumptions and presuppositions of the paradigm govern the choice of problems and the "correct" methods and criteria for evaluating the solution of such selected problems. By defining what is normal and natural, the paradigm acts as a blinder; the rules or ways of approaching problems operate more or less automatically and the researcher believes it to be the accepted course of events. The prevailing paradigm is a powerful force that determines the questions posed, the kinds of data considered relevant, and how data will be gathered, analyzed, interpreted, and related to theoretical concepts. With increasing anomalous data, however, the paradigm loses its effectiveness to account for significant novel events (anomalies), and is less able to function as an effective guide for the discipline. Eventually, the crisis caused by anomalous data introduces increased latitude in the rules of normal science to allow resolution of basic conflicts. This period of "extraordinary science" results in the emergence of a new paradigm better able to account for anomalous data. Thus, the discipline experiences a "paradigm shift" until all data are compatible within the theoretical framework.

The paradigm shift phenomenon is neither natural nor automatic in the face of anomalous data. The history of science suggests that established paradigms are typically held tenaciously and challenges are vigorously rejected (Toulmin, 1970; Watkins, 1970). Masterman (1970) argued that new paradigms are rarely accepted by rational persuasion; instead, the acceptance of new paradigms occurs only after the opposition is replaced. Barber (1961) presented examples to show that, although science espouses objectivity and openness, discoveries or ideas that challenge the dominant paradigm are not readily accepted. Examples include resistance to Young's wave theory of light by 19th century scientists faithful to the corpuscular paradigm; resistance to Mendel's conception of the separate inheritance of unit characteristics by biologists adhering to the prevailing paradigm postulating joint and total inheritance of characteristics; and resistance to Ampere's theory of magnetic currents by scientists who could not fit it into the prevailing Newtonian mechanical model (see deGrazia, Juergens & Stecchini, 1966; Koestler, 1971 for other examples).

The LD field presents alternative paradigms that compete for the allegiance of LD professionals. There exists a clear distinction between the behaviorist and cognitive (process) paradigms in LD (see Ysseldyke & Salvia, 1974). The behavioristic paradigm emphasizes objective descriptions of environmental events, operational definitions, and controlled experiments while the cognitive paradigm emphasizes internal information processing and programming. Adherents of the behavioristic paradigm seek antecedent environmental and situational events that can be related to denotable behaviors while cognitive investigators seek to construct a model of internal processes and structures that can lead to observed output. These contrasting paradigms lead to different questions and different ways of designing and conducting investigations (see Katahan & Koplin, 1968, for an analysis of these paradigms in psychology). Each paradigm determines how its "facts" are to be interpreted. With regard to the behavioristic paradigm, Kessel (1969) noted that "the behaviorist's presuppositions have led to a choice of phenomena and methods that render his position basically irrefutable: It is hardly likely that the human being will reveal 'higher order' activities when his eye blink or knee jerk are being conditioned, or when he is learning to associate pairs of nonsense syllables" (p. 1003). For example, behaviorists treat higher mental processes as "confounding variables" and can thus maintain behavioristic presuppositions by controlling the "confounding variables." Hence, at all stages of the research process, bias is introduced in accordance with the favored paradigm from initial hypotheses formulation, to research design, to data analysis, and, finally, to interpretation and conclusions.

Validity of LD Definition Components

As suggested earlier, the work of Strauss and Werner has been most influential in explicating an LD paradigm. Through experimental investigation and conceptual exposition, the Strauss and Werner paradigm includes (in varying degree) the following postulates: LD fits a medical model (implying something is wrong with the child); LD is associated with (or caused by) neurological dysfunction; LD academic problems are related to psychological process disturbance, most notably in perceptual-motor functioning; LD is associated with academic failure as defined by discrepancy notions; and LD cannot be due primarily to other handicapping conditions. Thus, the Strauss and Werner paradigm provided the foundation for "normal science" in LD, and the resulting fundamental postulates regarding the nature of LD were incorporated into LD definitions. As can be seen in the definitions reviewed earlier, these postulates are maintained either implicitly or explicitly in LD definitions right up to the present. The question arises: How valid are these postulates? If research disputes the validity of these postulates, then the Strauss and Werner paradigm must be questioned as the fundamental theoretical orientation of the LD field.

Locus of the Problem

The Strauss and Werner paradigm suggested that the locus of the problem was within the affected individual and represents a medical (disease) model. The medical model considers the disorder as emanating from some underlying cause. The analogy is made to physical medicine in which germs, viruses, or other insults interfere with normal functioning and lead to the production of symptoms. The approach seeks the source of difficulty within the individual rather than within the social ecology of that individual. It is assumed that the removal of the source of difficulty results in improvement, irrespective of the social context of intervention. The disease model, thus, implies that symptoms cannot be dealt with directly because they are simply manifestations of the cause and, consequently, symptom alleviation is not significant because it does not treat the real problem, that is, the underlying cause.

The assumptions underlying the medical model have been criticized and its utility challenged (Bandura, 1969; Hewett, 1968; Macmillan, 1973; Szasz, 1974; Ullman & Krasner, 1965). For problems in education like LD, little evidence exists suggesting solely a biophysical basis for the disorder (Owen, Adams, Forrest, Stolz, & Fisher, 1971).

On the treatment side, MacMillan (1973) suggested that the medical model defines intervention parameters which are not relevant for education. Although the data collected from a medical model perspective may be of interest, it is typically of little heuristic value in developing an appropriate educational prescription, since educational interventions focus upon symptoms which do not have a one-to-one correspondence with causes. As such, the medical model minimizes the value of psychoeducational intervention which focuses upon symptom relief rather than the removal of causes (Schmitt, 1975).

Besides concerns over diagnosis and treatment, Scheff (1966) suggested that the medical model creates more problems than it cures. One problem surrounds the conservative strategy associated with the medical model. Unlike the legal dictum of innocent till proven guilty, the medical perspective reverses that assumption and presupposes pathology unless normality is proved conclusively. Although appropriate for physical illness, the strategy is questionable for a school-based problem like LD. With the "safe side" tipped towards the assumption of underlying illness, the question arises as to the effects of labeling and the stigma associated with the labeling. Hobbs (1975) has outlined negative consequences of the LD label, specifically, the implication of a specific neurological condition which is damaging to the child, frightening to parents, and confusing to the school.

The negative effects of labeling are also related to the "self-fulfilling prophecy." MacMillan (1973) noted that most special education labels imply a deficit or deficiency and it is unclear how that deficit label affects the individual so labeled, as well as others who respond to that label. Consequently, expectations for the labeled child may be negatively influenced by the label's connotations.

For a phenomenon as complex as LD, the medical model fails to capture that complexity since the role of environmental variables is not considered. The LD child operates within a social system that may be either a positive or negative influence on the manifestations of LD. A complete description of LD thus requires an evaluation of environmental factors for their impact on the child (Forness, 1981a). The medical model, by focusing upon within-subject variables, provides an incomplete picture of the multiplicity of problems associated with LD.

Thus, conceptions of LD were drawn from the medical model; the locus of disability was assumed within the child and therapeutic efforts were directed at changing the child. This was unfortunate since the medical model proved to be of limited utility since it stresses disease and chronicity, and was unduly pessimistic. The LD field requires conceptualizations that replace disease with difference, chronicity with transiency, and pessimism with optimism.

Physiological Correlates

The most prominent physiological correlate of LD is central nervous system (CNS) dysfunction. The original brain damage syndrome (Strauss & Lehtinen, 1947) was extended to include children with relatively borderline disturbance suggestive of a brain damage syndrome. The organicity was reduced to a subclinical level with less overt manifestations and resulted in the diagnostic category "minimal brain dysfunction" (MBD) (Clements, 1966; Wender, 1971).

Although there has been a tendency to view MBD as a syndrome (Paine, 1962; Wender, 1975), statistical evaluations assessing the validity of an MBD syndrome have provided little evidence for the existence of a single homogeneous syndrome (Becker, 1974; Crinella,

1973; Routh & Roberts, 1972; Schulman, Kaspar, & Throne, 1965). For example, Paine, Werry, and Quay (1968), using information on medical history, neurological examination, EEG findings, psychological tests, and behavior ratings, found low correlations between the data collected under the five headings. It was concluded that the pattern of abnormalities observed in MBD children was the result of complex interrelationships among underlying dimensions emanating from innate, traumatic, and psychosocial variables. In a related study, Werry (1968) concluded that "these multidisciplinary measures do not tap a single unitary dimension of 'minimal brain dysfunction (MBD)', but rather a series of developmental dimensions each, or any combination of which may be impaired in MBD" (p. 15). It was then recommended that, because of the lack of empirical support for any medical statements about MBD and CNS impairments, the dysfunctions should be described in psychoeducational rather than neurological terms. Yet, the diagnostic category of MBD was elevated to the status of a hypothetical class of CNS impairments which subsumed smaller discrete and overlapping subsets of behavioral and academic problems (Clements, 1966; Laufer & Denhoff, 1957; Wender, 1971).

Although the symptoms of MBD fail to form a unitary cluster, if an etiological factor common to MBD children could be demonstrated, then support would be rendered for the concept of MBD as a discrete entity. In a review of genetic, perinatal, and constitutional factors in the etiology of MBD, Stewart (1980) concluded that a wide variety of causative agents have been implicated in producing MBD. Similarly, Martin (1980) reviewed the evidence suggesting environmental variables as possible etiological agents, and concluded that many possibilities exist which prevent a clear picture of their role in the genesis of MBD from being portrayed.

The diverse etiologies proposed for MBD have received varying degrees of empirical support, but none has been demonstrated to be etiological for all MBD children. The variety of causes suggested for MBD makes no single etiology sufficient to explain causation in MBD children but, rather, implies a multifactorial and heterogeneous etiology. Thus, the heterogeneity of causative factors does not support the view of MBD as a single entity.

Implicit in the conceptualization of a syndrome is a specific deficit which underlies the condition. The nature or location of the CNS dysfunction that presumably results in MBD symptoms, however, has been subject to a variety of speculations. Implicated as the basic MBD problem has been temporal lobe dysfunction (Ounsted, Lindsay, & Norman, 1966), diencephalon dysfunction (Laufer & Denhoff, 1957), cerebellar and vestibular dysfunction (Frank & Levinson, 1973), cortical and subcortical imbalance (Eveloff, 1970), delayed lateralization of brain function (Orton, 1937; Satz & Sparrow, 1970), disorders of brain metabolism (Shaynitz, Cohen, & Shaynitz, 1978; Shetty, 1971; Silver, 1971b; Wender, 1976), underarousal (Zentall, 1975), and maturational lag in the CNS (Dykman, Ackerman, Clements, & Peters, 1971; Kinsbourne, 1973). No one theoretical formulation has proved more valid than any other and, thus, the idea of a single deficit underlying the MBD condition is not supported.

The weight of the evidence casts much doubt about the existence of an MBD syndrome. The heterogeneity, in terms of symptoms, etiologies, and sources of dysfunction, precludes simple interpretations of MBD. The tendency to treat MBD as a homogeneous entity leads to fallacious generalizations and inappropriate treatment programs.

Diagnostic Issues in MBD

The lack of an identifiable MBD syndrome results in confusion because the term is loosely defined in terms of behavior and inferred etiology. The definition of MBD is more speculative than definitive, resulting in tentative speculations regarding the diagnosis of MBD. The MBD concept described by Clements (1966) implied the existence of (1) severe learning and behavioral disabilities, (2) average intelligence, and (3) impairment in perception, language, conceptualization, memory, and control of impulse, attention, and motor function. These implications represented necessary yet insufficient conditions. The sufficient condition surrounded the presumptive inference that the learning or behavioral disabilities manifested by impairment in behavioral–cognitive performance were related to deviations in CNS function.

The evolution of MBD to a concept presumptive of CNS impairment but diagnosed on the basis of purely behavioral signs was open to criticism. Bax and MacKeith (1963) objected to the disease connotation of MBD and the reliance on behavioral signs alone. Benton (1973) argued that MBD must be termed as a behavioral concept since it is defined by behavioral features, not by infrabehavioral evidence of CNS impairment. In fact, functional disorders, either in the realm of academic, behavioral, or cognitive performance, provide no valid basis for inferring impairment in CNS functioning.

A major source of difficulty surrounds the "minimal" adjective attached to the MBD concept. The implications of "minimal" are subtle neurological signs which presumably define MBD. Such behaviors as hyperactivity and distractibility are supposedly "minimal" signs but these same behavioral patterns are also observed in children whose primary problem might be cerebral palsy, mental deficiency, or severe epilepsy, whose "troubles are minimal neither as regards their behavior nor as regards their neurological signs" (Koupernik, MacKeith, & Francis-Williams, 1975, p. 122). In fact, real brain injury may be present without the presence of any functional abnormality (that is, minimal sign). Yet, as Benton (1973) pointed out, "a child (or an adult) cannot have minimal brain dysfunction without showing behavioral abnormalities, since the designation, in fact, means behavioral deviation" (p. 29).

The behavioral deviations, however, do not provide evidence of neurological involvement. In fact, when the neurological status of MBD-labeled children is examined, the majority of findings provide little support for CNS dysfunction underlying LD problems. Cohn (1964), for example, was unable to find a correlation between minimal signs and MBD. In a complete medical and psychological examination of 100 children with suspected MBD, Kenny and Clemmens (1971) found that "the final diagnosis *MBD* is more contingent upon symptomatology and the results of psychological studies than any specific medical, neurologic, or electroencephalographic findings, since no significant commonality results from these findings" (p. 277).

The weight of the evidence is negative with respect to evidence of CNS abnormality in MBD children. The failure to find "hard signs," unequivocal evidence of CNS impairment, makes it difficult to conclude that LD is related to neurological impairment. The presence of "hard signs" would be indicated by abnormalities in either cranial nerves or cerebellar, extrapyramidal, motor, or sensory functions. In the absence of "hard signs," abnormal findings in the form of "soft signs" have been taken as evidence of CNS impairment. The notion of minimal, border-line, equivocal, or "soft" neurological findings indicative of cerebral dysfunction was advanced by Bender (1957) in a description of specific reading disability. The concept has since been used as evidence of CNS dysfunction in children manifesting a variety of learning and behavioral disorders (Kennard, 1960).

Although little evidence was found supporting CNS impairment on the basis of "hard signs," there are studies finding "soft signs" in samples of MBD children (Hertzig, Bortner, & Birch, 1959; Kenny & Clemmens, 1971; Lucas, Rodin & Simson, 1965; Nichols & Chen, 1981; Schain, 1970). For example, Hertzig et al. (1969), in their neurologic study of "brain-damaged" children, found that only 29% revealed "hard signs" while 90% showed "soft signs." This finding is in a sample presumably referred on the basis of independent medical information of the presence of brain injury. Similarly, in a prospective study of an MBD sample of nearly 30,000 children, Nichols and Chen (1981) found actual neurological abnormalities in only 3% of an LD subgroup. Of 10 neurological symptoms (soft signs), only three (abnormal tactile finger recognition, impaired position sense, and poor coordination) were found significantly more in the LD group. In their study of 76 LD children, Owen et al. (1971) included a classical neurological examination and found only 3 of the 76 children showed definite signs of CNS damage. This led to the conclusion that "organic damage per se could not be considered a major causative factor in the learning problems" of LD children (Owen et al., 1971, p. 64).

The interpretation of "soft signs," however, is fraught with difficulties. A major difficulty surrounds the lack of age-related normative data for most soft neurological signs. The theoretical basis of soft signs has also been challenged. Ingram (1973) suggested that soft signs are diagnostic of soft thinking. Barlow (1974) supported a "hard line" on soft signs since it is entirely possible that soft signs may either disappear or change in the course of development. In fact, maturation can result in the restoration of function even in the face of prenatal or paranatal insult to the CNS. At best, soft signs may be interpreted as evidence of neurological immaturity (Schmitt, 1975). The presence of soft signs is not uncommon in children under age 7 and, therefore, should not be considered abnormal prior to that age (Hart, Rennick, & Klinge, 1974; Kinsbourne, 1973).

Attempts to differentiate LD and normal children on the basis of soft signs have shown negative findings (Adams, Kocsis, & Estes, 1974; Copple & Isom, 1968; Hart et al., 1974). In the Adams et al. (1974) study, only two of nine soft signs were significantly depressed in an LD group but the magnitude of difference was not great enough for clinical usefulness. The number of soft signs was found to be almost equal in underachievers and a control group (Hart et al., 1974). In fact, the number and combination of soft signs could not predict which children were having the most difficulty with schoolwork, which negates the assumption that the presence of a cluster of soft signs is of greater importance (Hart et al., 1974). Schmitt (1975) has also pointed out that the number of soft signs required to prove an organic cause is unknown. The evidence is thus clearly suggestive that LD children cannot be reliably distinguished from normally achieving children on the basis of soft neurological signs.

Thus, soft signs are no more reliable than behavioral symptoms as indications of either the existence or nature of underlying CNS disorder. Because the child has been initially referred because of learning and behavior problems, Ingram (1973) suggested that any soft signs elicited are far more likely to be interpreted as "positive," that is, indicative of CNS damage when this is an unwarranted assumption. Soft signs may be indicative of a child's difficulties but do not explain them as suggested by Touwen and Sporrel (1979), "The attempt to explain disorders of complex behavior only on the basis of neurological minor signs testifies to an objectionable kind of reductionism" (p. 529).

The diagnosis of MBD is frequently supported by evidence of electroencephalographic (EEG) abnormalities. The EEG, however, represents only a crude measure of brain activity, and some of the abnormalities frequently reported are controversial or questionable (Hughes, 1978; Satterfield, 1973; Schmitt, 1975). The clinical relevance of abnormal EEGs in MBD is problematic. Although EEG abnormalities are considered relevant, few studies report their prevalence in a blindly rated control group (Wender, 1971). A further complication is the fact that many MBD children (approximately 50%) are neurologically intact: "There is no doubt that the syndrome can appear with the total absence of neurological signs or symptoms or EEG abnormalities" (Wender, 1971, p. 28). The interpretation of EEG findings is complicated by changes associated with maturation (Pond, 1963), the finding of a low correlation between EEG findings and other indices of neurological dysfunction (Paine, et al., 1968; Schulman et al., 1965), the unreliability in clinical interpretation of EEG records (Freeman, 1967), and the limited success in relating EEG abnormalities to specific learning or behavior problems (Grossman, 1966; Paine, 1965). In reviewing the evidence, Freeman (1967) concluded that, "The EEG appears to be regarded with more awe than it deserves. It is not very reliable, and there are many technical problems in its use with children . . . . The marriage of convenience between the EEG and special education has never been a very happy one. The available evidence suggests that, until more definitive information is available, a trial separation, or at least a platonic relationship, would be more appropriate" (pp. 69–70). Thus, the EEG does not represent a simple and clear-cut measure of neurological functioning providing a single index of CNS integrity.

The diagnosis of MBD has also been attempted on the basis of psychological test data. For example, deficiencies on perceptual, particularly visual–motor, tests, and verbal–performance discrepancies on IQ tests have been suggested as diagnostic of MBD. Yet, the evidence suggests that differentiating LD children on the basis of test data, as either demonstrating or not demonstrating MBD, is not particularly useful when the primary concern is either cognitive function or academic achievement (Black, 1973; Edwards, Alley, & Snider, 1971; Hartlage & Green, 1971).

Using psychological test data for the purposes of dichotomous classification (MBD vs not-MBD) is of limited value since using the presumption of neurological difficulty as a factor differentiating MBD from non-MBD is meaningless. The reason is found in what Yates (1954) termed "empirical engineering," the fact that diagnostic tests have evolved prior to the development of an adequate theory of brain functioning upon which they could be based. The test data do not indicate particular signs and symptoms because the heterogeneity in MBD children presents a variety of neurological difficulties differing in type and localization, resulting in a variety of neurological and psychological signs. Herbert (1964) and Coles (1978) have reviewed the tests used in diagnosing MBD in children, and almost all failed to approach acceptable standards of psychometric efficiency for diagnostic tests. Consequently, test data cannot be taken to indicate particular signs and symptoms of MBD (Denckla, 1973).

Ross (1976) discussed methodological dilemmas in research, testing the assumption of a causal relationship between MBD and LD. Consequently, the MBD–LD hypothesis has been established as a self-evident entity before sufficient evidence has been collected to justify continued use. This "creeping reification" (Von Hilsheimer, 1973) results in MBD demanding respect in its own right without the necessary foundation to establish the concept's actual significance (Wolff & Hurwitz, 1973). Although MBD may possess validity for medical disciplines, the educational usefulness of the MBD diagnosis has been questioned (Barnes & Forness, 1982; Bateman, 1974). Birch and Bortner (1968) pointed out that, " . . . children with this syndrome do not come to our notice because they have damaged brains, rather, they come to attention because they represent individuals with behaviors that are deviant and because they are unresponsive to usual methods of rearing, training, and education" (p. 8). In discussing MBD and education, Cohen (1973) reached the conclusions that: (1) labels such as MBD are useless since they were referred not for neurological conditions but rather an inability in academic areas, (2) behaviors, not constructs, are real since the difference between one MBD child and one who is not is found in learning behavior, not neurological constructs, and (3) for educational purposes, etiology should be ignored since the antecedent conditions leading to academic failure are usually irrelevant to educational methods.

The concept of MBD which has evolved over the past 50 years remains as confused today as when it was first introduced by Strauss and Lehtinen (1947). Gomez (1967) suggested that MBD represents "maximal neurologic confusion" since the concept is an inference regarding some unknown brain deviation based upon either academic or behavioral signs. Such an inference is illogical and unwarranted.

The legacy of Werner and Strauss, however, has ingrained the idea of CNS impairments being the basis of LD. Until the LD field is willing to evaluate critically the MBD concept, it will probably be mired in false conceptualizations. Sprague (1976), in a provocative analysis of MBD entitled "Counting Jars of Raspberry Jam," recounted the story of how the British Foreign Office became upset because a regiment fighting Napoleon in Spain was not able to account for all jars of raspberry jam consumed. The Duke of Wellington responded that he could either train an army of clerks to account for all the raspberry jam to the satisfaction of Foreign Office accountants or an army of fighting men to defeat Napoleon, but he could not do both. It appears that regardless of the weight of evidence, the LD field continues to "count jars of raspberry jam" with regard to the relationship of MBD to LD.

Psychological Process Deficiency

Most definitions of LD suggest deficiencies in basic psychological processes as fundamental deficits. The psychological process disturbance orientation of the LD field, particularly in terms of perceptual–motor dysfunction, has resulted in the situation wherein LD is conceptualized as a problem at the process level which disrupts academic learning. Information is not related directly to academic achievement, but is processed through an intermediate level which allows for academic achievement. Thus, processes must be intact for academic learning to occur since received information must first be processed in order to be useful for the acquisition of academic knowledge.

Mann (1979) outlined the historical course of process concepts in education from its beginnings in philosophical foundations (Plato, Descartes, Hobbes, Locke, Berkeley, Rousseau, Kant), through its first application in special education (Itard, Seguin, Montessori), to its articulation in theory and practice by Orton, and culminating in the mid-twentieth century with the work of Strauss and Werner. Strauss and Werner (Strauss & Kephart, 1955; Strauss & Lehtinen, 1947; Werner, 1948) laid the foundation for process concepts in LD which were later refined and extended (Barsch, 1967; Chalfant & Scheffelin, 1969; Frostig & Horne, 1964; Getman, 1965; Kephart, 1964; Wepman, 1964) and incorporated into definitional proposals (Cruickshank, 1981; Wepman, et al., 1975). As a matter of fact, the current definition of LD in federal law begins with the phrase "specific learning disability means a *disorder in one or more of the basic psychological processes* . . . " (italics added, *Federal Register*, December 29, 1977, p. 65083).

Psychological processes represent abilities which are not observable; consequently, ability deficits must be distinguished from performance deficiencies manifested in assessment devices. This is the test–trait fallacy (see Tryon, 1979). Abilities are never measured directly and, therefore, represent hypothetical constructs. As such, construct validity (Cronbach & Meehl, 1955) must be demonstrated before presumed ability deficits may be used to explain performance differences. Little empirical support has been rendered for the constructs (abilities) assessed by process tests (Mann, 1971), making it difficult to determine whether measured performance differences are the result of "real" ability differences or the method of measurement. Mann and Phillips (1967) questioned "fractional" approaches to intervention in which there is differential analysis of abilities (hypothetical constructs), assumed to be related to academic achievement. Objection was raised to the view of the LD child as a collection of discrete and isolated constructs which are deficient rather than a wholistic, unitary organism.

A critical examination of the two major techniques for substantiating and validating fractional practices (factor analysis and validity studies) found little empirical support for the constructs assessed by "fractional" tests. Although some functions can be precisely and operationally defined in objective realities, more complex functions (e.g., perceptual–motor behaviors) cannot be validated as specific, independent entities. Besides the difficulties with test validity, the "fractional" approach also assumes that behavior assessed is directly related to basic processes in the LD child being evaluated and that the assessment results give an indication of the amount and quality of the process possessed. But Mann and Phillips (1967) term this the stimulus error; that is, "of directly identifying test responses and the processes they putatively represent with the names of the tests which elicit and supposedly measure them — an exercise in tautology, not scientific procedure" (p. 315). The quarrel is not with assessment of curricular abilities (reading, arithmetic, and the like), which are tested with achievement measures, but with differential psychoeducational assessment wherein the tests "are abstractions fleshed out and reified in psychometric garb as real 'processes'" (Mann, 1971, p. 6).

Besides philosophical and ideological rhetoric assailing the perceptual deficit hypothesis, empirical evidence is available which suggests, at best, a weak relationship between perceptual difficulties and impaired academic performance. Based upon historical precedent and clinical evidence, it has been assumed that LD is intimately linked to perceptual deficits which, in turn, result in achievement problems.

But little empirical support has been rendered for the assumption that perceptual difficulties underlie academic problems. The relationship of both auditory perception (Hammill & Larsen, 1974b; Kavale, 1981) and visual perception (Kavale, 1982b; Larsen & Hammill, 1975) was found to be of insufficient magnitude to validate the assumption that perceptual skills underlie academic achievement, although they may be useful as factors in the prediction of, for example, reading ability. Even when auditory and visual perception were considered together, Kavale and Forness (1984a) found no appreciable increase in the proportion of explained variance in reading achievement. The relationships were further confounded by the role of intelligence. When IQ was held constant, there was a substantial suppression in the magnitude of the relationships, suggesting that perceptual skills share a large common variance with intelligence in their relationship to reading abilities.

The inability to integrate one modality function with another modality (intersensory integration, cross-modal perception, intermodal transfer) has been suggested as a major process deficit in LD (Ayres, 1968; Birch & Belmont, 1964, 1965; Chalfant & Scheffelin, 1969). Freides (1974) criticized the literature on methodological grounds, which confounded the interpretation of a unique disability in intersensory processing rather than a generalized processing deficit. Kavale (1980a) found that, although the average correlation between auditory-visual integration and reading for normal readers was .346, it dropped to .209 for LD readers, which indicated that auditory-visual integration accounts for only 5% of the variance in reading ability.

Thus, the assumption of a relationship between perceptual abilities and academic achievement has not received empirical support. The association accounts for relatively small proportions of the variance in the relationship of perceptual abilities and academic ability. A majority of the variability in the relationship is attributable to factors other than perception. If LD were a basic process disturbance, particularly in perception, then a relationship of a greater magnitude might be expected. Since this expectation was not found in the empirical findings, which suggests a limited association, the hypothesis of perceptual deficit being the primary process disturbance must be questioned. As Hammill (1976) pointed out, the debate is not about the concept of perceptual variable as either physiological realities or hypothetical constructs, but rather the way the perceptual concepts are applied to LD. The evidence does not justify the notion of LD as a process disorder in perceptual-functioning and, while tradition has implanted the notion, it requires modification for LD to break the bonds of its past.

The perceptual deficit hypothesis, that LD subjects exhibit inferior perceptual functioning when compared to normal subjects, has been challenged. Although finding conceptual differences in groups selected on the basis of scholastic achievement and perceptual-motor achievement, Bibace and Hancock (1969) found no differences attributable to the level of perceptual-motor achievement. These results were immediately challenged (Journal of Learning Disabilities, 1969), which reveals the strong theoretical orientation of the LD field toward the assumption of perceptual-deficit as the primary difficulty. Its entrenchment in the LD field was reaffirmed by Cruickshank (1981a, b),who differentiated LD from environmentally determined problems of learning by defining LD as neurologically based perceptual processing deficits. In criticizing the broadening of LD to include problems never originally conceptualized as LD per se, Cruickshank (1981b) reemphasized the basic perceptual processing deficits of LD by suggesting "learning disabilities as an integral part of the neurological system giving rise to the S-R bond is perceptual" (p. 121).

Thus, while perceptual-motor deficiencies may be present, they are often minor contributors to learning (Bateman, 1969; Cohen, 1969). Empirical support for this assumption is found in studies which revealed that, although LD readers may exhibit perceptual deficiencies, reading ability is not related to the degree of perceptual deficiency (Black, 1974a; Camp, 1973; Fisher & Frankfurter, 1977; Hare, 1977; Stanley, Kaplan, & Poole, 1975; Zach & Kaufman, 1972). Likewise, studies which examined subgroups of poor readers suggest that those with perceptual deficiencies comprise only a very small percentage of all disabled readers (Boder, 1973; Denckla, 1972; Lyon & Watson, 1981; Mattis, 1978; Satz & Morris, 1981). A major difficulty in the perceptual deficit hypothesis is its failure to acknowledge that other factors might contribute to a deficit. For example, cognitive confusion alone may account for the perceptual deficits shown by LD children (Downing, 1979). Thus, a general inadequate approach to learning tasks may be reflected in poor performance on perceptual tasks as well as other academic tasks. This hypothesis is similar to Torgesen's (1977) view of the LD child as an inactive learner. The emphasis is upon performance problems rather than ability deficits. The low performance of LD children on many tasks is attributable to the failure to employ appropriate or efficient learning strategies rather than to structural or capacity limitations (Torgesen, 1980).

The failure to find perceptual deficits underlying academic abilities led Vellutino, Steger, Moyer, Harding, and Niles (1977) to pose the question, "Has the perceptual deficit hypothesis led us astray?" and Fisher and Frankfurter (1977) to ask, "Where's the perceptual deficit?" Thus, the empirical evidence does not justify the notion of LD as a process disorder, at least, in perceptual-motor functioning.

Academic Failure

Strauss and Lehtinen (1947) assumed the presence of academic difficulties when it was suggested that, "the response of the brain-injured child to the school situation is frequently inadequate, conspicuously disturbing, and persistently troublesome" (p. 127). The emergence of LD as a category of special education found academic failure as a primary component. Beginning with Bateman (1965) and reaffirmed in Public Law 94-142 (1975), the most common and accepted characteristic of LD has been underachievement. Definitions of LD, either by connotation or denotation, postulated a discrepancy between expected and actual achievement. Most typically, the discrepancy involves the score on a test of measured intelligence and the score on a test of measured educational achievement. These scores are then incorporated in a formula which provides an index indicating the amount of discrepancy. Although such formulae are in wide use, there is an expressed uncertainty among many professionals regarding the interpretation of discrepancy data at an applied level (Hoffman, 1980).

At a superficial level, determining a discrepancy would appear straightforward, but closer examination reveals complex issues and problems. Among those problems are the meaning of both actual and expected achievement. "Actual" achievement is most often based upon scores from standardized achievement measures whose psychometric properties have been questioned (Salvia & Ysseldyke, 1981). Problems surround, for example, the assumption that tests with the same labels measure similar functions (Goolsby, 1971; Kelley, 1927), the fact that scores have been found to be partially dependent upon the test series used (Jenkins & Pany, 1978; Richardson, DeBenedetto, & Christ, 1978), difficulties with norming (Lennon, 1951), intrasubject variability (Bernard, 1966), and scoring difficulties, specifically grade-equivalent scores (Stanley & Hopkins, 1981).

Expected achievement is generally related to intelligence test. Intelligence, however, includes a variety of definitions (Boring, 1923; Cleary, Humphreys, Kendrick, & Wesman, 1975; Terman, 1916) and theories (Cattell, 1963; Guilford, 1967; Jensen, 1970; Spearman, 1927). Intelligence represents a hypothetical construct and should not be perceived as an innate, fixed entity representing capacity (McClelland, 1973; McNemar, 1964). Additionally, intelligence test scores reveal considerable variability (Honzik, Macfarlane, & Allen, 1948; Hopkins & Bracht, 1975; McCall, Appelbaum, & Hogarty, 1973) and reveal a high correlation with achievement measures (Coleman & Cureton, 1954; Gallagher & Moss, 1963; Stanley & Hopkins, 1981).

The difficulties in defining actual and expected achievement are reflected in conceptions of discrepancy (Thorndike & Hagen, 1977). Underachievement as defined by a discrepancy is not synonymous with low achievement (Lavin, 1965) and is complicated by the less-than-perfect correlation between aptitude and achievement (Thorndike & Hagen, 1977). Thorndike (1963) discussed the substantial influence of measurement error in discrepancy formulations:

1. Although a high correlation exists between MA and academic achievement, it is not a perfect correlation, suggesting that the tests measure similar abilities but not identical ones.

2. The lack of a perfect correlation implies that errors of measurement, the combination of factors which precludes getting exactly the same results from measures of the same function or measures of different functions, will alter the relationship between expected and actual achievement. Thorndike (1963) provided a formula for calculating the standard deviation of a set of discrepancy scores given by

$$SD_e = S_c \sqrt{1 + r_{pc}^2 - r_c - r_p r_{pc}^2}$$

where

SD_e = standard deviation of discrepancy scores due to error of measurement in predictor and criterion,

S_c = standard deviation of criterion scores,

r_{pc} = correlation between predictor and criterion measure,

r_c = reliability of criterion measure,

r_p = reliability of predictor measure.

If the average values representing the components of the equation are used, the influence of errors of measurement can be demonstrated. Using 1.00 grade unit as the average standard deviation of achievement scores (S_c) for 6th graders in a particular school, .90 as the average reliability for the predictor test (r_p), .80 as the average reliability of the criterion measure (r_c), and .70 as the average intercorrelation between aptitude (IQ) and achievement measure (r_{pc}), the standard deviation of discrepancies arising purely from errors of measurement would be

$$
\begin{aligned}
SD_e &= 1.00 \sqrt{1 + (.70)^2 - .80 - .90(.70)^2} \\
&= 1.00 \sqrt{1 + .49 - .80 - .44} \\
&= 1.00 \sqrt{0.25} \\
&= 0.50
\end{aligned}
$$

Thus, the substantial influence of measurement error can be calculated. As Thorndike (1963) stated

> if *nothing* but the errors of measurement in the predictor and criterion were operating, we could *still* expect to get a spread of discrepancy scores represented by a standard deviation of half a grade–unit. We would *still* occasionally get discrepancies between predicted and actual reading level of as much as a grade and a half. This degree of "underachievement" would be possible as a result of nothing more than measurement error. (p. 9)

3. The basic unreliability of the criterion measure will produce errors of measurement resulting in random, unsystematic, and unpredictable discrepancies. There is, however, another source of error termed "criterion heterogeneity" which is associated with systematic variation associated with external facts about the criterion. Consequently, when data from different schools, different programs, or different teachers are combined, the likely result is the introduction of heterogeneity into the criterion; that is, the same score may represent different real levels of performance in different subgroups.

4. Although aptitude (IQ) is the most prominent factor in predicting achievement, there are other stable and relatively unmodifiable factors influencing the relationship between predictor and criterion. Such factors as sex, race, or socioeconomic status, while not direct causes of high or low achievement, may function as additional predictors of achievement but are typically not included in the determination of a discrepency.

A consequence of these difficulties is the phenomenon of regression (Crane, 1959; Thorndike, 1963; Yule, Rutter, Berger, & Thompson, 1974), the tendency of individuals who obtain a certain score (either high or low) on one measure to obtain, on average, a score nearer to the population average on the other test when the two tests are positively correlated. McLeod (1979) demonstrated the regression effect by showing little relationship between academic achievement and intelligence because of regression effects; for children in the high IQ range, their average achievement will be lower than expected while children in the low IQ range had higher average achievement than expected. For example, the average achievement level (expressed as an educational quotient) would be 123.6 for children in the IQ range 130–139 ($\overline{X}$ = 134.5), not the expected 134.5, while children in the IQ range 70–79 would have an average achievement of 83.9, not the expected 74.5. Thus, as a statistical artifact, the high aptitude group will appear primarily to be "underachievers" and the low aptitude group to be "overachievers."

Among the more popular procedures for determining discrepancy are mental-age methods (Harris, 1961; Horn, 1941), discrepancy quotient methods (Bond & Tinker, 1967; Monroe, 1932; Myklebust, 1968; USOE, 1976), transformed-score discrepancy methods (Erickson, 1975; Hanna, Dyck, & Holen, 1979), and regression discrepancy methods (McLeod, 1979; Shepard, 1980; Woodbury, 1963). Each method, however, possesses inherent difficulties. Problems with mental-age methods (Ullman, 1969), discrepancy quotient methods (Algozzine, Forgnone, Mercer, & Trifiletti, 1979; Macy, Baker, & Kosinski, 1979; Spache, 1969), transformed score discrepancy methods (Shepard, 1980), and regression discrepancy methods (Cronbach, Gleser, Nanda, & Rajoratnam, 1972; Shepard & Smith, 1981) limit their usefulness. All methods were found not to yield identical levels of expected achievement, particularly at the extreme ends of the IQ continuum (Bruininks, Glaman, & Clark, 1973; Forness, Sinclair, & Guthrie, 1983; Simmons & Shapiro, 1968) and to reveal large standard errors of estimate (Dore–Boyce, Misner, & McGuire, 1975; Yule, 1967). These problems make the discrepancy component of LD problematic (Hanna, Dyck, & Holen, 1979). Thus, what appears to be a straightforward matter is fraught with both conceptual and statistical difficulties. The presumed primary characteristic of LD, underachievement, is a complicated concept not easily measured or defined. Psychometric procedures for the determination of underachievement possess problems which call into question the validity of such procedures. Consequently, the accuracy of discrepancy formulas is distorted by considerable error, making the data of limited utility in deciding the presence or absence of LD. The primary component, task failure, in the form of academic learning difficulties, presents a variety of unresolved issues, which makes the discrepancy component of LD problematic.

Exclusion Component

Most LD definitions suggest that LD must not be primarily the result of other handicapping conditions. The origins are found in Strauss and Lehtinen's (1947) diagnostic criteria for minor brain injury wherein endogenous MR was excluded by the criterion that "the immediate family history indicates that the child comes from a normal family stock and that he is, in general, the only one of the sibship so affected" (p. 12).

The exclusion component was necessary initially to establish LD as a separate and discrete category of special education. As the "new kid on the block," LD required an identity of its own in order to provide funding and legislation for program implementation. Without an exclusion clause, the LD field would have been faced with the problem of overidentification; clearly, all children experiencing academic difficulties were not LD. Thus, with the parameters of LD in a state of flux, the initial incorporation of an exclusion clause was a necessary step for the emerging LD field.

Problems arose, however, since the exclusion clause became a primary defining characteristic of LD. With the principal criteria for LD designation subject to debate, the situation evolved into a state where LD was not defined so much by what it was but rather by what it was not. This is an unfortunate circumstance since it is a negative characterization rather than a positive one delineating the actual characteristics of LD.

In some cases, a clear differentiation between LD and other areas of special education is both practical and desirable. For example, sensorimotor handicaps (hearing disorders, visual impairments, and physical disabilities) represent long-established categories of special education with discrete parameters and prescribed intervention approaches. Although children represented in these categories possess learning problems, the difficulties are directly attributable to the primary deficit area. Learning problems would be expected but the resulting difficulties would not fit a definition of LD regardless of how narrow or broad that LD definition. Consequently, service delivery systems specifying physical and material modification should allow for optimal learning within the limits of the primary deficit areas. Although the child may experience problems in learning, there would probably be little heuristic value in a "multiply handicapped" concept involving a sensorimotor deficit plus LD. Difficulties in learning are inherent in conceptualizations about sensorimotor handicaps since the primary deficit will alter the normal course of learning. Thus, the exclusion of sensorimotor handicaps from the LD designation is appropriate and provides for less confusion surrounding the LD concept.

The exclusion component is less appropriate and more confusing, however, when the excluded categories represent individual differences in learning and behavior. The major difference surrounds the fact that the primary deficits are related to the acquisition of knowledge and skill, that is, learning. When the categories of mental retardation (MR), behavior disorders (emotional disturbance) (BD), and cultural–economic disadvantage (CD) are considered, a common factor related to learning deficits would fit the parameters circumscribing the LD category. Although a primary deficit area may be specified (e.g., mental subnormality, emotional disturbance), it becomes difficult to differentiate the influence of the primary deficit and its negative consequences on learning ability.

Hallahan and Kauffman (1977) considered LD, MR, and BD within a behavioral rather than a categorical framework and concluded that these traditional categories revealed more similarities than differences. Empirical support was found in the similarities among the three categories on cognitive, affective, and demographic variables (Gajar, 1979, 1980) and the inability to differentiate reliably LD from BD and MR on the basis of diagnostic test data (Webster & Schenck, 1978).

Average intelligence has been requisite for inclusion in the LD category but empirical evidence has reported that anywhere from 25% to 40% of labeled LD children were depressed in intellectual functioning (Ames, 1968b; Kirk & Elkins, 1975; Koppitz, 1971; Smith, Coleman,

Dokeck, & Davis, 1977). Gajar (1979) found that the distribution of IQ scores for LD, BD, and MR groups were all below the population mean while Belmont and Belmont (1980) suggested that LD represents only a subgroup of a broader classification of "slow learning." Finally, the functional similarities of LD and EMR have been noted (Neisworth & Greer, 1975). With respect to both genotype (underlying) conditions and phenotype (surface) dimensions, there exists substantial overlap between the LD and EMR categories for both causal conditions and subsequent performance problems.

Although the presence of social–emotional problems is assumed to be the primary defining characteristic of the BD category, there is increased awareness of the social–emotional difficulties manifested in LD children (Bryan & Bryan, 1977; Kronnick, 1981). Empirical evidence has suggested that a substantial proportion of LD children manifest behavior problems (Coleman & Sandhu, 1967; Koppitz, 1971; Wright, 1974) and that difficulty exists in distinguishing reliably LD and BD on the basis of behavioral profiles (Barr & McDowell, 1972; Hartlage, 1970; McCarthy & Paraskevopoulos, 1969).

The primary defining variable of academic underachievement, while found in LD, is also found in both MR (Meyen & Hieronymous, 1970; Schwarz, 1969; Schwarz & Cook, 1971) and BD (Forness, Bennett, & Tose, 1983; Kavale, Alper, & Purcell, 1981; Morse, Cutler, & Fink, 1964; Wagonseller, 1973; Wright, 1974). Additionally, the learning profiles exhibited by LD and BD were found similar (O'Donnell, 1980; O'Grady, 1974).

In sum, these findings indicate that LD does not exist in a "pure" form. The confounding influence of major defining variables makes differential diagnosis among the three mildly handicapping conditions difficult. The LD group cannot be distinguished on the basis of either lowered intellectual levels or social–emotional problems associated with the EMR and BD categories, respectively, and, conversely, is not unique with regard to the presence of academic retardation. Consequently, the exclusion clause is not supported for either the EMR or BD conditions and should be reassessed to include the possibility that these conditions can exist concomitantly with LD.

Besides the diagnostic categories of EMR and ED, the exclusion clause eliminates from LD classification children whose problems are primarily the result of environmental, cultural, or economic disadvantage (CD). Although the CD child has been included under special education classification (Hewett & Forness, 1983), a majority of the special education literature does not include the CD child. The CD child is primarily served by federally funded *Title* programs, but these are usually mandated under guidelines and provisions different from special education. The emphasis is most often upon compensatory education while special education is more concerned with remedial education.

Although children whose problems are primarily the result of CD are eliminated from LD consideration, conditions in CD environments have been suggested as placing a child at high risk for academic failure and LD (Hallahan & Cruickshank, 1973; Hallahan & Kauffman, 1976). It has also been argued that inadequate previous instruction might also result in poor academic performance and that these factors are likewise not always excluded prior to the diagnosis of LD (Forness, 1982). The similarities between LD and CD were described by Herrick (1973) while Kavale (1980b) suggested a strong association between LD and CD because of: (1) environmental factors associated with CD leading to CNS deficits which in turn, lead to LD, and (2) CD correlates leading directly to LD. Negative influences surrounding CD include: (1) prenatal and paranatal risks, (2) prematurity, (3) malnutrition, (4) greater incidence of disease and accident, and (5) deprivation (a constricted environment, or lack of proper amounts and types of stimulation) which all increase the likelihood of CNS dysfunction. Besides the greater probability of CNS dysfunction, the negative environmental circumstances may result directly in learning impairments which are indistinguishable from the cognitive, perceptual, linguistic, and information processing behaviors considered the primary characteristics of LD. Thus, the problem is most properly viewed as a complex interrelationship among the phenomena of LD, MBD, and CD as shown in Figure 3-2.

The finding that approximately 75% of LD children reveal reading problems as a primary deficit (Kirk & Elkins, 1975; Koppitz, 1971) and that approximately 87% of LD children receive remedial instruction in reading (Sartain, 1976) results in difficulties differentiating LD and reading disability (RD) (Artley & Hardin, 1976; Gaskins, 1982; Hartman & Hartman, 1973; Jakupcak, 1975). Analysis reveals no substantive differences with respect to either etiology, identification, and intervention between LD and RD (Kirk, 1975; Lerner, 1975; Wallace, 1976). Any distinctions appear to be false dichotomies related to territorial integrity rather than substantive issues (Bryant, 1976; Senf, 1975).

The evidence does not support the exclusion clause found in LD definitions. The substantial overlap among defining parameters of the excluded categories and LD prevented any clear differentiation. Consequently, since the excluded conditions are more like LD than different, exclusion is a weak presupposition in LD definitions.

A Victim of Its Own History

Analysis of the definitional components of LD finds a variety of anomalies but no major paradigm shift. A partial explanation is found

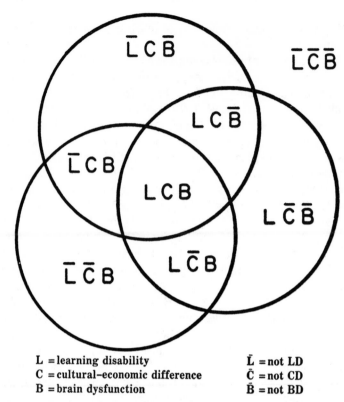

L = learning disability   L̄ = not LD
C = cultural-economic difference   C̄ = not CD
B = brain dysfunction   B̄ = not BD

FIGURE 3-2 Proposed Relationships Among Learning Disabilities, Cultural-Economic Difference, and Brain Dysfunction

in the fact that the prevailing paradigm (Strauss and Werner) biases the research process from initial problem formulation to final interpretation of findings. Scheffler (1967) suggested that there is often an attempt to prove rather than modify a theory which results in an "unconscious" focusing on supportive data and relative neglect of data not in harmony with the theory. This is found in cases where the prevailing paradigm makes researchers overlook events that are incongruent, such as the failure of physicists to recognize the positron (Hanson, 1963), or conversely, make scientists "see" nonexistent phenomena like N rays after the discovery and acceptance of x rays (Rostand, 1960).

Thus, paradigms refer to general beliefs and methods that sometimes may bias the investigative processes. Although biases within an accepted paradigm are often considered, biases inherent in the paradigm itself may also be present. Within a paradigm, investigators differ with respect to favored theories or hypotheses and, while the scientific community is ready to debate the merits of respective biases within an accepted paradigm, the biases inherent in the paradigm itself are much more difficult to observe and to debate. Consequently, procedures and conclusions based on biases in a paradigm itself are usually not open to questions and, for the LD field, the Strauss and Werner paradigm is not only accepted but has become orthodoxy.

The consequences are reflected in an inability of the paradigm to solve basic problems (e.g., definition). The failure to define the basic phenomenon (LD) represents a dismissal of the problem in favor of problems viewed as possessing more foreseeable solutions. But the failure to define the phenomenon in question suggests that the LD field is essentially mired at a stage of development making it equivalent to astrology or alchemy. Grossman (1978) explicated the consequences of a failure to provide a comprehensive definition and discussed the lack of a paradigm shift in LD. There was, however, no explanation of why the LD field has not experienced a paradigm shift.

The history of the LD field reveals that the seminal work of Strauss and Werner evolved into the present-day LD field through the efforts of their colleagues and students who incorporated the paradigmatic assumptions of Strauss and Werner into basic conceptualizations about the nature of LD. The individuals involved represent key figures in shaping the fundamental thinking in both the emerging and present-day LD field. The historical linkages in the LD field have been outlined (Farnham–Diggory, 1978; Hallahan & Cruickshank, 1973; Hallahan & Kauffman, 1976; Haring & Bateman, 1977) and are illustrated in a "family tree" diagram shown in Figure 3-3.

The linkages shown are irrefutable in some instances, more tenuous in others, but everywhere suggestive of the profound influence of Strauss and Werner on people and events in the evolution of LD. Consequently, there exists a bias toward the Strauss and Werner paradigm and no discernible paradigm shift which prevents resolution of the definitional problem. Since paradigms are always relative to the assumptions, preconceptions, and models existing at the time of conception (Feigl, 1970), the Strauss and Werner paradigm, while appropriate for an early stage of LD development, no longer possesses the relevance necessary for advancing LD towards a more scientific status.

The primary components of LD definitions based upon historical precedent and clinical validation, particularly the influential work of Strauss and Werner, simply do not withstand critical scrutiny. Although widely accepted as "truth," these components are not supported by the evidence. Therefore, they are not valid assumptions about LD and support the view of LD as a "victim of its own history" in the sense that ideas no longer cogent are perpetuated by present linkages to the seminal work of Strauss and Werner.

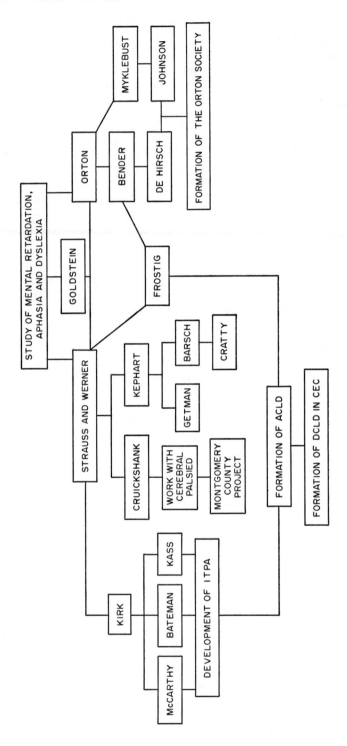

FIGURE 3–3 The "Family Tree" Outlining the Genealogical Development of the LD Field

Lessons from the History of Another Syndrome

A possible solution to the definitional problem might be found be examining these same issues in another syndrome with at least some similarity to LD. The area of mental retardation (MR) immediately presents itself and has been discussed in terms of its relationship to LD (Tarjan & Forness, 1979). Like LD, mental retardation is a condition affecting a significant number of school-age children, is multi-etiological, with exact physiological or psychological causes often not determined, is defined partly by certain exclusionary features, is associated with academic failure, and is diagnosed in school years by reliance on similar psychological measurements in adaptation (achievement) and potential (IQ). Its definition has likewise been subject to scientific controversies in recent decades, most notably the inclusive concept in which MR was seen as an unchangeable condition (Doll, 1941), the introduction of sociocultural etiologies (Hurley, 1969), IQ testing of ethnic minorities (MacMillan & Meyers, 1980), and underidentification of children at upper levels of MR (MacMillan, Meyers, & Morrison, 1980).

The history of MR suggests, however, that paradigm shifts have indeed resulted in definitional adjustments (Scheerenberger, 1982). Official *American Association of Mental Deficiency* (AAMD) definitions of MR have, in fact, shifted five times in the past 25 years (MacMillan, 1982). The current definition indicates that MR "refers to significant subaverage general intellectual functioning resulting in or associated with impairments in adaptive behavior and manifested during the developmental period" (Grossman, 1983). Note that etiology, physiological or psychological correlates, chronicity, and prevailing scientific models are not included in this definition. Emphasis is thus on two coexisting criteria: low IQ and low adaptation. Both criteria further rely on operational guidelines, such as two standard deviations below the mean on a standardized, individually administered test of intelligence and specific areas to be considered in adaptive behavior, including academic achievement during the school years.

Such a two-dimensional definition could indeed be similar to that of LD. The principal difference is that both these criteria are significantly subaverage in MR whereas, in LD, adaptation (achievement) is subaverage while IQ is not. The remaining distinction suggests that the MR definition allows the condition to coexist with certain other conditions which an LD diagnosis traditionally and correctly excludes: gross physical or neurological handicaps, uncorrected impairments in auditory or visual acuity, serious emotional disturbance, and sustained lack of environmental or instructional opportunity. Note that the last two conditions of poor opportunity are difficult exclusionary decisions in LD, but Forness (1982) has detailed how these can at least be approached.

What would remain, then, is a definition of LD that would essentially acknowledge the paradigm shifts discussed herein, shifts similar in some instances to those which the MR definition has so admirably accommodated in recent years. The definition of LD would thus stress significantly subaverage academic impairment, IQ in the normal range, and exclusion of the conditions named above. This diagnosis would thereby differ from one recently proposed by the *NJCLD* (Hammill, Leigh, McNutt, & Larsen, 1981) in which LD could coexist as a disorder secondary to mental retardation, sensory impairment, and social or emotional disturbance. Although specific disabilities might indeed occur as a part of the learning problems of such handicapping conditions, it does not seem necessary to include children thus affected in the LD category for research or eligibility purposes; but it does, however, remain quite important to address their particular needs in individual educational plans.

Agreement on acceptable operational guidelines for these criteria would still be difficult to obtain but not as difficult as before. The most problematic would undoubtedly be that of discrepancy, that is, what constitutes a *significant* difference between low achievement and normal potential at different age levels. The least difficult should be that of determining an underlying physiological or psychological process deficit, since that consideration would now be eliminated. Thus, LD is defined simply as a discrepancy between normal potential and achievement not explained by obvious physical, neurological, sensory, emotional, or experiential deficits.

Other guidelines could likewise be addressed to avoid false-positive diagnoses, such as the use of *individual* IQ and achievement tests, low performance on more than one test of achievement, and acknowledgement that LD could indeed coexist with a behavioral or conduct disorder (as opposed to serious emotional disturbance) (see Kavale, Alper, & Purcell, 1981). This last issue would also be problematic but might perhaps be resolved by resorting to an operational definition of LD "with or without behavior disorder," much in the same fashion that psychiatric diagnostic procedures now operate (Forness & Cantwell, 1982) (e.g., as in the case in the diagnosis of what is termed "attention deficit disorder," ADD, in which the diagnosis is further specified as "ADD with" or "without hyperactivity"). Whether such a distinction in LD is possible or even necessary may not be clear until after further research and experience with the principal LD diagnosis as proposed above is accumulated.

Conclusion

The LD field faces a fundamental problem of definition that was hypothesized to be the result of historical influences. The failure to modify LD definitions has made LD a victim of its own history, unlike MR, which has adapted to its historical changes. The genealogical evolution of the LD field has nonetheless led to its establishment as an important category of special education but has also led to unique problems, namely the perpetuation of paradigmatic assumptions no longer fundamental to the characterization of LD. The primary components of LD definitions were not supported by empirical evidence and represented reified concepts masquerading as actualities.

Consequently, to accomplish resolution of the definitional problem, the LD field will have to break the bonds of its past and not resist modifying the prevailing (Strauss & Werner) paradigm. Such an action, as has happened in the field of MR, will represent the stage of "extraordinary science," resulting in a paradigm shift allowing new concepts to be incorporated into definitional statements. The ultimate result may be redress of definitional problems and LD definition reaching consensus.

4

Philosophical Perspectives on the Science of Learning Disabilities

Learning disability (LD) at its most fundamental level is the study of disability in learning. As such, the purpose of research in LD is the steady extension of knowledge about difficulties in acquiring academic knowledge. This knowledge should coalesce into theories that serve as a basis for research and conceptualization in the science of LD. Theories are intellectual devices representing structured relations linking two or more variables plus appropriate limiting conditions under which the relations will hold. The structured relations in theories are based upon the assumption of an unbroken chain of causal relations between (and among) variables. (These causal relations take two basic forms: if the *necessary* conditions for an event to occur can be established, a theory can be created in the form "no X unless Y under condition C," or if the much stronger, but more difficult to establish, *sufficient* conditions for an event to occur can be determined, a more powerful theory is produced in the form "if X, then Y under condition C." The limiting conditions (C) are essential, though usually suppressed, aspects of theories. Theories based on necessary conditions for change can be used only to prevent change (e.g., necessity of teaching for the child to learn so as not to be LD). When the sufficient conditions for change are known, an intervention strategy can be developed that produces change (e.g., specific deficits are remediated by specific intervention strategies). Any assertion to the effect that an LD child can be treated by "something" implies knowledge of the sufficient conditions for that "something" to occur and this is the assumption underlying present theories of LD.

Although this meaning of theory corresponds to usage in the physical science (Braithwaite, 1955; Nagel, 1961; Toulmin, 1960), it approaches theory development from a different direction that involves human purposes (e.g., understanding of LD). Theories attempt to provide an instrument for reasoned action that can provide an unbroken chain of connections between specific actions (i.e., LD) and consequences in the real world. The actions may cause a change or suppress it; in either case, they have the effect of making the phenomenon different. Reasoned action depends upon the ability to supply reliable answers to three basic types of questions: What caused a particular change to occur? How can a particular aspect of the environment be changed? What will follow if a specific action of change is introduced into the system? Theories supply a set of working assumptions whereby the nature of an adequate response to each question can be determined.

The Soft Nature of LD Theory

Unfortunately, LD theories have not provided the basis for criticizing, justifying, arguing, and improving the responses to basic questions concerning LD. Wong (1979a) reviewed the role of theory in LD and concluded that research based on early theories of LD has generally been unproductive for enhancing understanding of LD. The earlier LD theories were viewed as narrow and inadequate. In a later paper, Wong (1979b) outlined more recent theories of LD that were assumed to avoid the conceptual and methodological difficulties that plagued earlier LD theories. Finally, Wong (1979c) assessed the research and educational implications of recent theories of LD. Although these valuable analyses serve to demonstrate the rudimentary and fragile nature of LD theory, they did not provide an explanation of the reasons why LD theories remain "soft" in the sense of being, for the most part, scientifically unimpressive and technologically unproductive. The need for better LD theories is hardly debatable.

The weakness in LD theory does not seem to be necessary; it is not a function of some innate difference in phenomena or methods but is better accounted for by a short history and a limiting tradition. Although the history question has been addressed (see chapter 3), the tradition of theory building in LD has not been addressed. It is, therefore, the purpose of this chapter to examine critically the nature of theories in LD, to suggest why they are inadequate, and to offer suggestions for improving LD theory to improve its scientific status.

The Development of LD Theory

Theories of LD do not follow the pattern found in the developed physical sciences. For the developed physical sciences, theories typically face two choices: acceptance or rejection (at least in the sense embodied in Kuhn's, 1970, idea of extraordinary science and paradigm shifts).

This approach is noninductive and nonrational since there exists an incommensurability between dislodged theories and those which have taken (or are in the process of taking) their place. Theories in LD, however, reveal a different sequence of events: an initial period of enthusiasm, a period of attempted application to real situations, a period of growing disillusionment when validation studies produce negative results, a period of puzzlement over inconsistent and unreplicated findings, a period of multiple excuses by theory proponents (and counterattacks by theory opponents), and, finally, a period when interest wanes and the theory fades into the background. Nevertheless, there exists the strong probability that the theory will be only temporarily dislodged and will reappear in some form (either intact or modified). The reappearance suggests no incommensurability in the face of an alternative theory but, rather, an attempt to correlate theories into contingent dependencies that neither accepts nor rejects a theory per se.

The primary difficulty with this "come and go" nature of LD theories is that such an attitude is antithetical to scientific theory building (Stegmuller, 1976). This unscientific stance is an impediment to progress since the result is not theorizing but most usually acrimonious debate that develops more along political than scientific grounds (e.g., the controversy over psychological processes and process training). The developed sciences are characterized by cumulative knowledge based upon a critical posture wherein facts are submitted for evaluation and, if acceptable, pooled into a more accurate description of the phenomenon (e.g., an LD paradigm). This process allows for scientific progress.

The LD field, unfortunately, has been marked by an "authority syndrome" that is antagonistic to the critical tradition of science. In chapter 2 we demonstrated how invalid concepts about LD have been promulgated because of the uncritical acceptance of early LD paradigms. The LD field has been marked by cults (or schools of thought for a less pejorative term) which often withdraw into metaphysical belief systems that defy the critical questioning necessary for establishing paradigmatic assumptions critical to scientific progress. If an LD theory is impervious to any criticism based on contrary evidence, then it is devoid of scientific content since it proves true no matter what happens. If evidence is favorable, good; and if it is unfavorable, it is simply interpreted to mean its opposite — good once again. But as Popper (1959) emphasized, the content of a scientific theory essentially consists of what it excludes, that is, in the things that it says do not happen. A theory that excludes nothing reveals nothing since it does not narrow expectations: as far as such a theory is concerned, anything at all might happen and be perceived as true.

The Validation of LD Theory

The theories of LD discussed by Wong (1979a, b) represent a variety of substantive and methodological positions regarding the nature of LD. Some are conceptually exciting but technologically weak (or vice versa) but all have a common feature with the physical sciences: they were originally developed with little emphasis on notions of statistical significance testing. As clinical evidence became less rewarding, theoretical notions about LD became more reliant on attempts to refute the null hypothesis as the method for corroborating substantive theories of LD. This procedure is basically unsound, is poor scientific strategy, and is the reason that LD theories remain "soft."

The reliance on statistical significance testing (Fisher, 1956, 1966, 1967) leads to methods of theory validation that do not either prove or disprove theories. Theories are validated neither through an inductive-empirical system of logic based on facts (see Hempel, 1955; Wright, 1957), nor through a system of axioms based on operational definitions (see Carnap, 1969; Reichenbach, 1968). Theory validation for these logical positivists is based on the induction of general empirical laws from a set of observations that are formally stated using "pure logic." Theories then consist of a set of induced general laws about observable phenomena which, coupled with a set of particular observations of phenomena, allows for the deductive prediction or explanation of associated empirical phenomena (Braithwaite, 1955).

The theories, however, have not been validated as universal in scope because their foundation is based only on past and present observation and future projections cannot be made with certainty. This deterministic aspect is a function of the pure logic used since it is constrained within a formal structure. Thus, if logic begins with general true statements, the conclusions arrived at, when they are combined with particular statements, must necessarily be true. This is not validation.

Although pure logic is assumed to arrive at universal conclusions, the logical positivists ignore the problem of where general laws come from. Logic is again the answer, though for this problem inductive logic is used (Reichenbach, 1968). But this is not an adequate solution since it simply hides an empirical generalization under the label "logic." Inductive reasoning proceeds from particular observations to a general statement of associations that are still tied to the past and present and does not allow projection of its relevance to the future. Although the particular statements upon which it is based may be "true," it is not possible to know whether the general statement is true. If the general statement is not necessarily true, neither are the conclusions that can be drawn from its use. This "pure logic" cannot draw necessary conclusions by deduction from inductive general statements.

The possibility of using induction to arrive at general laws has been subject to critical attack (Feyerabend, 1962; Hesse, 1966; Scriven, 1958, 1962; Sellars, 1956). It is claimed that scientific explanation is simply not so amenable to neat logical treatment as claimed. The deductive schema oversimplifies the process since it subsumes a finished body of laws. But this is seldom, if ever, the case; this ideal is achieved only in systems where all relevant variables are accurately specified and thus represent "perfect knowledge" (Bergmann, 1957; Brodbeck, 1962). For explanatory efforts in LD, however, explanation requires the interplay of experimental hypotheses, factual language, and theoretical construction which are contextually interrelated. Thus, theoretical systems are both incomplete (imperfect) and dynamic in that events themselves may cause some theoretical modification. By focusing solely on observables, a hypothetico–deductive system maintains its simplicity and integrity but the resulting lawlike statements are both inaccurate and incomplete descriptions of the particular events to which they presumably apply.

It is also the case that inductive inferences in a hypothetico–deductive system cannot be "probable" or specified in terms of probability. Clearly the universality of a general law cannot be a matter of "degree" or the law would not be universal; it cannot be sometimes true and sometimes not. Brodbeck (1962) suggested that there is no general logic by which scientific laws can be constructed but instead the result of "obscurantist criteria" that include creative intuition and the feel for conceptual context rather than pure logic. But if general empirical laws are arrived at through some mental operation, then the result only represents another label for generalizing from particular observations.

Within the hypothetico–deductive tradition, the classic treatment of the logic of deductive explanation, according to Hempel (1952) involves the use of a set of general laws $L_1, L_2, L_3, \ldots, L_n$, a set of statement of observed events, $C_1, C_2, C_3, \ldots, C_n$, and E, a sentence containing the predicted or explained event which is arrived at deductively from the premises (L_s and C_s). Prediction and explanation are thus both consequences of the use of deductive logic, going from premises including empirical generalizations and particular observations to a conclusion involving an event to be explained or predicted. But if a general law (L) is simply a generalization (or an induction from previous observations), any additional C_s simply add to the law itself and cannot be used deductively to predict or explain E, which itself can be no more than a test of the truth or falsity of the general law. A general law, L, if it is indeed a consequence of generalization, is less sure than particular observations, C_s, on which it is based; consequently, even if E_s could be explained by deduction, the explanation would be less sure than the observations on which it was based.

The problem is that laws based on empirical generalization contain no more than the observations themselves, and explanation is reduced to nothing more than a statement of what is (or more accurately, what was). Such laws are causal explanation of the form A has been observed with B, and B is said to be explained by the observation of A. But if B does not occur when A occurs, the law is not universal. This is because the causal connection itself cannot be observed so the observation is incomplete and the connection remains tentative. Nothing is predicted or explained if the event itself is more certain than the law supposedly explaining it. The event is the test of the theory, not a prediction from it. Thus, no empirical generalization can act as a major premise in a hypothetico–deductive system since it can never be used deductively to explain or to predict.

Although statistical explanation involving the application of "probabilistic" relational statements to particular events are also included as a type of scientific explanation by logical positivists, their structure is analogous to deductive explanation. This is the case, since a general relational statement and a specific factual statement (data) are used to derive a conclusion about a specific fact. For example, an explanation of Billy Jones' recovery from a bacterial infection would include the following:

Premise A: The probability of recovery from a bacterial infection when treated with an antibiotic is close to 1.

Premise B: Billy Jones was given large doses of antibiotic.

Conclusion: The probability that Billy Jones will recover from the bacterial infection is close to 1.

Hempel (1952) termed this concept a probability statement like Premise A a "statistical law" but this suffers from the same logical problems as other "general laws." Prediction and explanation cannot be made; Billy Jones either does or does not recover, which either increases (slightly) or decreases (substantially) the probability value. Such a statistical relationship is as unsure as a causal relationship since its value varies with the event it is supposed to predict and is also altered by it, while the event itself cannot be predicted with any certainty. The statistical explanation based on the findings of LD research are of this type, except that our "probability" values are usually much lower then 1. A doctor may use an antibiotic on Billy Jones with some hope for recovery since it has been used many times with considerable success, but we have no such confidence in our LD statistical findings. Knowledge of empirical association is often used in practical situations but it *explains* nothing. In the above-mentioned example, knowledge consists of nothing more than knowing (1) many children who take an antibiotic recover from bacterial infections, (2) Billy Jones was given an antibiotic, and (3) Billy Jones recovered (or did not recover) from the infection. These statements are not inductive (as Hempel termed it) because it involves no general statement, and is not even deductive (in the more usual hypothetico-deductive terminology) since it is based on no major premise. Thus, logical positivism turns science into "empirical science" based on a faulty hypothetico-deductive model; any attempt to construct science in accordance with such thinking ends in simplistic empiricism.

How then should theories be tested? Theories are best validated through the methodological viewpoint proposed by Popper (1959, 1968, 1972) wherein the notions of falsifiability and corroboration are central themes. Since there are always alternative explanations of any given set of data and since it is always possible that inconsistent data might turn up, no conclusions that go beyond the data can be proven. The only possibility is that they can be falsified by finding data which are inconsistent. Thus, inductive conclusions are not verifiable, only falsifiable. Scientific theories are viewed as universal statements (all Y's are Z) that can be falsified by a single contrary instance. In this way, a theory is corroborated to the extent that it is improbable and has withstood severe tests which subject it to grave danger of refutation. In a more formal system refutation is demonstrated in the implicative syllogism ($[H{\rightarrow}O]$ and $\sim O{\vdash} \sim H$) (Popper's modus tollens — i.e., a method of reasoning from a hypothetical proposition according to which if the consequent be denied the antecedent is denied, e.g., if A is true, B is true; but B is false; therefore A is false).

Once a theory is proposed, empirical findings are compared with theoretical predictions and a decision is made on whether the "fit" can be taken as confirmation or falsification. Thus, the fate of theory is the result of such testing, but theories vary in the extent to which they can be tested. A theory is testable in principle if it predicts that at least one logically possible empirical generalization will not be found to be true in fact, and the more such predictions it makes, the more readily testable it is. In other words, a theory is highly testable in principle when it can be shown to be false by any of a large number of logically possible empirical findings and when only one or a few such findings can confirm it. In this sense, a theory thus obtained would describe the phenomenon as precisely as possible and allow for the maximization of scientific progress. When the notion of falsifiability is applied to theory validation, Popper (1959) suggested that the process is analogous to trial by jury, wherein the truth of a theory is decided according to rules of evidence and procedure, and to sentence by a judge, wherein the fate of the theory is determined.

It is the characteristics of falsifiability that make a theory scientific (as opposed to logical or metaphysical), and not any inductive support or any degree of probability calculated from empirical date. The primary criterion of choice between theories is in terms of "degree of falsifiability;" the riskier the test the better, since a good theory is one that has stood up to tests designed to falsify it if it is, in fact, false. Popper (1959) termed this *corroboration*. An illustration based upon the hypothetical Kavale–Forness Theory of LD will provide an example. Suppose that we predict from our LD theory that 3% of the school population will be LD. If this turns out to be the case, our predictive success would not be particularly impressive. Our colleagues would probably not be any more impressed if we predicted that more boys than girls (3:1) will be LD even if the sex differences in prevalence are highly significant ($p < .001$). If our LD theory predicts that 300 children in a school district of 10,000 will be LD and exactly 300 children are found to be LD, then our colleagues might take notice of our theory but might attribute its predictive success to coincidence and good luck. But suppose that we predict beforehand which 225 boys and 75 girls will be LD and, in fact, these are the 300 children found to be LD. The Kavale–Forness LD theory is now somewhat more impressive. But now further suppose that we predict which of the 225 boys and 75 girls will fall into the mild, moderate, and severe classifications of LD and also predict their primary area of deficiency (within reasonable tolerance). The Kavale–Forness Theory of LD must now be noticed because it possesses considerable verisimilitude ("truth-likeness") (Popper, 1959; see also Bunge, 1964; Popper, 1976).

The concept of verisimilitude is an ontological, not an epistemological, concept that should not be confounded with notions of probability levels as evidence or proof (as Fisher might argue). In terms of statistical concepts, a better analogy can be drawn with Bayesian statistics (except for the demand of low rather than high prior probability) to reach the concept of expectedness (Pap, 1962), which specifies how many and how much LD would be found. Because such prediction is commonplace in the physical sciences, a theory of this sort is not extraordinary; but a theory (of LD or any behavioral phenomenon) that makes precise predictions and correctly constrains narrow intervals or point values out of a wide range of possibilities is a strong theory.

The State of LD Theory

Although no LD theory even approaches this state, the complex nature of LD and extensions of Popper's conceptualizations demand a refined procedure for theory building and testing. Most theories of

LD offer a single condition paradigm wherein a single antecedent state (e.g., attention deficit, perceptual-motor disability) results in a single consequence (i.e., LD). This rendering of LD theory is too simplistic (Applebee, 1971; Wiener & Cromer, 1967) because there is no definition of LD that recognizes it as a unitary disorder. Learning is too complex a phenomenon to be viewed as a unitary process and the constructs used to define the single condition (e.g., perception, attention, memory, language) do not possess sufficient validity. Compounding these difficulties is the typical methodological procedure of basing theoretical statements on obtained differences between normal and LD subjects. But Cronbach (1957) pointed out the paradoxical situation found in the fact that what is one researcher's subject matter is another researcher's error term.

An LD sample is likely to differ not only with respect to the strength of the variable but also how the variable was developed and organized. These individual differences are usually not considered, since groups are most usually selected on the basis of exclusionary parameters that makes LD a residual disorder (i.e., that aspect of underachievement not explained). As the selected LD subsamples are found to possess some new associated deficit area, the previously identified deficits may or may not be present. This situation indicates both an ambiguity about the nature of LD and a complexity around the nature of LD brought about by a confounding of variables associated with the LD phenomenon.

The nature of LD demands a multiple condition paradigm that addresses the complexity surrounding the phenomenon. Such a paradigm, however, is not simply a linear combination of elements found in single condition paradigms but, rather, a multivariate and interactive stochastic configuration. This type of theory possesses the advantage of reducing heterogeneity but the disadvantage of increasing the number of parameters needed to define LD.

A behavioral system like LD is usually conceived as having three classes of variables: (1) variables that are manipulable, (2) variables that are not manipulated but, rather, held constant in an effort to exclude them from influencing the system under study, and (3) variables that are random and contribute to either measurement error or sample variance. But, when a multiple condition paradigm is attempted for a phenomenon like LD, it is likely that a nonnegligible class of variables that are not random but systematic (and, in turn, are influenced by other variables both inside and outside the system) are likely to operate. These *nuisance variables* (Meehl, 1970; see also Fisher, 1966) exert considerable influence of outcomes, but it is rarely possible to measure either their magnitude or direction. Thus, nuisance variables are statistically and causally indeterminate.

When combined with indeterminant construct validity (for manipulable variables) and sample heterogeneity, this indeterminism affects the causal structure of the system. Even in complex systems, there exists causal structures and boundary conditions wherein slight differences (truly random events) tend to "wash out" and cancel effects. This situation is termed *convergent causality* (Langmuir, 1943; see also London, 1946) and permits confidence in the stability of predictive values. On the other hand, there are systems (e.g., LD) in which slight differences in the exact character of the initial conditions are, in fact, amplified over the long run. This *divergent causality* can distort predictive accuracy in an essentially unknown fashion. Since the large number of variables necessary for theorizing about LD are neither independent nor equal contributors to the system, the number of nuisance variables also increases; these variables then interact with each other to produce divergent causality. This situation makes LD theory more idiographic than nomothetic since the inductive subsumption of particulars is more difficult than in the physical sciences.

LD Theory and Context—Dependent Stochastologicals

A multiple condition paradigm might be conceptualized as similar to Cronbach and Meehl's (1955) nomological network to designate the system of laws assumed to exist between theoretical entities themselves, and between theoretical entities and their observable indicators. The "network" indicates a structured system wherein the nodes represent the postulated theoretical entities, while the strands represent the lawful relationships hypothesized to hold between them. This network is systematic because its semantic base (i.e., the overlap in the propositions' inner components) allows for the formal derivation of logical chains from the shared terms to observational statements. The network is also empirical because subsets of theoretical terms are directly coordinated with terms designating observable predicates ("operational"). Despite one's position on a particular matter (e.g., processes and process training), it is true that physical sciences differ from an enterprise like LD in the fact that (in part) they demand an objective conception (in the positivist sense) of the protocols that describe observations (i.e., reliable and replicable).

The nomological network in a field like LD is only correlated directly in a few instances and is thus not operational throughout, since some nodes and strands are connected with an observational base only through other subregions of the network (see Hempel, 1952). The nomological network designates strict laws or "nomic necessity" in a logical sense (Johnson, 1964) but the lawlike relationships in LD are rarely (if ever) of this strict, logically structured variety. Instead, LD "laws" are correlations, tendencies, probabilities, and the like that Meehl (1978) has termed *context-dependent stochastologicals* (an analog to nomological). Although the problems of stochastologicals are not new to LD (see *Journal of Special Education*, 1976, for a symposium on research problems in LD), the limitations of such a probabilistic law network is not readily apparent until we decide to test our theories. When theories are corroborated solely with observational data based on percentages, correlations, or significance tests, it is difficult (or impossible) to determine whether some empirical data refute a theory or even whether two sets of data are inconsistent. The only certain statement is that such context-dependent stochastologicals (statistics) should not be the same in different studies investigating the same problem. Although certain, it is neither terribly interesting nor a good test of theory. (It does become interesting when the data are too consistent, as was the case in Burt's kinship correlations which were practically identical, even though derived from different tests and samples.)

Because of the indeterminate nature of LD, the observed statistical dependencies are always, to some degree, contingent upon the ecological setting (Barker, 1968; Lewin, 1951) in which the measurements were obtained. With the failure to provide a comprehensive causal theory (as expressed in the nomological network) of LD that provides insights into both the magnitude and direction of ecological influences, it is impossible to compute the numerical changes expected in statistical dependencies collected from either different populations or settings. Consequently, it is even difficult to determine whether, for example, the difference between two correlations is attributable simply to fluctuation resulting from random sampling (as might be assessed in a simple cross-validation procedure) or whether the differences are attributable to the particular contexts, which involves the more complex problem of external validity. In the first instance, it is possible to use standard statistical procedures to decide whether study X "replicates" study Y but the second instance is associated with no standard statistical procedure. Although seemingly empirical, context-dependent data are really more qualitative since they provide only general insights (i.e., it seems to fit).

Its qualitative aspect, however, provides little confidence that the shift in statistical dependency is a strong signal for theory refutation. Hence, there are no "ball park" figures that indicate either corroboration or refutation of theoretical statements. For example, what conclusion might be drawn if the Forness–Kavale Test of LD correlates .60 with IQ and .50 with *SES* in California, but .35 and .65

with IQ and SES, respectively, in New York LD students? Besides rationalizations related to context dependencies (e.g., different LD definitions), there is nothing in these differences that reflects cogently on theoretical conjectures.

In the physical sciences, although probability concepts (in theories) and statistical distributions (in data) may appear, they often are eliminated in the course of deriving a nomological network until closure is achieved in a substantive theory. Even when statistical notions remain in the predicted observations, the resulting numerical values are typically not context dependent, and if they are, precise experimental manipulation is usually possible. But the strong context dependency of LD makes it very unlike the physical sciences. The problems involve basic dissimilarities like knowing even all the contextual influences. Even if known, problems still exist in delineating the functional form of contextual influences with numerical values for the parameters. Thus, context dependencies introduce essentially unknown elements into the theoretical system. The result is a reliance on probability statements that vary with different contexts. This variability precludes any final probability statements, which means any claims to precision evaporate in the refuge of stochastic processes. The other methods used to excuse imprecision — standard deviation, standard error, and confidence intervals, for example — make it difficult to quantify contextual variables and keep them essentially unknown elements. Since sample sizes in LD research (unlike physical science) do not guarantee a close fit between theoretical and observed frequencies (as predicted from the Bernoulli theorem), the question remains as to whether context-dependent stochastologicals represent real influences or extraneous influences that need to be either controlled, incorporated into, or eliminated from theoretical systems.

LD Theory and Operationalism

The consequences of these problems are found in the difficulty of providing rigorous and explicit definitions for theoretical LD concepts. The variability and unpredictability of LD means it is not a body of "perfect" knowledge characterized by complete and closed procedural laws (i.e., a temporal sequence of events) wherein the value of any one variable at any time can be calculated by means of such laws (Bergmann, 1957; Brodbeck, 1962). Rather, LD is a body of "imperfect" knowledge marked by open concepts where understandings are neither complete nor closed. The indeterminate nature of LD means that LD possesses no procedural laws. To compensate for either incompleteness or lack of closure (or both), the "openness" in LD is usually sidestepped by either operationalism (if a tough-minded scientific stance is taken) or fuzzy verbalisms (if an artistic or literary orientation is taken). Because the LD field most often assumes a tough-minded scientific stance, operationalism is a common phenomenon in its theories.

Operationalism is concerned with the formation of empirical categories that can be determined by carrying out a set of systematic operations. A basic assumption is that empirical categories can best be defined by the operations used to observe the experiences to be included in the categories. The purpose of operational procedures is to structure operations so that different results can be assigned numerical values. When a succession of similar operations can be performed on a succession of similar objects, with each different result being assigned a different numerical value, the aggregate of all those possible values is called a *scale*. The scale, in turn, is supposed to represent a *concept*. Thus, the concept of visual perception is what the visual perceptual test measures. Like empiricists, operationalists have confused concepts with observations. If visual perception is defined as an empirical entity, the operations of the visual perceptual test are also then observational. As such, it cannot enter into mathematical relations with other concepts in a scientific law. In fact, operationalists, like empiricists, view scientific laws as consisting of causal empirical relations between observables (see Bridgman, 1927; Campbell, 1957).

Operationalist approaches have had a negative impact on the LD field because it has consistently (and persistently) been used as a *method*, whereas in the physical sciences operationalism has been used only to interpret already established measurement procedures. Scientific measurement is not dependent on any empirical technique but is a consequence of a mathematically exact theory. To explain, predict, and manipulate the relations between observables, a scientific knowledge system uses concepts (nonobservables) theoretically related in laws (abstract inventions). If laws are to have any empirical use, they must be abstractively related to observables through their concepts. Abstractively relating a concept to particular empirical observations may be termed an empirical interpretation of a concept. Measurement is a means by which a concept is empirically interpreted. Concepts are not observables and empirical measures thus cannot be definitions of concepts. In sum, the idea of operational definitions is contradictory to the meaning of concepts in science.

In a field like LD, operationalism has been the justification for the development of scaling techniques, and is the reason why we encounter discussion of the "measurement problem" in LD. For LD, the measurement problem is usually discussed in relation to "validity" and "reliability." The validity issue addresses, for example, the question, "How can we know that our attention measure really measures attention?" But the question is really meaningless since it is evident that an operational viewpoint suggests that attention can be no more than its operations for measurement. Obviously, it must measure attention because "attention is what it measures." The question of reliability is usually concerned with whether the same group will score similarly at two different times (also involved might be questions of ordering and stability). This question is also meaningless because no empirical group is ever the same at two different times. Additionally, operational procedures for scaling are not very precise and thus all subsequent empiricist procedures of association will only compound error. Because such scales are not scientific measures, their scope is limited to the population studied; therefore, any attempt to induce beyond the population studied is not possible.

From a scientific point of view, it makes no sense to establish exact measurement unless it is theory based. Operationalism represents an empiricist attempt to understand scientific measurement but is really a nonrational interpretation of scientific measurement. The result is a method that produces low levels of relationship with limited scope, while scientific measurement allows for the production of laws with high levels of relationship and broad limits. To explain this limitation of empiricism, the fault is assumed to lie in the measurement problem. Yet, this same measurement problem is the result of operationalism. The outcome is a tautology that moves the LD field in a disorganized mass of justification, assumption, and incantation.

The rigor found in the physical sciences is not possible in LD because of the intrinsic nature of the subject matter, that is, its multidimensional and context-dependent nature which defies a fully determinate rendering of its structure and causal relationships. The openness found in LD may take three forms that may all be present in the same theoretical conjecture (Meehl, 1977; see also Hempel, 1970). These include (1) openness arising from its indefinite extension of operational indicators of a construct, (2) openness associated with individual indicators because they are probabilistically, rather than nomologically, linked to the theoretical construct, and (3) openness associated with the fact that theoretical constructs are often delineated by a contextual definition, that is, by their role in the nomological network rather than a rendering of its own internal structure. For a phenomenon like LD, explicit definition of theoretical constructs is seldom achieved in terms of the initial observational variables but, rather, through a process of theoretical reduction. This is not to suggest, however, that LD researchers must become "reductive materialists" where a concept is synonymous with expressions of general logic (Nagel, 1961). The process of concept formation involves a *symbolic* representation aimed at formulating relations between indicators of a concept, so that one set of indicators can be taken as a reliable, rather than absolute, sign of the indicators. Thus, although LD concepts are often quite vague or fuzzy, every attempt would be made to be precise and explicit about that very conceptual fuzziness in order to provide, at least, partial closure rather than the pretentiousness found in operational definitions.

The creation of new concepts that may be important for LD theory does not require operationalism, that is, the requirement for theoretical constructs to be anchored to the data of observation. Strict operationalism is not a necessary condition for scientific significance and meaningfulness of a proposition. This "ultraoperationalism" is restrictive and narrow, and is probably not even possible in the physical sciences (Feigl, 1956). A theory begins with the description of a phenomenon that is then grouped and classified. The process of grouping and classifying is based upon abstract ideas, suggesting that even foundation concepts possess a measure of uncertainty (i.e., imperfect). Concepts gain increased clarity (i.e., completeness and closure) through observation that leads to modification in an attempt to make them more "perfect" but, at the same time, remaining logically consistent.

MacCorquodale and Meehl (1948) indicated that concepts originally introduced in LD as intervening variables, that is, conventionalized designations for a class of observable properties (e.g., perception, attention, memory, and so on) become hypothetical constructs when there are modifications that make them more logical and perfect. These hypothetical constructs, however, are inadmissable in theory (unlike intervening variables) because they require the existence of entities that cannot be validated. In reality, all the conditions in which intervening variables become manifest cannot be specified, since their statement involves open concepts and requires an infinite series of conditions to be tested. Most LD concepts are, thus, theoretical abstractions which give generic names to categories of psychological phenomena contained in hypothetical functions. Thus, hypothetical constructs or "fictitious concepts" (Hempel, 1952), although only having a tenuous relationship with observation, represent the introduction of creativity into theory construction that allows for useful theoretical abstractions even if they are only indirectly confirmable (Feigl, 1956). The rationale is based upon the assumption that "a term is fruitful only if it encourages changes in its own meaning; and, to some considerable extent, this is incompatible with operational definition" (Scriven, 1956, p. 113).

It is probably the case that concocting quick and easy operational definitions for LD concepts does more harm than good since they usually lack theoretical interest and technological power (Loevinger, 1957). The reason is that an ultraoperational approach fails to account for the complexly determined nature of LD. The classical experimental situation, wherein control is exercised over everything but a single operationally defined variable, is inappropriate. But when design complexity is increased in multivariate studies that simply operationalize many variables, the result is probably overdetermination. This makes it difficult to evaluate the relative weights of the multiple factors leading to the behavior (i.e., LD).

The same behavior may be determined by a combination of variables (i.e., *A . . . Z*) and may appear superficially the same when *A* is the primary variable or when *Z* is the dominant factor. Not only are identical LD behaviors produced by a variety of variables, but the configuration within even the same individual leading to identical LD behaviors may vary over time (see Forness and Kavale 1983a, 1983b, for a review of these issues).

In order for theory to be tested, operationalism necessitates the identification of elements of the hypothetical abstract statement with observation of particular events in the real world. For example, the LD notion of discrepancy is often operationalized to provide rigor in definitional statements. The abstract notion that discrepancy is defined by the difference between expected and actual achievement can be given psychological significance if expected and actual achievement can be specified in a way that permits their measurement. Although seemingly plausible, major problems are encountered in attempting to measure either expected or actual achievement (see chapter 2). The usual solution is to identify each theoretical entity with something already measured (i.e., intelligence tests and achievement tests). By fiat, the theoretical entities have been measured and a bit of simple subtraction is assumed to reveal the presence or absence of a discrepancy. Unfortunately, the situation is not so simple; inherent problems are found in (1) the reliability and validity of each individual measure, (2) the reliablility and validity of the concept "discrepancy" because of the imprecision produced by context-dependent stochastologicals (most notably the phenomenon of regression), and (3) the failure to specify (or include) the influence of intervening variables in the nomological network (e.g., *SES*, motivation, instruction, and the like) (see Forness, 1982; Forness, Sinclair, & Guthrie, 1983).

The usual response is to validate the discrepancy index by correlating it with school grades, for example, and not surprisingly, a significant correlation is found in 358 children; that is, those with the largest discrepancy also show the lowest grades. This is not theoretical verification but rather a low grade of psychometric engineering. Validation of this type substitutes the appearance of rigor for explicit theoretical derivation. By masquerading under the guise of operationalism, discrepancy so defined can only be regarded as a delusion. There is no theory in the sense of an explicit and non-self-contradictory system, but only the appearance of one. The procedure of quantifying variables (e.g., test scores) only serves the purpose of disguising poorly realized conceptions, such as equating expected achievement with the score on an IQ test. A concept like expected achievement is too complex to be quantified in a simplistic operational manner which, seemingly rational, is obviously meretricious. Even though the LD field appears committed to scientific theory, the result is actually anti-theoretical and intellectually unappealing.

LD Theory and Multiple Validation

Recall that Popper's view of science focuses on the single negative instance that falsifies a theory. But the complexity of LD, in terms of its multivariate structure and context–dependent relationships, suggests that no LD theory of any power or sophistication is ever refuted by a single counter instance. Duhem (1954) pointed out that the schema ($[H{\rightarrow}O]$ and $\sim O\}{\vdash}\sim H$) was an oversimplification (see also Grunbaum, 1960; Quinn, 1969; Wedeking, 1969). A single hypothesis is never tested in isolation, but, rather, against a whole network of auxiliary hypotheses plus the empirical rendering of the conditions describing the experimental protocol. Therefore, a better representation of falsification is the more complicated schema ($[\Sigma H{\rightarrow}O]$ and $\sim O\}{\vdash}\sim \Sigma H$). Thus, when observation is in disagreement with prediction ($\sim O$), then the only legitimate conclusion is that one of the hypotheses (e.g., H_1) in the system was false; which particular hypothesis was refuted can never be determined with complete assurance.

This rendering suggests that the act of falsification is inherently ambiguous. In order to falsify a particular hypothesis, the veracity or plausibility of all other hypotheses entering the experiment must be assumed. For every hypothesis tested, there arises a more complicated auxiliary network via the assumptions that were necessarily entertained in order to conduct the experiment.

Falsification is also ambiguous in another sense. Suppose there exists a single hypothesis entailing O and the results of a test produces $\sim O$; the conclusion $\sim H$ is justified if and only if it can be shown that there is no set of auxiliary assumptions (A) that can "'save the original hypothesis" (i.e., there exists no A such that $[H$ and $A]{\vdash}\sim O$). This is not to suggest that for every H it is possible to find a set of auxiliary hypotheses A that would allow H to be saved but, rather, those who deny H must show that there does not exist an A which would make H compatible with O (Laudan, 1965). Unless no suitable A is demonstrated, there is justification in believing in the power of H even in the face of seemingly disconfirming evidence. Thus, hypothesis testing (i.e., the gradual elimination of false ideas through tests) possesses a fundamental openendedness.

Yet another complication enters even the simple schema ($[H \rightarrow O]$ and $\sim O \vdash \sim H$), since data (O's) cannot be collected without having presupposed some prior theory with respect to what is being observed. Thus, observations are not theory free; the theoretical set strongly influences what can be and what is observed. "'Seeing" is an activity of the mind, not solely of the eyes (Hanson, 1970).

Most usually, in LD research data are collected and then subjected to interpretive comments (e.g., theory) which is appropriate for clinical inquiry but not scientific inquiry. The primary characteristic of this procedure is interpretation after observation (postdictive), rather than the testing of predictive theoretical hypotheses. Merton (1957) termed these *post factum explanations*, and, although designed to "'explain," they differ logically from a situation where observations are utilized to derive new hypotheses to be either confirmed or refuted by new observations. The primary difficulty with such explanations is that they are indeed consistent with a given set of observations since only those hypotheses in accord with observations are selected for interpretation. In a case like LD theory, such post factum hypotheses are also ad hoc in the sense of having only a slight degree of prior confirmation. The consequence is a spurious sense of adequacy in theory construction because alternative hypotheses (possible equally consistent with observation) are not explored by being tested by new observation. The method of post factum explanation does not lend itself to falsifiability.

The implications of auxiliary hypotheses(and ambiguity) in subjecting the main substantive theory to danger of refutation have been incorporated into more complex schema (Feyerabend, 1962, 1965, 1971; Lakatos, 1970, 1974a, 1974b). First, because hypotheses (H) are formulated as a function of theory (T) (i.e., $H \approx H[T]$ and $O = [H,T]$), where O is a function of both H and T, then $\{(H[T] \vdash O[H,T]$ and $\sim O[H,T]) \rightarrow \sim H(T)\}$. But Feyerabend (1970) argued that theory testing can be "incestuous": If theories and hypotheses influence what is observed, then the possibility exists that observation, instead of challenging the theory and the hypotheses under investigation, will simply be viewed as compatible with the elements being tested. The theory and hypotheses may serve only to screen out the most critical or negative observations ($\sim O$).

Since observations can only be made through theories and hypotheses upon which the observations are based, and if observations may unintentionally reinforce rather than challenge the theories upon which they are based, the solution rests on the process of developing strongly competing alternative theories for every phenomenon. For example, if a theory is conceptualized as the combination of a series of propositions, then the task is to discover at least two competing theories (e.g., T_1, T_2) such that their intersection produces an empty set ($T_1 \cap T_2 = 0$), indicating that they possess no common elements. Not only should theories have as little in common as possible ($T_a \cap T_b = 0$) but should also be dialectical opposites (i.e., $t_{ab} \textcircled{b} t_{bc}$) so that when common components are removed, the test observation modus tollens ($\sim O_c$) uncovered by one theory (T_c) will provide a strong challenge to the predictions of the other theory (i.e., O_a from T_a). When all these ideas are considered in a schema for falsification, the following emerges

$$\{(\Sigma H[T] \vdash O[\Sigma H, T] \text{ and } \sim O[\Sigma H, T]) \rightarrow \sim \Sigma H(T)\}$$

—if and only if no alternative (i.e., ΣH_a, T_b) can be found that "saves" $\Sigma H(T)$.

Auxiliary Hypotheses and LD Theory

The primary difficulty in a field like LD is the fact that the auxiliary hypotheses, as well as the boundary conditions of the system, are frequently (or perhaps always) as problematic as the theory (T) itself. For example, suppose the role of attention in word recognition is investigated by asking two groups of LD children identified on the basis of WRAT reading scores to determine whether words flashed in a tachistoscopic presentation are real or nonsense. For the experimental group, a buzzer is sounded to orient the child to the screen while the control group is not given this orienting stimulus before presentation. If negative empirical results are obtained, what can be said about whether the main substantive theory concerning attention and word recognition has been falsified? Or is it the case that only the auxiliary hypotheses (e.g., that the WRAT is a valid indicator of LD or that a buzzer increases vigilance in LD subjects) have been falsified? Perhaps other conditions were not met (e.g., variables related to visual perception, memory, stimulus value, and so on) that provided for an invalid test.

The problematic nature of auxiliary hypotheses in LD is due, in part, because they are more difficult to validate than in the physical sciences. The looseness of the nomological network allows for a much greater range of possible auxiliaries than found in the physical sciences. Additionally, the physical sciences usually reveal a more intimate connection between substantive theory (T) and the derivation of auxiliary hypotheses. The physical sciences appear to possess auxiliary hypotheses that are, at least, part of a set of core concepts. When these core concepts are absent (as in LD), the auxiliary hypotheses must be considered ad hoc. In the LD field, no such intimate connections exist (in the nomological network), and almost never a relation that leads to direct theoretical derivability. Thus, the auxiliary hypotheses in LD must stand on their own since almost nothing conjectured about the substantive theory (T) can assist appreciably in developing auxiliary hypotheses (e.g., a hypothesis indicating that the Bender-Gestalt is useful for detecting minimal brain damage). The situation where auxiliary hypotheses are merely compared to T in setting up a test of T makes it difficult for LD researchers to fulfill a basic falsifiability requirement, that is, to state a priori what would constitute a strong falsifier. For this reason, Duhem (1954) was critical of the notion of the "crucial experiment" for testing theory. No single test can resolve theoretical controversies for the following reasons: first, because specific hypotheses cannot be isolated from the presumptive failure of the total theory and, second, because any given hypothesis of the theory can be modified so as to alter the theory's testable consequences.

The implication is that there exists no obligation to deny basic theoretical assumptions if, at a given point in time, they cannot be subjected to critical tests of refutation. Rather, research should be directed at improving the fit between theory and observation by developing or modifying auxiliary hypotheses. In this way, auxiliary hypotheses encroach on the theoretical center only when no alternate assumptions are derivable that will have any appreciable effect. Thus, research requires a continuing program rather than focusing on single "critical" studies. Research is focused on auxiliary hypotheses in which theory is fit to data; they are also what is discarded when observation proves negative. Evaluation is not concerned with the capacity of the theory to explain observation, but whether the research efforts are progressive or degenerative (Strike, 1979). A progressive procedure validates theory by introducing auxiliary hypotheses that are not overly ad hoc in relation to the substantive theory, are parsimonious, are consistent, are precise, and, in conjunction with the substantive theory, result in the expansion of the observational base. A degenerative program is, on the other hand, more ad hoc, less parsimonious, uses inconsistent assumptions, and does not expand the observational base. These features make it difficult to assimilate problematic new phenomena, resulting in a theoretical system which is inconsistent, vague, or vacuous.

Testing LD Theory: An Example

An example will reveal the difficulties and complexities of adequate and appropriate theory testing in LD. Suppose we wish to test our "Theory of selective motivational deficit in perceptual interaction for the cognitive integration of visual attention." Each component (i.e., motivation, perception, cognitive integration, visual attention) may be assessed by a "sign" that has some stated construct validity. These assessments might be combined into some quantitative estimate to reveal how an LD group might differ from a normal comparison sample on these signs. Such numerical estimates, however, will fluctuate not only from test unreliability and random sampling, but also from some unknown degree of systematic bias (nuisance variables). All the LD subjects will not average the same scores on the indicator variable (e.g., ITPA, MMFT, Frostig DTVP, or any other test that might be chosen) and may even fall within the average range (at least when standard error is considered). But if the LD sample is reasonably LD, then there must be something inherent in its performance that distinguishes it from the normal comparison group that allows it to be designated LD and perform poorly. Unfortunately, there is no way to ascertain the relative contribution to each theoretical component in making any particular child LD, although the total theory predicts it to be the reason why a child is LD.

This situation is not hopeless if data from previous findings are used to "fine tune" the actual numbers in an attempt to provide reasonable close agreement between previous empirical findings and present conjectures about the relative contribution of each theoretical component to LD. An example is found in the methods of quantitative synthesis (Kavale, 1983; Kavale & Glass, 1981) (see chapter 2), wherein general outcomes are rendered across individual empirical findings. These general outcomes are embodied in the "effect size" statistic that transforms study findings into standard deviation units that provide an expectation about average performance for the phenomenon under study. The outcome is a rough average for each theoretical component, realizing that it is the best possible estimate at this point with data based on different LD groups, who despite differences, were all designated LD. Given that the theoretical components are combined into a single psychometric sign, it is possible to make numerical predictions about how the LD group should vary from the normal control group. These predictions are also computed for other LD samples in an effort to obtain sufficiently large samples.

The substantive theory (T) ("Theory of selective motivational deficit in perceptual interaction for the cognitive integration of visual attention"), when conjoined with auxiliary hypotheses (H) concerning the psychometric validity of each component, and assuming that the proper conditions (C) have been met (i.e., the diagnostic validity of our samples), can generate point predictions that are in danger of being refuted ("high risk") but only when the conjunction ($T+H+C$) is considered the "theory" under test. If the theory is not refuted modus tollens by the empirical data, then it is corroborated since it has escaped falsification, despite the high risk of making .numerical point predictions.

The primary problem is that Popper's views demand that it be stated, before doing any research, what would count as a strong basis for rejecting the theory. If the theory is taken to be the substantive T only, rather than the psychometric auxiliary hypotheses (H) and diagnostic conjectures (C), then the test is not really legitimate as a method of falsification. If the empirical findings do not support the predictions, the T is not abandoned; instead, three alternatives emerge: T is incorrect, H is incorrect (i.e., the tests were not reliable and valid), or C was incorrect (i.e., the diagnoses were not trustworthy).

The difficulty is that LD theory is permeated with auxiliaries and varying conditions so that any hypothesis generated is really based on a conjunction ($T+H+C$). In the strictest sense, it is a violation of the basic Popper position that substantive theory will be viewed favorably when the observations produce results forecast but will not be dismissed when they do not. This amounts to taking the position "heads I win, tails you lose." If the observations are as predicted, then the results support all three aspects of the conjunction ($T+H+C$) and the main substantive theory (T) remains problematic. Thus, no theoretical hard core is substantiated.

The reason is again found in the fact that the LD field lacks the intimately linked inner connections between the components (i.e., $T+H+C$) and it would stretch the imagination if the substantive theory T should have low verisimilitude while the two (unrelated) components of H and C are so delicately balanced that they generate the same numerical predictions generated from the combination (i.e., $T+H+C$) thus giving H and C relatively high verisimilitude. Such a precise counterbalancing of theoretical errors, while not impossible, is highly implausible. Thus, despite the fact that it appears to be hedging when the substantive theory T is not falsified by "bad" results, it is not unreasonable to be, at least, somewhat pleased in theory building when some antecedent observational pattern (i.e., high risk point values) is successfully predicted and confirmed from the conjunction ($T+H+C$).

LD Theory and Statistical Significance Testing

Earlier, it was suggested that theory testing is not best approached through the statistical significance testing procedures developed by Fisher. But the question arises as to why this is so, particularly since it appears that the LD researcher's use of the null hypothesis is an application of Popper's view in contexts where probability plays a major role. In reality, it is not because the testing of the null hypothesis in LD as a means of "corroborating" substantive theories does not subject the theory to risk of refutation modus tollens; the problem is that such a test provides only a feeble risk. The calculated probability in this instance is merely a description of uncertainty based on what has been observed. This is absolute indeterminism at the observational level. Consequently, "probabilistic" generalizations are only "probably" true or false, since they can never be verified or falsified by observation. Theories of LD, as well as the presumed theoretical risks to which they are subjected when the method involves significance testing, are not like testing the Kavale–Forness Theory of LD by seeing how well it predicts the number of males and females falling into a level of severity dimension as well as area of deficit. That is a statement of general empirical knowledge, an empirical generalization, which is based on the observation of similarities and consists of a classification of those similarities according to the criteria by which they are said to be similar. Instead, significance tests make testing the Kavale–Forness Theory like determining whether there are any LD children, whether there will be 3% of the school population LD, or whether there are more males than females LD. That is because such LD findings are not general knowledge; they deal with averages and proportions that are descriptive of particular samples only. In fact, regardless of the sample size, the resulting findings are always a descriptive particular. An average, for example, does not reflect similarities but summarizes a range of differences. Consequently, LD findings are not general—they are instead particularistic descriptions which say nothing about other particulars.

These differences are attributable, at least partially, to the fact that the null hypothesis, taken literally, is always false (see Morrison & Henkel, 1970, especially the papers by Hogben, Bakan, Lykken, & Rozeboom). This is the case because any dependent variable (e.g., academic achievement) in LD will always be a function of a sizable but probably finite number of contributing influences. In order for two groups (i.e., LD versus normal) to be exactly equal on such a dependent variable, it must be imagined that they are exactly equal or precisely counterbalanced on all the contributing influences in the causal chain (which is probably never the case).

Because the null hypothesis is almost always false in LD, the probability of refuting it is contingent almost exclusively on the sensitivity of the experimental design – its logic, the construct validity of the measures, and most importantly, the sample size, which determines statistical power. These features suggest that with a large enough sample and adequate reliability in measures, the null hypothesis will always be falsified, regardless of the truth of the substantive theory. There is, of course, the possibility of a null hypothesis being falsified in the wrong direction, which would indicate that, as power increases, the probability of a corroborative result approaches .50. But if a theory has no low verisimilitude, then the probability of refutation by obtaining a significant difference in the wrong direction also approaches .50. This status quo does not at all resemble the situation desired for theory testing using Popper's methodology. Besides high verisimilitude, theories must also provide powerful measurement techniques wherein there exists some certainty in ascertaining the boundary conditions of the theoretical system. Meehl (1967), however, has pointed out a paradox: improvement in measurement (i.e., accuracy) in the physical sciences tends to subject the theory to greater risk of refutation modus tollens, whereas improved precision in measurement in a field like LD, where theories are tested with the null hypothesis, usually decreases the risk of refutation. This is because it is not the individual characteristics of LD samples that are quantified when these samples are measured but, rather, only examples of general properties which are presumed inherent within the selected LD sample. Heisenberg discovered that the simple act of measurement can have substantial effects on the thing measured in the physical sciences but the implication has yet to be accommodated within LD methodology, even though it applies here with particular force, most obviously because of the human elements involved. Thus, the more prolific the measurement in any LD research, the greater the number of possible distortions built into the research design. These distortions, in turn, prevent the presuppositions underlying the inferential statistics applied to the obtained measurements. Consequently, a significant statistical test in LD provides weak corroboration of theory because the procedure subjects theory to only slight risk of refutation.

Neither is theory testing improved through the use of many significance tests rather than one instance. This is best illustrated in review articles that attempt to verify theory through "vote counting" methods (Light & Smith, 1971) wherein a study may have three possible outcomes: the relationship may be statistically, significantly positive, or significantly negative, or show no statistical significance in either direction. The number of observations falling into each category is tallied and the category containing the plurality of studies is declared the "winner." The theory is thus tested by conclusions based upon the winning category. If, for example, theory X of LD has a batting average of 7:3 on 10 significance tests in a contingency table, it is generally concluded that theory X appears well supported (but with the usual caution "further research is needed to explain the discrepancies"). In Popper's view (and more generally the view of science), this is an inappropriate way to reason because it lacks a logical basis. These procedures fail to recognize the orthogonality between confirmation, which involves an inference (usually invalid) about the third figure ($\sim O$) of the implicative syllogism (this means that such inductive inferences can be objectively wrong even though the procedures were correct), and refutation (involving the fourth figure, i.e., $\sim H$) which gives the modus tollens its robust position in inductive inference. Thus, the significantly negative statistics do theory X of LD far more harm than the positive statistical tests do it good.

The problem is not simply a statistical matter; theory testing by using statistical significance is also inadequate from a scientific perspective. The difficulties transcend technical debate (e.g., whether marginally significant higher order interactions should be pooled in the error term, whether varimax rotation should be used, whether communality estimates should be made differently, whether the covariance matrices were not sufficiently homogeneous, whether the sums of squares should be partitioned under fixed or random assumptions, whether the units of statistical analysis coincide with experimental units, or whether the correlation relationship is based on data that are bivariately normally disturbed). These are statistical problems but have very little to do with scientific methods of theory verification. In attempting to validate theory through a contingency table based on statistical significance, the process is not testing theory but, rather, only the imposition of a theoretical "sense" through rather trivial substantive constructions based on properties of the statistical power function.

The Logic of Statistical Significance Testing

Statistical significance testing is based on Mill's (1872) system of logic to discover whether events (e.g., X and Y) are causally connected. The canons may be depicted as follows in the method of joint occurrence

$$X, A, B, C \rightarrow Y$$
$$X, \bar{A}, \bar{B}, \bar{C} \rightarrow Y$$
$$\bar{X}, A, B, C \rightarrow \bar{Y}$$

where events X and Y appear to be connected such that whenever X is present, Y follows. Since events rarely (if ever) occur in isolation, other events (i.e., A,B,C) occur along with X in order for Y to occur. The task of experimentation is to establish whether X is both necessary and sufficient for the occurrence of Y, as illustrated in the method of joint occurrence.

In considering the basic schema $X, A, B, C \rightarrow Y$, it is the case that no amount of repeated application will allow for confidence about which particular factors X, A, B, C, Y to put into this schema in the first place. Application of the schema presupposes that it is known what should be subjected to the schema. The schema is only capable of demonstrating that the particular array of X, A, B, C, Y can be tested to determine whether X and Y stand in causal relationship to one another. But it may be the case, however, that it is not the occurrence of these alone that cause Y, but some other factor D not included. The method thus presupposes prior knowledge of a finite set of factors. This assumption, however, is problematic because of the difficulty in knowing the nature of the finite set of factors on an a priori basis.

The Mill's schema is best illustrated in the analysis of variance (ANOVA) procedure wherein $X, A, B, C \rightarrow Y$ are depicted in the familiar ANOVA table with X, A, B, C as independent variables and Y the dependent variable. It allows an answer to the following question: Are changes in X, A, B, C accompanied by statistically significant changes in Y? The answers may be equivocal, however, because they are based upon the assumption that there are no interactions between A, B, and C, either among themselves or between them and X and Y. The complex relationships between the primary theoretical concept (in this instance X) and the auxiliary hypotheses (in this case A, B, C) make it difficult to specify distinct levels of X and A, B, C in an unambiguous manner and, consequently, to make a precise determination of the extent to which any particular level of X (e.g., x_i) and A (e.g., a_j), for example, contribute to Y (e.g., y_{ij}). Further, if factors X and A, B, C are not distinct, then it becomes difficult to determine precisely which of the two factors X and A contributes to the presence of Y. There is a confounding of effects.

Campbell and Stanley (1969) have discussed the problem of confounding. In their simplest schema, $X \rightarrow Y$ is depicted as follows

$$O_1 \; X \; O_2$$
$$O_3 \; \bar{X} \; O_4$$

At a given time, t, a set of observations O_1 is obtained. Next, condition X is introduced to see if X has produced a change (O_2) in the original observation O_1. In this schema, X is the causative agent while Y is represented by the difference $O_2 - O_1$. The schema $O_3 \bar{X} O_4$ determines whether the absence of X ($\bar{X}$) causes no change between O_4 and O_3; $\bar{Y} = 0 = O_4 - O_3$ or $O_4 = O_3$ (no change). To control for the possible effects of confounding, Campbell and Stanley (1969) outlined two classes of phenomena that should be considered. The first is internal validity: Did, in fact, the conditions (the X) make a difference? The second is external validity, which involves the question of generalizability. (Internal validity assumes more importance when the goal is theory verification.) Internal validity is concerned with whether or not there are factors other than X in schema, $O_1 X O_2$, causing a difference ($O_2 - O_1$) in Y. If there are other factors besides X, then, unless their potential confounding influence is recognized, it will be incorrectly concluded that it was X that produced a difference between O_2 and O_1 when, in fact, it was some other factor (essentially unknown).

The form of such statistical significance testing is based upon the assumption of precision and accuracy in measurement. If the basic schema ($X, A, B, C \rightarrow Y$) is viewed as a basic and valid representation and explication, then it must be shown that the factors X, A, B, C were enumerated precisely and accurately (i.e., logically) and then also determined, in a precise and accurate fashion (i.e., reliably), the degree to which each factor contributes to Y. Unfortunately, the reliability of LD measurement is rarely precise enough to meet the required assumption. Meehl (1978) suggested that problems of measurement are worsened by the practice of "step-wise low validation." This practice involves using one investigation to "validate" a particular instrument and another study to validate some other instrument, and then the two instruments are correlated in an effort to validate a substantive theory. In reality, little (if anything) has been accomplished. For example, consider that *Kavale's ID Test of Learning Disability* has a validity coefficient of perhaps .40 (against a reasonably definitive criterion). Now suppose that the *Forness Underachievement Index* has the same validity (.40) when considered against its criterion variable. Next is an attempt to corroborate the Kavale–Forness LD theory by demonstrating that the two instruments (each having been "validated") correlate at .40, which, for argument's sake, is highly significant ($p <$ .001). This is simply not an adequate test of a theory. Even if each instrument if very reliable (.90), the proportion of construct valid variance for each measure is about 20% of the reliable variance and the same for their overlap when correlated with each other. Interpretation in such a situation is problematic since, without other information, it is probable that the correlation between measures occurs in a region of each one's components that has little connection to the criterion variables used in validity studies that were the basis for theory testing.

These comments should not be taken as an indictment against statistical significance testing; it is simply not appropriate for theory testing in a field like LD because (to return to an earlier example) a theory that splits seven for and three against is spurious and would clearly be viewed as such in the physical sciences. The problem for LD is based partially on a failure to distinguish between substantive theory and statistical hypotheses (Bolles, 1962; see also Binder, 1963; Grant, 1962). There exists a tendency to assume equivalence between these statements in making inferences. The substantive theory is a hypothesis about the causal structure of the phenomenon in terms of the relationships underlying its entities and processes; the statistical hypothesis is a more restricted and operational conjecture about the value of a parameter (e.g., mean). Statistical hypotheses are thus statements about population distributions that are tested to determine if they should be rejected or nullified (hence, null hypothesis) in favor of an alternative hypothesis. This alternative hypothesis, however, is not part of the causal structure of the phenomenon and suggests nothing about the status of the substantive theory. Although the null hypothesis is often stated in terms of the elements in the experiment, those elements are not entailed in the actual test, which is concerned only with the likelihood of randomness of the data.

The probability expressed in a significance level might be termed auxiliary probability, in contrast to "intrinsic probability" inherent in most scientific hypotheses (Camilleri, 1962). Auxiliary probability refers to a relationship between a sample and a population in terms of the relative frequency with which sampling error will lead to an incorrect decision to reject the null hypothesis, while intrinsic probability provides reference to a relationship between variables expressed in probabilistic terms. Braithwaite (1955) made a similar distinction between a universalistic hypothesis (not all A's are B's) and a probabilistic hypothesis (a proportion of A's are also B's). When theories are tested with significance tests, both auxiliary and intrinsic probability nature are involved, but the obtained level of significance (auxiliary probability) provides no substantive insight into the validity of theoretical formulations. This is because it is erroneous either to define substantive importance in terms of intrinsic probability or to confuse auxiliary and intrinsic probabilities by allowing the former to determine what will be minimally meaningful or acceptable for the latter. The practice of using statistical significance as either a necessary or sufficient criterion for confirmation or refutation of theory is not appropriate, since the findings are not "significant" but, rather, only "signify" a basis for rejecting the null hypothesis. This means simply that it is unlikely that the differences in, let's say, scores on a visual perceptual measure reveal anything about what particular association is not random. Any inference made of an association between variables cannot result from the test of the null hypothesis itself, but must come from elsewhere, primarily from the intent in experimental design and control. The test of significance is really no more than a legitimization for an association either already evident by inspection or already intended by the nature of the design.

Fisher developed procedures for statistical significance testing in agronomy which is quite different from a field like LD. In agronomy, the logical distance (i.e., the difference in meaning or content) between the auxiliary hypothesis (H) and the substantive theory (T) is minimal. For example, suppose that the problem is to determine whether putting fertilizer on the ground will assist in raising more soybeans. Because soil receives its nutrients from the soil, if the statistical null hypothesis is refuted (that plots of soybeans with fertilizer do not differ in yield from plots without fertilizer), then the alternative hypothesis is proved—that there is a difference between these two sorts of plots. The substantive conclusion, given such a difference, is that the fertilizer made the difference. Fisher could assume such an association because the experimental objects (seeds) were developed according to the dictates of scientific theory (genetics), and were essentially the same. This sameness makes Fisher's induced associations actually not the result of any induction but, rather, the demonstration of an expected isomorphism. Such a situation, in which the content of the substantive theory is logically identical with the alternative hypothesis that was refuted by the significance test, is entirely different from the situation in LD. In LD, our empirical subjects are not the same; we can only randomize our selection of subjects and hope that it is relevant, whereas Fisher had perfect control making his experiment's confirmations of established laws. Theory X of LD is not equivalent (or anywhere near equivalent) to the alternative hypothesis. Many sorts of competing explanations are available to explain the non-null statistical difference. As a result, the LD researcher can take little reassurance about the use of significance tests from knowing that Fisher's approach has been useful in studying the effect of fertilizer on crop yields. In fact, the use of random samples for induction to populations is an implicit recognition within LD that test–retest methods will not lead to universally true relationships. Induction from a sample to a population is indeed justified, but scientific laws having the characteristic of unlimited scope can never be developed through these statistical methods. It may be that the brilliance of the techniques and procedures of generalization developed by Fisher has masked its triviality under the illusion of quantitative rigor, and inhibited the search for stronger tests for theory validation. Consequently, efforts have not been directed at concocting substantive LD theories that will generate stronger consequences than merely "the X's differ from the Y's."

If there is a certain discomfort with this position in the LD field, then an examination of any textbook in theoretical physics or chemistry will provide some proof, since one can search in vain for a statistical significance test. This is certainly not the case in the theoretical LD texts that are literally filled with inferential statistics. The difference lies in the fact that the power found in physical science theory does not come from exact assessment of probabilities that a difference exists, nor from the presumed verbal precision of "operational definitions" in the embedding context. The power comes from two other sources: the deductive capacity of the formal theory and the accuracy of the measuring instruments. These sources are powerful because the logic of mathematics and experimental precision are conjoined, and not in the pretentious verbal "pseudorigor" typical of theory in LD. The physical sciences develop sufficiently powerful theory for generating point values that are then plotted to determine the extent to which "the results are in reasonably good accord with theory." For theory validation, it is always more valuable to show approximate agreement of observations with a theoretically predicted numerical point value, than it is to compute a "precise" probability that a parameter merely differs from some other parameter value. (Of course, the probabilities are not precise in significance testing because of the falsity of the assumptions generating the table values and the varying robustness of inferential tests under departures from these assumptions.)

An Approach to Testing LD Theory

It seems clear that a new view of the epistemic structure of LD is required in terms of theory construction and theory validation. A model depicting the main features of such a model is presented in Figure 4-1 (as adapted from Mitroff & Kilmann, 1978). The model is entered at Step I (*reality*) wherein a problem situation surrounding a phenomenon is viewed as requiring explication for the purposes of prediction and explanation. Thus, we might wish to know who will be LD and perhaps why. Once the problem is described, the next step consists of formulating a *conceptual model* (Step II) of the problem by defining it in the most basic and broadest terms. Thus, the problem is viewed from a macroperspective, rather than an exact and detailed microperspective. For the LD field, what is required is a conceptual

THE EPISTEMOLOGY OF LD THEORY

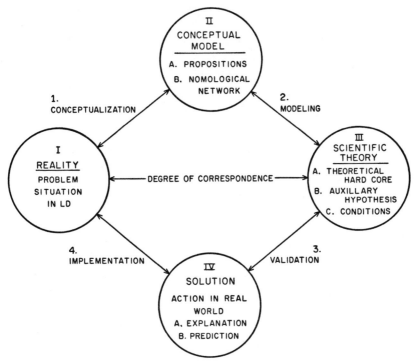

FIGURE 4-1 The Epistemology of LD Theory

model along the lines proposed for a meta-theory of psychoanalysis (see Rapaport, 1960; Rapaport & Gill, 1959). This meta-theory attempts to state the structure of psychoanalysis "from the inside" by distinguishing four classes of propositions that are used to provide psychoanalytic explanation in terms of dynamic, economic, structural, genetic, and adaptive points of view.

A conceptual model should present a framework from which the latent causal composition of the phenomenon is conjectured. The conceptual model should approach the properties of a nomological network (Cronbach & Meehl, 1955) in the sense of providing an integrated set of propositions. For a field like LD, the conceptual model probably cannot be formally derived (in a mathematical sense) but, rather, must be based upon analogy and metaphor (Hesse, 1966; see also Black, 1962; Carnap, 1950). In this way, the conceptual model will possess an intrinsic value related to understanding (Toulmin, 1972).

Although strongly predictive, conceptual models are not justified by choice criteria (i.e., strength of inductive support, falsifiability, and simplicity) (Hesse, 1966) and thus once established, attention should be directed at developing a detailed and precise formulation termed a *scientific theory* (Step III). This theory differs from pure logical theorizing because some of its propositions can be coordinated with empirical data to produce facts. This type of theoretical conjecture possesses an explicitness and rigor as well as an attempt to provide a detailed articulation with reality. The theoretical assumptions are not meant to be fanciful, or incredible, or lacking contact with other aspects of reality. They should be part of a larger framework of knowledge that increases the understanding of the complex, interactive nature of LD.

Both features are necessary because substantive theory itself rarely entails anything about experience directly. Any empirical prediction is not derived from a single theoretical conjecture but, rather, from a system of assumptions including the auxiliary hypotheses necessary for describing the phenomenon. Because of the presence of auxiliary hypotheses, substantive theory should not be denied because it cannot be mapped onto experience. Rather, theory testing in LD should involve a series of tests that attempt to improve the fit between theory and experience by modifying (or developing new) auxiliary assumptions, allowing such modification to encroach upon the substantive theory only when no alternative of lesser scope is either appropriate or available. Thus, the scientific model is really comprised of three components: (1) the theoretical hard core—a systematically interrelated set of assumptions that functions to set the norms that determine what counts as confirmation or refutation; (2) auxiliary hypotheses—assumptions which map the theoretical hard core into observation and represent the normal focus of empirical work (the substantive theory being assumed to be true) to be either accepted or rejected when observations prove negative; and (3) observation—the various data about the state of the world.

The scientific model may be conceptualized as a process involving informational components, methodological controls, and information transformations. These components may be mapped as shown in Figure 4-2. In translation, Figure 4-2 indicates that individual observations are specific and essentially unique pieces of information, whose synthesis into the more general form denoted by empirical generalizations is accomplished by measurement, sample summarization, and parameter estimation. These empirical generalizations, in turn, are pieces of information that can be synthesized into a theory via concept formation, proposition formation, and proposition arrangement. A theory (the most general piece of information) is transformable into new hypotheses through the method of logical deduction. An empirical hypothesis is an information item

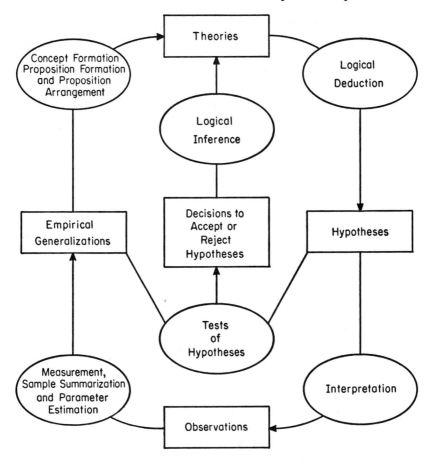

FIGURE 4-2 The Scientific Model

that becomes transformed into new observations via interpretation of the hypothesis into observables. These new observations are transformable into new empirical generalizations (again, via measurement, sample summarization, and parameter estimation), and the hypothesis that occasioned their construction may then be tested for conformity to them. Such tests may result in a new informational outcome—namely, a decision to accept or to reject the truth of the tested hypothesis. It is this that gives either confirmation, modification, or rejection of the scientific theory. Within this framework, the scientific process may be divided into interrelated components. For example, the left half of Figure 4-2 represents inductive construction of theory from, and understanding of, observations, whereas the right half represents the deductive application of theory. Similarly, the top half of Figure 4-2 may be termed theorizing, via the use of inductive and deductive logic as method, whereas the bottom half represents what is typically meant by doing empirical research, with the aid of "research methods."

The result of this process is a middle range theory (Merton, 1957). On one end are weak theories that simply amalgamate statistics of relatively little significance. Because such theories are based on either obvious hypotheses or hypotheses so unrelated to other hypotheses, the mindless accumulation of statistical validations offers no substantive insight into a phenomenon like LD. On the opposite end, there are strong theories that are based on highly theoretical constructions that actually transcend empirical data. Although presenting a formidable structural framework, such strong formulations have little value for understanding LD because they are essentially untestable for either technical or logical reasons. A middle range theory, on the other hand, occupies an intermediate ground between what appears trivial and what is not subject to testing. Consequently, the theory is testable and, if validated, presents a heuristic device for gaining insight into LD.

At this point, differences emerge between the usual course of LD theory and the present view. Instead of probability notions found in inferential statistics for testing LD theory, theory validation should focus more upon consistency testing (Meehl, 1965). From the scientific model, formulas for estimating the theoretical quantities of interest are derived (e.g., the proportion of LD in a given school population, the mean values of the LD and non-LD classes, and the optimal cutoff score on each indicator for classifying LD individuals). But it must be realized that such predictions may be false (i.e., the indicators used may have low validity, or the conjectures may be more correlated than desired, and so forth). Additionally, even if the basic formal structure postulated is approximated by the state of nature (i.e., the conjectures about LD are true), it may still be the case that some systematic bias is present in one of the indicators due to nuisance variables (e.g., SES differences).

Whether the postulated formal structure is unsound or the numerical values found in samples are seriously in error, a method of checking the data internally is needed to find out whether these possibilities are true. This is done by deriving theorems within the formal structure, specifying how various numerical values (observed or calculated from the observed) should be related to each other. Additionally, the same conjectures are used to establish robustness in terms of the tolerable departures from the postulatled conditions. With the values determined, the primary question becomes: How sensitive are the consistency tests to sample departures from the parametric truth in excess of the tolerance allowed?

Statistical significance testing for theory validation results in a microapproach wherein a single schema null hypothesis is tested for a single parameter such as

$$Ho: \mu = \mu$$
$$H_1: \mu \neq \mu$$

In testing these values, a particular course of action (A_a) is chosen so as to be maximally efficient for achieving some preferred objective for the parameter values (e.g., sample size, alpha level). In this way, the usual Type I and Type II errors of statistics associated with choice A_a are minimized. Thus, the probability of choosing some other course of action (A_b) when A_a is "true" should be minimal (i.e., $p(A_b/A_a)$ = minimum while conversely $p(A_a/A_b)$ = maximum).

Within a statistical significance testing paradigm for theory validation, attention is directed at minimizing Type I and Type II errors. But much more important is the minimization of Type III errors (Mitroff & Featheringham, 1974), defined as the probability of attempting to solve the "wrong" hypothesis instead of the "right" hypothesis. By "right" (or correct), the emphasis is on more theoretically interesting or "conceptually rich" hypotheses (see Davis, 1971). For LD theory, it is more important to determine the correct schema (in the sense of theoretical fruitfulness) rather than minimizing Type I and II errors. As Tukey (1962) suggested, "Far better are approximate solutions to the right problem than an exact solutions to the wrong one" (p. 53).

Consistency testing, on the other hand, results in testing multiple schema hypotheses (H_c) to determine whether multiple observations provide data demonstrating that

$$H_c: \Sigma[V(O_1) = V(O_2)]$$

where $V(O_1)$ and $V(O_2)$ are the obtained values for multiple observations of the hypothesized conjectures.

For H_0 and H_1 in significance testing, Type I error is defined as p (rejecting H_0/H_0 is true) while Type II error is defined as p (rejecting H_1/H_1 is true). In terms of H_c, Type III error (i.e., solving the wrong hypothesis instead of the right hypothesis) can be defined in two ways where, in the first case, if $V(O_1) \neq V(O_2)$ when indeed $V(O_1) = V(O_2)$, or, in the second case, if $V(O_1) = V(O_2)$ when $V(O_1) \neq V(O_2)$. Thus, Type III error directs attention towards refutation; if it is conjectured that $V(O_1) = V(O_2)$, then the test is directed at showing that a case can be made for $V(O_1) \neq V(O_2)$, while if $V(O_1) \neq V(O_2)$ is conjectured, then the refutation test attempts to show that $V(O_1) = V(O_2)$.

The consistency tests involve procedures for assessing H_c (depending upon the particular conjecture). The procedure consists of testing $\Sigma[V(O_1) - V(O_2)]$ to determine whether the differences between $V(O_1)$ and $V(O_2)$ are "consistent" (within the tolerance range). This goes beyond significance testing because multiple values of O_1 and O_2 (rather than single parameter values, e.g., $\bar{X}, r$) are computed in order to entertain the different theoretical possibilities for $\Sigma[V(O_1) - V(O_2)]$. The purpose of computing $\Sigma[V(O_1) - V(O_2)]$ is not to determine with exact precision "what is" but, rather, "what if"—what would be confirmed or refuted if such and such were the case?

Consistency tests provide a much more powerful test of LD theory than the weak null hypothesis (e.g., "more boys than girls are LD" or "LD children have more visual–perceptual problems") found in significance testing. Especially when multiple nonredundant estimates of the same theoretical entity are made in what Feigl (1970) refers to as "triangulation in logical space," a more valuable test of theory is achieved through these approximations than a so-called exact test of significance. This is because LD findings possess no phenomenological status within a statistical significance testing paradigm for theory validation. The result is a lack of theoretical meaning which is often covered up by a blanket of legitimizations that include the notions of (1) uniqueness—LD is a unique occurrence and, hence, objective testing by different investigators at different points in space and time is impossible, (2) value-character—LD subject matter is value loaded which makes objectivity theoretically impossible, (3) selective focus— LD investigators select their methodology which precludes a common focus and hence objectivity, and (4) complexity—LD phenomena are much more complex than natural phenomena and thus cannot be studied by the logical methods of science. But, in reality, there is no absolute distinction between physical and behavioral uniqueness; some aspects of physics are equally "complex." Consequently, complexity appears to be an apology for the state of our LD theory and something of a speculation, since there are no formal mechanisms for comparing the inherent complexity of one phenomenon with that of another. Scriven (1956) suggested that the difference is assumed to be in the relatively greater complexity of the simplest phenomena that need to be accounted for in, for example, an LD theory compared to a theory in the physical sciences. Consequently, a field like LD must develop higher-order theories in order to even speculate on the critical variables that need to be isolated for sound generalizations. Thus, these legitimizations provide convenient excuses for the LD field not achieving scientific status. But Scheffler (1956) rejected these and analogous arguments about the presumed differences between physical and social science. Although not denying that the current state of LD theory is in a much more primitive state than the physical sciences, it can be concluded that there exist no theoretical barriers to the advance of scientific study of LD. There are, of course, practical problems to overcome and increased theoretical ingenuity required, but these are the obstacles that are met everywhere in scientific research. Theoretically, science can be applied to LD.

If the scientific theory is verified, then the substantive conjectures may be applied to the initial problem situation for the purpose of taking action on it. This process is termed *implementation*, and it constitutes the action-taking aspect and specifies the strategies for mapping the substantive theory on the real world. The model is completed by a path from reality to scientific theory that provides insight into the degree of correspondence between reality and a representation of reality (Hesse, 1966).

Conclusion

A considerable change in the LD field's attitude toward theory testing is required to see that the concepts *rational* and *statistical* are not equivalent. With most of us trained in the tradition of statistical significance testing, a shift in perspective is needed to accept the fact that qualitative converging evidence can make a stronger case for validating substantive theory than the weak kinds of quantitative nonconverging evidence usually represented in inferential statistics. Nevertheless, it may be true that the nature of the subject matter in LD does not permit theories with sufficient conceptual power to yield the types of strong tests required in the Popper tradition. Clearly, some aspects of LD are not presently testable (in a rigorous and realistic fashion) because the required intermediate technology found in auxiliaries and methods does not exist. Yet, philosophers of science have made the point that there are theories in the physical sciences that were untestable when first propounded because the conceptual and technological developments necessary for making the required observations were not available.

Thus, substantive theory in LD need not be testable right now. The proper tests must be developed over time in a program that reveals continuity and feedback. When it is realized that the most powerful aspects of LD are found in the atheoretical realms of psychometric prediction and behavior modification, it is clear that LD theory must perhaps begin at the level of low-order inductions and proceed from that point. It will then be possible to develop the conceptual richness (not found in the atheoretical realms) that allows for the possibility of LD theory being falsified. Only then will LD theory become scientific.

5

Theoretical Perspective on the Nature of Learning Disabilities

Since its inception, the LD field has wrestled with the problem of providing theoretical insights that might enhance the understanding of the basic nature of LD. Early theoretical concepts usually proposed single-paradigm causes (e.g., Delacato's, 1966, neurological organization, Birch & Belmont's, 1964, intersensory integration, Kirk's, 1971, psycholinguistic deficits, Clement's, 1966, minimal brain dysfunction, Myklebust's, 1964, psychoneurological learning disability, Kephart's, 1960, perceptual–motor mismatch, Frostig's, 1972, visual perceptual problems, and the like). Later conceptualizations (e.g., Ross', 1976, selective attention deficit, Vellutino's, 1979, verbal deficit hypothesis, and so on), although broader in scope than earlier theories, remained basically singular notions providing theoretical statements with a narrow focus.

These theoretical statements postulated the basic nature of LD to be intrinsic to the child and generally did not incorporate speculation about extrinsic influences as either primary or secondary contributions to the nature of LD. With the realization that LD represented primarily a school-based problem, there was increased attention paid to extrinsic variables, particularly related to schooling and the teaching–learning process (e.g., Cohen's, 1968, notion of dyspedagogia, Adelman's, 1971, interactional model, Bateman's, 1974, teaching disorders, and the like). Yet, these conceptions are also, in a sense, unidimensional since they focused on deficient aspects of the teaching–learning process as the primary cause of instructional failure, but did not incorporate the contribution of intrinsic variables in the nature of LD. More recent theoretical statements have provided a more comprehensive perspective than is found in single-paradigm notions that stress either the process or the educational conceptualizations discussed earlier. An example is Torgesen's (1977) *inactive learner* notion suggesting that the LD child lacks efficient learning strategies. By postulating a generalized performance deficit underlying LD, Torgesen's, (1977) view can probably incorporate both intrinsic and extrinsic variables, but the nature of the interactions producing passive learners were not specified.

The many competing theories of LD usually result in the conclusion that LD has no single cause but has a multivariate etiological structure. Assuming that LD is a product of many causes does not excuse us from providing a comprehensive perspective that incorporates as many notions regarding etiology as possible. Therefore, the purpose of this chapter is to provide a framework for viewing the causes of LD that integrates a variety of theoretical positions regarding both school learning and the nature of LD.

Models of School Learning

The relationship between student learning outcomes and theories of learning, teaching, and instruction has produced a vast research literature documenting its complexity (Dunkin & Biddle, 1974; Gage, 1976; Stephens, 1967). In an effort to harness this complexity, models of school learning have been proposed that provide a framework for viewing the interrelationships among variables producing student learning (Bennett, 1978; Berliner, 1979; Bloom, 1976; Cooley & Leinhardt, 1980; Harnischfeger & Wiley, 1976; Fredrick & Walberg, 1980). Although these models emphasize different aspects of the teaching–learning process, they all derive from a common root found in Carroll's (1963) model of school learning, in which major constructs were defined in terms of time (i.e., time spent learning or time needed to learn). Carroll (1963) conceived the degree of learning as a function of the ratio of the amount of time the learner actually spends on the learning task to the total amount of time needed. Thus:

$$\text{Degree of Learning} = f\left(\frac{\text{time actually spent on task}}{\text{time needed to learn}}\right)$$

Although time is considered the critical variable, those elements represent a wide array of constructs that determine the amounts of time required. For example, time *needed* for learning is determined by (1) aptitude, (2) ability to understand instruction, and (3) quality of instruction, while time actually *spent* in learning is determined by (1) opportunity, and (2) perseverance.

The models derived from Carroll's (1963) formulation attempt to expand and to amplify the determinants of both time variables. Bloom (1976), for example, included under aptitudes two types of prerequisites: cognitive entry behaviors and affective entry behavior. Cognitive entry behaviors may be general (i.e., intelligence) or specific (i.e., prerequisites for accomplishing individual learning tasks). Affective entry behaviors typically include both task-specific attributes (e.g., attitude towards curricular area) and more general affective characteristics (e.g., attitudes towards school, self-concept) that correspond to Carroll's (1963) notion of perseverance.

The model proposed by Cooley and Leinhardt (1980) attempted to expand the concept, quality of instruction, by positing four components that intervene between initial student performance and criterion performance that explain variation in school outcome not accounted for by students' mental abilities and attitudes. The classroom processes include (1) opportunity — which follows Carroll's (1963) notion of how time is spent; (2) motivators, including student behaviors and attitudes that encourage learning; (3) instructional events involving the content, frequency, quality, and duration of instructional interactions; and (4) structure, related to the level of organization of curricular variables.

Besides focusing on curricular variables, the "structure" factor may be expanded to include the entire setting for instruction. These contextual variables have been incorporated into a model that examines school and teacher variables that influence student achievement (Centra & Potter, 1980). The variables include (1) school district conditions (e.g., size, fiscal resources, pupil–teacher ratio, staff services, facilities), (2) within-school conditions (e.g., administrative and instructional organization, class size, school ambience), and (3) teacher characteristics (e.g., qualifications, experience, subject knowledge, teaching knowledge, expectations, attitudes).

A primary contextual component is related to the quantity of schooling, which focuses on the actual amount of schooling (i.e., days and hours), and time allocated to curriculum activity (i.e., classroom management, transition time, seatwork, whole-class instruction, small-group instruction, individual instruction) (Hyman, Wright, & Reed, 1975; Wiley, 1976). Models (viz., Bennett, 1978; Harnischfeger & Wiley, 1976) emphasizing the quantity of schooling variable also incorporate the idea of total active learning time as in the Carroll (1963) model. Within a similar framework, Berliner (1979) developed a model that indicates achievement to be a function of student aptitudes, teacher behavior, and classroom learning. The classroom learning component is defined by academic learning time (ALT) whose four elements include (1) time allocated to instruction, (2) time engaged in instruction, (3) student success rate, and (4) task relevance (see Stallings, 1980). The quantity of ALT is, in turn, a function of the classroom instructional processes and total classroom environment.

Analysis of Models of School Learning

The models of school learning all suggest that learning is the result of a complex amalgamation of factors. At the most general level, learning can be thought of as the product of three classes of variables: student attributes, environmental influences, and instructional features. *Student attributes* include general elements such as (1) cognitive abilities that include both aptitude (Hopkins & Bracht, 1975; McCall, Appelbaum, & Hogarty, 1973) and achievement (Bracht & Hopkins, 1972; Hilton, 1979), (2) psychomotor abilities (Cratty, 1981; Keogh, 1981), (3) affective characteristics (Hamachek, 1978; Kifer, 1975; Ringness, 1975), and sex (Garai & Scheinfeld, 1968; Maccoby & Jacklin, 1974). Besides these general characteristics, individual differences in learning ability are also related to more specific variables like (1) locus of control (Fanelli, 1977; Joe, 1971), (2) achievement motivation (Atkinson & Feather, 1966; McClelland, Atkinson, Clark, & Lowell, 1953), (3) cognitive style (Sigel & Coop, 1974), (4) conceptual tempo (Bentler & McClain, 1976; Kagan & Kogan, 1970), (5) psychological differentiation (Witkin, Moore, Goodenough, & Cox, 1977), (6) anxiety (Sarason, Lighthall, Davidson, Waite, & Ruebush, 1960; Speilberger, 1966), (7) attribution patterns (Weiner, 1977), (8) attitudes (Backman & Secord, 1968), (9) curiosity (Berlyne, 1965), and so forth. The *environmental* component contains elements related to general family characteristics (Freeburg & Payne, 1967; Hess, 1970; Hunt, 1961; Marjoribanks, 1972; Stevenson, Parker, Wilkenson, Bonneveaux, & Gonzalez, 1978; Werner & Smith, 1977), and educational environments (Anderson & Walberg, 1974; Marjoribanks, 1974; Walberg, 1976). The variable of *instruction* includes the elements of (1) instructional design (e.g., Bruner, 1966; Gage, 1978; Gagne, 1977; Glaser, 1976), (2) teacher behavior (Good, Biddle, & Brophy, 1975; Rosenshine, 1971, 1979; Rosenshine & Furst, 1973; Ryan, 1960; Walberg & Anderson, 1968), (3) classroom processes (Good & Brophy, 1978; Jackson, 1968), (4) instructional processes (Berliner & Gage, 1976; Joyce & Weil, 1972; Kuethe, 1968; Rosenshine, 1976), (5) expectations (Braun, 1976; Good, 1979; Rosenthal & Jacobson, 1968), (6) psychological context (i.e., school size, class size, grouping practices, classroom structure, and the like) (see Glaser, 1977; Glass, Cahen, Smith, & Filby, 1982; Gump, 1978; Krantz & Risley, 1977; Schwebel & Cherlin, 1972), (7) decision-making practices (Brophy & Evertson, 1976: Shavelson, 1976), (8) classroom management (Brophy & Putnam, 1979; Kounin, 1970; Schmuck & Schmuck, 1971), (9) curriculum structure (e.g., process, content) (Rubin, 1977; Tanner & Tanner, 1980), and (10) classroom interaction (Bennett, 1976; Withall & Lewis, 1963).

Relationship of Variables to School Learning

The models of school learning include domains and their related elements that conceptualize learning (L) as a function (f) of student abilities (S_i), environment (E_j), and instruction (I_k), where the environmental component (E_j) can be conceptualized as consisting of two parts: one emphasizing the home environment (E_{jh}), and the other the school environment (E_{js}). In sum, $L = f(S_i), f(E_{j[h+s]}), f(I_k)$. The question now arises as to how the domains might be related to learning. The most parsimonious model is additive and assumes no interaction between student abilities, environment, and instruction. This model would derive empirical weights (e.g., by regression analysis) for each term as follows:

$$L = f[(S_j) + (E_{j[h+s]}) + (I_k)]$$

The difficulty with this model (i.e., that learning is an additive function of student characteristics, home or school environment, and instructional variables) is findings indicating that the three domains are not independent and, in fact, interact with one another. For example, there is evidence for an S_iE_{jh} interaction (Bloom, 1964; Fraser, 1959; Lightfoot, 1979; Walberg & Marjoribanks, 1976), and S_iE_{js} interaction (Brophy & Good, 1974; Keeves, 1972; Walberg & Anderson, 1968), and S_iI_k interaction (Berliner & Cahen, 1973; Bracht, 1970; Cronbach & Snow, 1977; Messick, 1976), and $E_{js}I_k$ interaction (Cohen, 1972; Walberg, 1969; 1976), and, by implication, an $S_iE_jI_k$ interaction. By including the interaction components, the resulting multiplicative model assumes that student abilities, environment, and instruction interact with one another to afford a better prediction of learning than the first three terms alone. The expanded model would look like the following:

$$L = f[(S_i) + (E_{j[h+s]}) + (I_k) + (S_iE_{jh}) + (S_iI_k) + (E_{js}I_k) + (S_iE_jI_k)]$$

By including interactive terms, this learning model is more comprehensive and allows for greater specification of the components that influence learning.

The values accorded each term in the model can be viewed as a function of the interrelationships among the postulated elements for each domain. In the most general form, this equation expands to account for increasingly specific interactions that influence learning:

$$
X = [x_{ij}] = [x_1, x_2, x_3, \ldots x_n] =
\begin{bmatrix}
x_1 \\
x_2 \\
x_3 \\
\cdot \\
\cdot \\
\cdot \\
x_m
\end{bmatrix}
=
\begin{bmatrix}
x_{11} & x_{12} & x_{13} & \cdots & x_{1n} \\
x_{21} & x_{22} & x_{23} & \cdots & x_{2n} \\
x_{31} & x_{32} & x_{33} & \cdots & x_{3n} \\
\cdot & & & & \cdot \\
\cdot & & & & \cdot \\
\cdot & & & & \cdot \\
x_{m1} & x_{m2} & x_{m3} & \cdots & x_{mn}
\end{bmatrix}
$$

where X is the domain (e.g., S_i, E_j, or I_k) and x equals factors contributing to the domain. For the case of interaction

$$
XY =
\begin{bmatrix}
x_1 \\
x_2 \\
\cdot \\
\cdot \\
\cdot \\
x_n
\end{bmatrix}
\bullet [y_1, y_2, \ldots y_n] =
\begin{bmatrix}
x_1 y_1 & x_1 y_2 & \cdots & x_1 y_n \\
x_2 y_1 & x_2 y_2 & \cdots & x_2 y_n \\
\cdot & \cdot & & \cdot \\
\cdot & \cdot & & \cdot \\
\cdot & \cdot & & \cdot \\
x_n y_1 & x_n y_2 & \cdots & x_n y_n
\end{bmatrix}
$$

where XY is the interaction component (e.g., $S_i E_j$, $S_i I_k$, $E_j I_k$) and x and y are the factors contributing to the interaction component.

By postulating a general equation including the primary domains and their interaction, plus the relationships among the individual elements comprising the domains, it is possible to describe the complexity involved in school learning. Although these conceptualizations relate to major variables in school learning, they must now be related to the time factor, seen as a critical component of the models reviewed

(Fredrick & Walberg, 1980). Recall that Carroll's (1963) model proposed that

$$L_h = f\left[\frac{\text{(time actually spent on task)}}{\text{(time needed to learn)}}\right] = f\left[\frac{T_a}{T_n}\right]$$

If L_h is assumed to be related to academic learning time (ALT) and T_a is assumed to be related to influences on learning (extrinsic) while Tn is related to influences in learning (intrinsic) (Jensen, 1967), then the relationship between T_a and T_n can be conceptualized as defining the amount of time engaged in academic tasks (perseverance) as follows:

$$ALT = \begin{bmatrix} T_a < T_n \\ T_a = T_n \\ T_a > T_n \end{bmatrix}$$

The optimal situation would be where $T_a = T_n$ (indicating that the child is willing to persevere to the extent needed for learning); but this does not always occur because of changes in the value of either T_a or T_n or both. Because the time engaged in academic pursuits influences achievement (Denham & Lieberman, 1980), both $T_a = Tn$ and $T_a > T_n$ can be viewed as producing an optimal degree of learning while $Ta < T_n$ would be associated with a less than optimal degree of learning, since it has been found that increasing time on task does not alter the degree of learning or learning rate (Millman, Bieger, Klag, & Pine, 1983).

The variations in T_a and T_n can be accounted for by distributing the components of the general, multiplicative model in the Carroll scheme. For T_a, the components dealing with instruction and environment (particularly school setting) are most prominent while T_n is primarily affected by student ability and the interactions with environment (particularly home settings) and instruction. These relationships may be depicted as follows:

$$T_a = f[E_{j[h+s]} + I_k + (E_{js}I_k)]$$
$$T_n = f[S_i + (S_iE_{jh}) + (S_iI_k)]$$

If the $S_iE_jI_k$ interaction can be assumed to influence T_a and T_n equally, thus cancelling its effects, then these equations may be used to assign values to T_a and T_n. The outcome would be an expected value for T_a and T_n, that is

$$ALT = \frac{T_a}{T_n} = \frac{E(T_a)}{E(T_n)}$$

By using hypothetical expected values, it is possible to see how variations in T_a and T_n can affect ALT. If it is assumed that the optimal relationship is represented by unity, then different expected values would define ALT. For example, assuming $E(T_a) = 1$ and $E(T_n) = 1$ would result in

$$ALT = \frac{T_a}{T_n} = \frac{1}{1} = 1$$

which is the desired situation. Now, if $E(T_a) = 2$ and $E(T_n)$ remains the same (i.e., 1), then $ALT = 2$ indicating increased time on task. This increased perseverance (perhaps as a result of rewards) will not, however, produce more learning (see Millman, Bieger, Klag, & Pine, 1983). If, however, $E(T_n) = 2$ while $E(T_a)$ remained the same, then

$$ALT = \frac{1}{2} = .50$$

suggesting that academic learning time is decreased by one-half. Thus, the level of perseverance is reduced 50%.

Although T_a and T_n may vary with respect to the number of elements included in each component, the expected values could be adjusted for the actual number of elements included in a particular case. Nevertheless, the concept would remain the same and the optimal situation would be represented by a situation wherein $E(T_a)$ and $E(T_n)$ are equal so that the time spent on learning matches the time needed to learn.

A Model of LD

The model outlines above included factors that operate, for the most part, in "normal" learning and produce individual variation that is within the boundaries of average achievement. The explicit assumption is that children in school generally fall within parameters suggesting restricted values for T_n. For this reason, it is probable that the discrepancy between T_a and T_n would not vary over a wide range but would only reveal variation within circumscribed boundaries (i.e., defining normality). The primary reason for this is the dynamic nature of schooling which, for normal children, suggests that modifications in instruction (i.e., I_k) will be made periodically in an effort to bring equilibrium back to the equation (i.e., $ALT = 1$).

For normal children, it is probably the case that $E(T_n)$ would not reveal wide variation since it is constrained by factors which operate within "normal" boundaries. Consequently, a child may be near the top or bottom of a distribution but, nevertheless, remains within "normal" limits as shown in Figure 5-1. Thus, although variation may

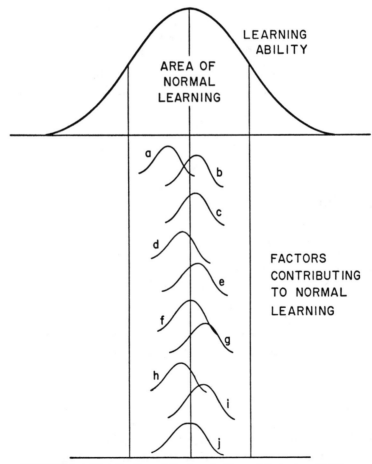

FIGURE 5-1 Distribution of Factors in Normal Learning Ability

be found in individual factors contributing to learning ability, if most fall within the boundaries delineated by normal learning (e.g., $\pm$ one standard deviation), then, on average, it will be the case that $T_a = T_n$.

Because LD is a school-based disorder recognized when a child fails to respond to instruction, experiences difficulty on academic tasks and, ultimately, fails to achieve as expected, a major contributor is the lack of response to instruction so that *ALT* is reduced significantly. Within the framework provided by T_a and T_n, LD can be conceived as an increasing disparity (i.e., discrepancy) between T_a and T_n. For T_n, the distributions of factors contributing to normal learning place the potential LD child at the lower end or below the area for normal learning as depicted in Figure 5-2.

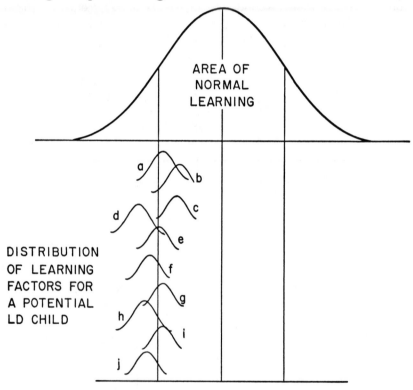

FIGURE 5–2 Distribution of Factors for a Potential LD Child

For a child with this distribution of learning abilities, instruction would have to be shifted to meet this child's needs. When the distribution of abilities places the child at or near the low end of the normal learning area, the value of T_a needs to be increased. Classroom instruction, however, is typically targeted at the mean since, on average, this will ensure that the greatest number of children will be in a situation where $T_a = T_n$. Thus, the value of T_a is not likely to reveal much variation in the average regular class, resulting in a mismatch in the case of some children, between actual instruction and needed instruction as shown in Figure 5-3.

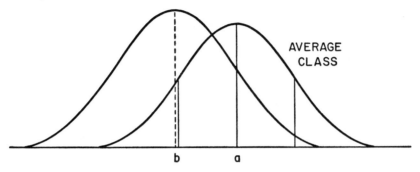

a = TARGETED LEVEL OF INSTRUCTION FOR THE AVERAGE REGULAR CLASS

b = LEVEL OF INSTRUCTION NEEDED BY A PARTICULAR CHILD

FIGURE 5–3 Instructional Levels for Average Regular Class and Potential LD Child

The result is a situation where $T_a < T_n$ within the normal learning situation and accounts for the approximately 16% of children who reveal limited perseverance with a consequent reduction in the degree of learning. The time actually spent on learning is reduced significantly because the two primary criteria (1) opportunity (time allowed for task), and (2) quality of instruction are not met (Bloom, 1980). Walker (1980) proposed a theoretical formulation based upon complexity that can be used to explain why the situation (i.e., $T_a < T_n$) is not likely to improve and is shown in Figure 5-4. The instructional mismatch shifts the optimal complexity level (where tasks are interesting and motivation is high) to a situation of "complexity overload" (where learning tasks are viewed as confusing and difficult, thus reducing motivation) that results in a child who quits trying and becomes discouraged (Walker, 1980). Thus, a vicious cycle is formed, and the consequences are found in reduced *ALT* when, in fact, the child actually requires an increase in T_a to allow for optimal learning based upon the increase in T_n. A number of developmental theorists posit such a situation, which is often overlooked in dealing with handicapped school children (Forness, 1973).

THEORY OF PSYCHOLOGICAL COMPLEXITY

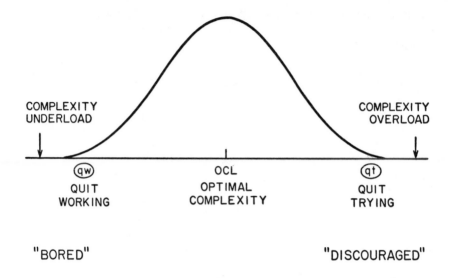

from Walker, 1980

FIGURE 5-4 Theory of Psychological Complexity

Although these notions account for the low achievement in about 16% of the population, how do the 5% or so of that group come to be classified as LD? Besides the elements involved in producing differences in student abilities (S_i) for normal learning, about one-third of the low perseverance group will have additional factors operating that interfere with their learning ability, thus comprising the 5% of the population known as LD. Among the factors assumed to operate in LD are (1) maturational lag (Ames, 1968a; Bender, 1957; Kinsbourne, 1973), (2) genetic variation (Owen, Adams, Forrest, Stolz, & Fisher, 1971; Silver, 1971a), (3) minimal brain dysfunction (Kinsbourne, 1983; Rie & Rie, 1980), (4) biochemical irregularities (Mayron, 1979; Weiss, 1982; Wender, 1976), (5) physiological differences (deQuiros, 1976; Green & Perlman, 1971; Steg & Rapoport, 1975), (6) neuropsychological variables (Gaddes, 1980; Knights & Bakker, 1976), (7) nutritional factors (Conners, 1980; Cravioto & DeLicardie, 1975), (8) perinatal events (Balow, Rubin, & Rosen, 1975–1976), (9) temperamental differences (Thomas & Chess, 1977), (10) ecological factors (Mayron, 1978), (11) cerebral specialization (Guyer & Friedman, 1975), (12) emotional/social differences (Bryan, 1981; Connolly, 1971; Kronnick, 1981), (13) linguistic deficits (Butler & Wallach, 1982; Vogel, 1975), (14) motor problems (Keogh, 1982), (15) visual perceptual problems (Frostig, 1975; Kavale, 1982b), (16) auditory perceptual problems (Kavale, 1981b; Wepman, 1975), (17) integrative deficits (Kavale, 1980a; Senf, 1972), (18) psycholinguistic deficits (Kass, 1966; McLeod, 1967), (19) cognitive disabilities (Keogh & Donlon, 1972; Myklebust, Bannochie, & Killen, 1971), (20) memory problems (Torgesen, 1978, 1982), (21) attention deficits (Keogh & Margolis, 1976; Kinsbourne & Caplan, 1979; Tarver & Hallahan, 1974), and the like.

These correlates of LD add another dimension to T_n that increases the time required by adding another factor to the components found in normal learning as follows:

$$T_n = f[S_i + (S_i E_{jh}) + (S_i I_k) + LD_c]$$

where LD_c equals correlates of learning disability and is obtained from

$$LD_c = [c_{ij}] = [c_1, c_2, c_3, \ldots c_n] = \begin{bmatrix} c_1 \\ c_2 \\ c_3 \\ \cdot \\ \cdot \\ \cdot \\ c_m \end{bmatrix} = \begin{bmatrix} c_{11} & c_{12} & c_{13} & \cdots & c_{1n} \\ c_{21} & c_{22} & c_{23} & \cdots & c_{2n} \\ c_{31} & c_{32} & c_{33} & \cdots & c_{3n} \\ \cdot & \cdot & \cdot & & \cdot \\ \cdot & \cdot & \cdot & & \cdot \\ \cdot & \cdot & \cdot & & \cdot \\ c_{m1} & c_{m2} & c_{m3} & \cdots & c_{mn} \end{bmatrix}$$

For LD, the model would look as follows:

$$ALT = \frac{T_a}{T_n} = \frac{f[E_{j[h+s]} + I_k + E_{js}I_k]}{f[S_i + S_i E_{jh} + S_i I_k + LD_c]}$$

where $E(T_a) = {<}1$ and $E(T_n) = {>}1$. To separate LD from low achievement, LD may be defined as the point where the discrepancy between T_a and T_n is of a magnitude that indicates little (if any) learning is taking place.

It would be difficult to specify precise values for the T_a-T_n discrepancy defining LD; but, if *ALT* were reduced to perhaps 10%–20%, then actual learning time would be so depressed in comparison to the optimal state (i.e., 100%) that the child would be certain to experience difficulty with academic tasks and to reveal little achievement gain over time. For example, consider the following values for T_a and T_n:

1. if $E(T_a)$ = .75 and $E(T_n)$ = 5, then $ALT = \dfrac{.75}{5} = .15$

2. if $E(T_a)$ = .50 and $E(T_n)$ = 4, then $ALT = \dfrac{.50}{4} = .125$

3. if $E(T_a)$ = .25 and $E(T_n)$ = 3, then $ALT = \dfrac{.25}{3} = .08$

4. if $E(T_a)$ = 1 and $E(T_n)$ = 6, then $ALT = \dfrac{1}{6} = .17$

These examples all point to the fact that both factors (T_a and T_n) may make a contribution to the etiology of LD. For the child who will be classified LD, it is probably the case that Tn will always be greater than one and its value will be contingent upon how much normal variation is present as well as the number of LD correlates operating. But as illustration No. 4 suggests, even under optimal instruction, the negative influences may be great enough to disrupt the amount of time engaged in learning.

Regardless of the values for T_a and T_n found for any particular child, if the discrepancy limits learning time to perhaps 20% of normal, then the child becomes essentially disassociated from the formal learning process. Within the school setting, instructional practices may not be satisfactory for a particular child, thus reducing the time actually engaged in academic tasks. Normal variation plus correlative conditions also increase the time required for academic learning. Such a mismatch produces a discrepancy that reduces *ALT* significantly and results in a child disassociating from school learning. This disassociation represents the foundation for LD.

Conclusion

The basic nature of LD has proven to be an elusive and vexing problem for the field. The many proposed hypotheses regarding the essence of LD have generally failed to provide a comprehensive and definitive statement regarding its essence. Almost every proposed hypothesis about LD provides only a singular viewpoint that emphasizes either intrinsic or extrinsic factors. Such models lack explanatory power for the full range of LD behaviors and result in oversimplification or, what Kaplan (1964) better terms, "undercomplication" in the sense that something important is being overlooked. The result may be a false sense of closure.

Although it provides useful descriptions for some possible antecedent events for LD, single paradigm formulations represent particular modes of representation that do not correspond to all elements (i.e., all LD children) of its subject matter (Nagel, 1961). Consequently, there has been a failure to provide a description of the nature of LD in general rather than of LD in particular. We have made the point elsewhere (Forness, 1981b; Forness & Kavale, 1983a, 1983b) that LD research is far too simplistic to be effective for practitioners, who must contend simultaneously with several variables that may affect their minute-by-minute instructional interactions with LD pupils.

Snow (1973) outlined the elements of theory construction for research on teaching and emphasized the role of *metatheory*, the description of theory itself. In such a sense, this chapter has presented a metatheoretical framework incorporating elements of school learning theory and LD theory to provide a structure for viewing the nature of LD. The analysis is grounded in what Pepper (1942) termed a *root metaphor* which, in this case, views the LD child as a disassociated learner. The resulting description is not a model (physical, semantic, mathematical, or theoretical) in the scientific sense (see Brodbeck, 1963) but is closer to what Black (1962) termed an *archetype*, that is, a systematic synthesis of ideas, by analogical extension, through which a domain is described to which those ideas do not literally apply. By combining knowledge of the normal teaching–learning process with information about correlative factors of LD, a "plausible topology" (Boulding, 1967) has been offered that perhaps more logically conceptualizes how some children disassociate themselves from academic learning and come to be termed LD.

It should not be viewed, however, as a metaphysical description of LD but, rather, as a heuristic device that possesses enough implicative power to be a useful speculative apparatus for explaining the basic nature of LD. As such, this framework is potentially useful both in research and in classroom practice. For example, in research, it may serve to pinpoint exactly where more research is needed or to describe the specific foci of ongoing research programs, such as those in the federally funded network of Learning Disability Research Institutes at the Universities of Columbia, Illinois at Chicago Circle, Kansas, Minnesota, and Virginia (see Kneedler & Hallahan, 1983). In the model or archetype just presented, some institutes, such as Illinois and

Minnesota, chose to focus on the interaction between the student and instructional techniques (S_iI_k). While no one institute seemed to make the home environment (E_{jh}) a principal effort of its investigation, the Illinois group did devote some study to the interaction between the home environment and certain instructional tasks $(E_{jh}I_k)$. The Minnesota Institute also conducted some studies to examine the question of academic learning time available for learning disabled children.

In classroom practice, the framework presented may bring some perspective, for both special education trainees and practicing teachers, to conflicting studies appearing in professional literature, or may pinpoint where existing research is or is not helpful in suggesting remedial strategies. For example, the large body of aptitude-treatment interaction literature $(S_i + I_k + S_iI_k)$ is quite often perplexing, with many studies finding an interaction and many others suggesting that none exists (Larivee, 1981). Part of the reason for this is quite likely the virtual absence of studies that examine the additional influence of classroom environment on this interaction $(S_i + I_k + E_{js} + S_iI_k + S_iE_{js} + E_{js}I_k)$. Arter and Jenkins (1977) have, in fact, alluded to this as a possibility. The lack of sufficient attention to the effects of home environment (E_{jh}) in published research likewise suggests that teachers must be especially cautious in interpreting research studies, and that they are left with little option but to exercise their own judgment in considering this variable when planning an individual child's program, since guidance from the research literature is relatively sparse here. On the other hand, literature has recently appeared that suggests a very important interaction between the early home environment and within-student characteristics $(S_i + E_{jh} + S_iE_{jh})$ that tempers the prediction that a specific neurologic etiology will ultimately be of use in early identification or in program planning for LD students (Keogh & Kopp, 1978).

In this text, we have shown how the field of learning disabilities not only rests on a rather shaky empirical foundation but has also come to embrace its own historical and philosophical perspectives far too uncritically to be either an effective science or a systematic practical endeavor. We have briefly presented alternative formulations of the science of learning disabilities that we hope will assist the field in focusing on the essential scientific variables, and upon their interactions, in order to provide a more complete foundation for the practice of teaching LD children.

EPILOGUE

Our goal in this volume has been to show that the important (and legitimate) study of LD can be called science in no significant sense, and the continued application of this misleading metaphor can only vitiate and distort research efforts. It should be understood that we are *not* saying that LD should not be empirical, that LD should not essay a tough-minded analysis of events, or that LD should not apply statistical (and mathematical) methods. We *are* saying that in studying LD, particularly in terms of notions like learning, language, cognition, perception, attention, motivation, information processing, and so on, concepts such as "law," "theory," "model," "measurement," "control," and the like do not behave sufficiently like their counterparts in the established sciences to justify their extension to LD science. To persist in the assumption that what LD is doing is science is to shackle the field with unrealistic expectations concerning generality limits of findings, predictive specificity and confidence levels, feasible research strategies, and modes of conceptual ordering. The consequences are found in the enaction of empiricism rather than the generation of significant knowledge. The pursuit of empiricism, although a highly sophisticated skill, has resulted, over some 50 years, in erecting a discipline whose hallmarks of scientific style have been: rigor by rigidity, experiment by exculpation, ratiocination by asseveration, proof by pronouncement, truth by trivialization, and progress by proclamation. These are not the qualities of a discipline based on science but, rather, one based on deceit. The few areas in which germane insight or hard discoveries have been possible under these less than scientific circumstances are viewed as pockets of sedition—or just not seen.

We hope our position is not seen as nihilistic; we do hope that the LD field will retreat from its intellectual imperialism which provides ever bolder claims and pretensions based upon presumed forms of rigorous inquiry. This "hard science" approach has proven illusory and results in empiricism when what is required is greater reliance upon philosophical analysis that reveals "what it makes sense to say" (Winch,

1958). When it is realized that LD's central problem is philosophical, that is, to account for the nature of LD phenomena in general, then we will be less inclined to take as empirical questions, what actually are a priori conceptual questions.

In reality, it is necessary to strike a balance between the "empirical" and the "conceptual." This is because the empirical nature of LD as embodied in its present empiricism is inherently conservative and unimaginative since it deals only with what is and what was (Sklar, 1975). On the other hand, because it assumes no empirical truths and is not restricted by them, science is inherently radical and imaginative. In this way, it is possible for such unscientific elements as creativity, art, and intuition to enter the scientific process. Yet, with its strict empiricism, the LD field has attempted to maintain Weber's (1949) concept *verstehen* (to understand), which attempts to eliminate experience by an emphasis upon objective and quantitative analysis. The prime error of LD has been to develop along a single methodological track, one that stresses mental abstraction to the neglect of experience in the sense of Dilthey's concept *erleben* (to experience) (see Hodges, 1944). Because of this emphasis, the word empirical has been transformed from its original meaning including practical, experimental, and experiential approaches as distinguished from approaches relying on abstract theory, especially scientific theory. It is the absence of the scientific element (real or supposed), then, and the presence of practical observation based on experience (not conclusions based on the statistical manipulation of aggregated data) which ought to be the distinguishing characteristics of empirical LD.

In its preoccupation with objective and value-free methods, the LD field has failed to recognize that modern science shows a concern for more qualitative, rather than quantitative, analysis. This is because of the realization that quantitative evidence is insufficient, since reality is no more than a projection of our own reality (Stent, 1975). Thus, experience is an integral part of a system like LD and cannot be separated by elegant statistical manipulations of data which are not matters of experience, per se. Polyani (1958) suggested that we rid ourselves of the "false ideal of objectivity" and suggested the importance of different forms of knowing including tacit knowledge, as distinct from hypothetico–deductive, approaches to knowledge. Thus, any scheme for generating and testing scientific knowledge must include what Kaplan (1964) termed *creative elaboration*, which idealizes the logic of science to show what it would be if it were extracted and refined by the context of experience. By acknowledging the influence of experience, our tasks in the LD field become more difficult because the knowledge achieved may become either more true or less true.

Consequently, our belief in the truth must remain provisional, as Popper (1968) so eloquently stated

> The demand for scientific objectivity makes it inevitable that every scientific statement must remain tentative forever . . . . It is not his possession of knowledge, or irrefutable truth, that makes the man of science, but his persistent and recklessly critical quest for truth (pp. 280–281).

But it is that quest which will make a science of LD.

REFERENCES

Adams, R. M., Kocsis, J. J., & Estes, R. E. (1974). Soft neurological signs in learning-disabled children and control. *American Journal of Diseases of Children, 128*, 614-618.

Adelman, H. S. (1971). The not so specific learning disability population. *Exceptional Children, 37*, 528-533.

Algozzine, R., Forgnone, C., Mercer, C., & Trifiletti, J. (1979). Toward defining discrepancies for specific learning disabilities: An analysis and alternatives. *Learning Disability Quarterly, 2*, 25-31.

Ames, L. B. (1968a). Learning disabilities: The developmental point of view. In H. Myklebust (Ed.), *Progress in learning disabilities* (Vol. 1). New York: Grune & Stratton.

Ames, L. B. (1968b). A low intelligence quotient often not recognized as the chief cause of many learning difficulties. *Journal of Learning Disabilities, 1*, 735-739.

Anderson, G., & Walberg, H. (1974). Learning environments. In H. Walberg (Ed.), *Evaluating educational performance: A sourcebook of methods, instruments, and examples*. Berkeley, CA: McCuthan.

Andreski, S. (1972). *Social sciences as sorcery*. London: Andre Deutsch.

Applebee, A. N. (1971). Research in reading retardation: Two critical problems. *Journal of Child Psychology and Psychiatry, 1971, 12*, 91-113.

Arter, J., & Jenkins, J. (1977). Examining the benefits and prevalence of modality considerations in special education. *Journal of Special Education, 11*, 281-298.

Artley, A., & Hardin, V. (1976). A current dilemma: Reading disability or learning disability? *The Reading Teacher, 29*, 361-366.

Association for Children with Learning Disabilities. (1967).

Atkinson, J. W., & Feather, N. T. (Eds.). (1966). *A theory of achievement motivation*. New York: Wiley.

Ayer, A. J. (1956). *The problem of knowledge*. Baltimore: Penguin.

Ayres, A. J. (1968). Sensory integrative processes and neuropsychological learning disabilities. In J. Hellmuth (Ed.), *Learning disorders*, (Vol. 3). Seattle, WA: Special Child Publications, 43-58.

Backman, C. W., & Secord, P. F. (1968). *A social psychological view of education*. New York: Harcourt, Brace & World.

Bacon, F. (1960). *Novum organon and related writings*. New York: Liberal Arts Press. (originally published 1620).

Balow, B., Rubin, R., & Rosen, M. (1975-1976). Prenatal events as precursors of reading disability. *Reading Research Quarterly, 11*, 36-71.

Bandura, A. (1969). *Principles of behavior modification*. New York: Holt, Rinehart & Winston.

Barber, B. (1961). Resistance by scientists to scientific discovery. *Science, 134*, 596-602.

Barker, R. G. (1968). *Ecological psychology: Concepts and methods for studying the environment of human behavior*. Palo Alto, CA: Stanford University Press.

Barlow, C. F. (1974). Soft signs in children with learning disorders. *American Journal of Diseases of Children, 128*, 605-606.

Barnes, T., & Forness, S. (1982). Learning characteristics of children and adolescents with various psychiatric diagnoses. In R. Rutherford (Ed.), *Severe behavior disorders of children and youth* (Vol. 5). Reston, VA: Council for Children with Behavior Disorders, 32-41.

Barr, K., & McDowell, R. (1974). Comparison of learning disabled and emotionally disturbed children on three deviant classroom behaviors. *Exceptional Children, 39*, 60-62.

Barsch, R. H. (1967). *Achieving perceptual-motor efficiency: A space-oriented approach to learning.* Vol. 1 of a perceptual-motor curriculum. Seattle, WA: Special Child Publications.

Bateman, B. (1965). An educator's view of a diagnostic approach to learning disorders. In J. Hellmuth (Ed.), *Learning disorders*; Vol. 1. Seattle, WA: Special Child Publications.

Bateman, B. (1969). Reading: A controversial view — research and rationale. In L. Tarnopol (Ed.), *Learning disabilities: Introduction to educational and medical management.* Springfield, IL: Charles C. Thomas.

Bateman, B. (1974). Educational implications of minimal brain dysfunction. *Reading Teacher, 27*, 622-668.

Bax, M., & MacKeith, R. (Eds.). (1963). *Minimal cerebral dysfunction.* Little Club Clinics in Developmental Medicine, No. 10. London: Heinemann.

Becker, R. D. (1974). Minimal cerebral (brain) dysfunction — clinical fact or neurological fiction? The syndrome critically re-examined in the light of some hard neurological evidence. *Israel Annals of Psychiatry and Related Disciplines, 12*, 87-106.

Belmont, I., & Belmont, L. (1980). Is the slow learner in the classroom learning disabled? *Journal of Learning Disabilities, 13*, 496-499.

Bender, L. (1957). Specific reading disability as a maturational lag. *Bulletin of the Orton Society, 7*, 9-18.

Bennett, S. N. (1976). *Teaching styles and pupil progress.* London: Open Books.

Bennett, S. N. (1978). Recent research on teaching: A dream, a belief, and a model. *British Journal of Educational Psychology, 48*, 127-147.

Bentler, P., & McClain, J. (1976). A multitrait-multimethod analysis of reflection-impulsivity. *Child Development, 47*, 218-226.

Benton, A. L. (1973). Minimal brain dysfunction from a neuro-psychological point of view. *Annals of the New York Academy of Sciences, 205*, 29-37.

Bergmann, G. (1957). *Philosophy of science.* Madison: University of Wisconsin Press.

Berliner, D. C. (1979). Tempus educare. In P. Peterson & H. Walberg (Eds.), *Research on teaching: Concepts, findings, and implications.* Berkeley, CA: McCuthan.

Berliner, D. C., & Cahen, L. S. (1973). Trait-treatment interactions and learning. In F. Kerlinger (Ed.), *Review of research in education.* Itasca, IL: F. E. Peacock.

Berliner, D. C., & Gage, N. L. (1976). The psychology of teaching methods. In N. Gage (Ed.), *The psychology of teaching methods: The 75th Yearbook of the National Society for the Study of Education, Pt. I.* Chicago: University of Chicago Press.

Berlyne, D. E. (1965). Curiosity and education. In J. Krumholtz (Ed.), *Learning and the educational process.* Chicago: Rand-McNally.

Bernard, J. (1966). Achievement test norms and time of year of testing. *Psychology in the Schools, 3*, 273-275.

Bibace, R., & Hancock, K. (1969). Relationships between perceptual and conceptual cognitive processes. *Journal of Learning Disabilities, 2*, 17-29.

Binder, A. (1963). Further considerations on testing the null hypothesis and the strategy and tactics of investigating theoretical models. *Psychological Review, 70*, 107-115.

Birch, H. G. (1964). The problem of "brain damage" in children. In H. Birch (Ed.), *Brain damage in children: The biological and social aspects.* Baltimore: Williams & Wilkins, 3-12.

Birch, H. G., & Belmont, L. (1964). Auditory-visual integration in normal and retarded readers. *American Journal of Orthopsychiatry, 34*, 852-861.

Birch, H. G., & Belmont, L. (1965). Auditory-visual integration, intelligence, and reading ability in school children. *Perceptual and Motor Skills, 20*, 295-305.

Birch, H. G., & Bortner, M. Brain damage: An educational category? In M. Bortner (Ed.), *Evaluation and education of children with brain damage.* Springfield, IL: Charles C Thomas, 3-11.

Black, F. W. (1973). Neurological dysfunction and reading disorders. *Journal of Learning Disabilities, 6*, 313-316.

Black, F. W. (1974a). Achievement test performance of high and low perceiving learning disabled children. *Journal of Learning Disabilities, 7,* 178–182.

Black, F. W. (1974b). The word explosion in learning disabilities: A notation on literature trends 1962–1972. *Journal of Learning Disabilities, 7,* 323–324.

Black, F. W. (1976). Cognitive, academic, and behavioral findings in children with suspected and documented neurological dysfunction. *Journal of Learning Disabilities, 9,* 182–189.

Black, M. (1962). *Models and metaphors.* Ithaca, NY: Cornell University Press.

Bloom, B. S. (1964). *Stability and change in human characteristics.* New York: John Wiley.

Bloom, B. S. (1976). *Human characteristics and school learning.* New York: McGraw–Hill.

Bloom, B. S. (1980). *All our children learn.* New York: McGraw–Hill.

Boder, E. (1973). Developmental dyslexia: A diagnostic approach based on three atypical reading patterns. *Developmental Medicine and Child Neurology, 15,* 663–687.

Bolles, R. C. (1962). The difference between statistical hypotheses and scientific hypotheses. *Psychological Reports, 11,* 639–645.

Bond, G., & Tinker, M. (1967). *Reading difficulties: Their diagnosis and correction* (2nd ed.). New York: Appleton–Century–Crofts.

Boring, E. G. (1923, June 6). Intelligence as the tests test it. *The New Republic,* 35–37.

Boulding, K. (1967). *The impact of the social sciences.* New Brunswick, NJ: Rutgers University Press.

Bracht, G. H. (1970). Experimental factors related to aptitude-treatment interactions. *Review of Education Research, 40,* 627–645.

Bracht, G. H., & Glass, G. V. (1968). The external validity of experiments. *American Educational Research Journal, 4,* 437–474.

Bracht, G. H., & Hopkins, K. D. (1972). Stability of general academic achievement. In G. Bracht, K. Hopkins & J. Stanley (Eds.), *Perspectives in educational and psychological measurement.* Englewood Cliffs, NJ: Prentice–Hall.

Braithwaite, R. B. (1955). *Scientific explanation.* Cambridge: Cambridge University Press.

Braun, C, (1976). Teacher expectations: Socio-psychological dynamics. *Review of Educational Research, 46,* 185–213.

Brenton, B. W., & Gilmore, D. (1976). An operational definition of learning disabilities (cognitive domain) using WISC Full Scale IQ and Peabody Individual Achievement Test scores. *Psychology in the Schools, 13,* 427–432.

Bridgman, P. W. (1927). *The logic of modern physics.* New York: Macmillan.

Brodbeck, M. (1958). Methodological individualisms: Definition and reduction. *Philosophy of Science, 25,* 1–22.

Brodbeck, M. (1962). Explanation, prediction, and "imperfect" knowledge. In H. Feigl & G. Maxwell (Eds.), *Minnesota studies in the philosophy of science: Vol. III. Scientific explanation, space, and time.* Minneapolis, MN: University of Minnesota Press.

Brodbeck, M. (1963). Logic and scientific method in research on teaching. In N. Gage (Ed.), *Handbook of research on teaching.* Chicago: Rand McNally.

Brodbeck, M. (1963). Meaning and action. *Philosophy of Science, 30,* 309–324.

Brophy, J., & Evertson, C. (1976). *Learning from teaching: A developmental perspective.* Boston: Allyn & Bacon.

Brophy, J., & Good, T. (1974). *Teacher–student relationships: Causes and consequences.* New York: Holt, Rinehart & Winston.

Brophy, J., & Putnam, J. (1979). Classroom management in the elementary grades. In D. Duke (Ed.), *Classroom management: The 78th Yearbook of the National Society for the Study of Education, Part II.* Chicago: University of Chicago Press.

Bruiniks, R. H., Glaman, G. M., & Clark, C. R. (1973). Issues in determining prevalence of reading retardation. *The Reading Teacher, 27,* 177–185.

Bruner, J. S. (1966). *Toward a theory of instruction.* New York: Norton.

Bryan, J. H. (1981). Social behaviors of learning disabled children. In J. Gottlieb & S. Strichart (Eds.), *Developmental theory and research in learning disabilities.* Baltimore: University Park Press.

Bryan, T., & Bryan, J. H. (1977). The social–emotional side of learning disabilities. *Behavioral Disorders, 2,* 141–145.

Bryant, N. (1976). Role conflict in providing services to learning disabled children. *Division for Children with Learning Disabilities Newsletter, 2,* 32–33.

Bunge, M. (Ed.). (1964). *The critical approach to science and philosophy: Essays in honor of Karl R. Popper.* New York: Free Press.

Butler, K. G., & Wallach, G. P. (Eds.). (1982). Language disorders and learning disabilities. *Topics in Language Disorders.* Rockville, MD: Aspen.

Camilleri, S. F. (1962). Theory, probability, and induction in social research. *American Sociological Review, 27,* 170–178.

Camp, B. W. (1973). Psychometric tests and learning in severely disabled readers. *Journal of Learning Disabilities, 6* 512–517.

Campbell, D. T., & Stanley, J. C. (1969). *Experimental and quasi-experimental designs for research.* Chicago: Rand McNally.

Campbell, N. R. (1957). *Foundations of science.* New York: Dover.

Carlberg, C., & Kavale, K. (1980). The efficacy of special versus regular class placement for exceptional children: A meta-analysis. *Journal of Special Education, 14,* 295–309.

Carnap, R. (1950). *Logical foundations of probability.* Chicago: University of Chicago Press.

Carnap, R. (1969). *The logical structure of the world and pseudo-problems in philosophy.* Berkeley: University of California Press.

Carroll, J. B. (1963). A model of school learning. *Teachers College Record, 64,* 723–733.

Cattell, R. B. (1963). Theory of fluid and crystallized intelligence: A critical experiment. *Journal of Educational Psychology, 54,* 1–22.

Centra, J. A., & Potter, D. A. (1980). School and teacher effects: An interrelational model. *Review of Educational Research, 50,* 273–291.

Chalfant, J. C., & King, F. S. (1976). An approach to operationalizing the definition of learning disabilities. *Journal of Learning Disabilities, 9,* 228–243.

Chalfant, J. C., & Scheffelin, M. A. (1969). *Central processing dysfunctions in children: A review of research* (NINDS Monograph No. 9). Washington, DC: U.S. Department of Health, Education, and Welfare.

Cleary, T., Humphreys, L., Kendrick, S., & Wesman, A. (1975). Educational uses of tests with disadvantaged students. *American Psychologist, 30,* 15–41.

Clements, S. D. (1966). *Minimal brain dysfunction in children. Terminology and identification* (NINDS Monograph No. 3, U.S. Public Health Service Publication No. 1415). Washington, DC: U.S. Department of Health, Education, and Welfare.

Clements, S. D., & Peters, J. E. (1962). Minimal brain dysfunction in the school-age child. *Archives of General Psychiatry, 6,* 185–197.

Cohen, E. (1972). Sociology and the classroom: Setting the condition for teacher–student interaction. *Review of Educational Research, 42,* 441–452.

Cohen, S. A. (1969). Studies in visual perception and reading in disadvantaged children. *Journal of Learning Disabilities, 2,* 498–507.

Cohen, S. A. (1971). Dyspedagogia as a cause of reading retardation: Definition and treatment. In B. Bateman (Ed.), *Learning disorders* (Vol. 4). Seattle: Special Child Publications.

Cohen, S. A. (1973). Minimal brain dysfunction and practical matters such as teaching kids to read. *Annals of the New York Academy of Sciences, 205,* 251–261.

Cohn, R. (1964). The neurological study of children with learning disabilities. *Exceptional Children, 31,* 179–185.

Coleman, J., & Sandhu, M. (1967). A descriptive relational study of 364 children referred to a university clinic for learning disorders. *Psychological Reports, 20,* 1091–1105.

Coleman, W., & Cureton, E. E. (1954). Intelligence and achievement: The jangle fallacy again. *Educational and Psychological Measurement, 14,* 347–351.

Coles, G. S. (1978). The learning disability test battery: Empirical and social issues. *Harvard Educational Review, 48,* 313–340.

Congressional Record Daily Edition (July 29, 1975). H 7755.

Conners, C. K. (1980). *Food additives and hyperactive children.* New York: Plenum Press.

Connolly, C. (1971). Social and emotional factors in learning disabilities. In H. Myklebust (Ed.), *Progress in learning disabilities* (Vol. 2). New York: Grune & Stratton.

Cooley, W. W., & Leinhardt, G. (1980). The instructional dimensions study. *Educational Evaluation and Policy Analysis, 2,* 7–25.

Copple, P. J., & Isom, J. B. (1968). Soft signs and scholastic success. *Neurology, 18,* 304–308.

Crane, A. R. (1959). An historical and critical account of the accomplishment quotient idea. *British Journal of Educational Psychology, 29,* 252–259.

Cratty, B. J. (1981). Sensory-motor and perceptual-motor theories and practices: An overview and evaluation. In R. Walk & H. Pick (Eds.), *Intersensory perception and sensory interaction.* New York: Plenum.

Cravioto, J., & DeLicardie, E. R. (1975). Environmental and nutritional deprivation in children with learning disabilities. In W. Cruickshank & D. Hallahan (Eds.), *Perceptual and learning disabilities in children:* Vol. II. *Research and theory.* Syracuse, NY: Syracuse University Press.

Crinella, F. M. (1973). Identification of brain dysfunction syndromes in children through profile analysis: Patterns associated with so-called "minimal brain dysfunction." *Journal of Abnormal Psychology, 82,* 33-45.

Cronbach, L. J. (1957). The two disciplines of scientific psychology. *American Psychologist, 12,* 671–684.

Cronbach, L. J., Gleser, G., Nanda, H., & Rajoratnam, N. (1972). *The dependability of behavioral measurements: Theory of generalizability for scores and profiles.* New York: Wiley.

Cronbach, L. J., & Meehl, P. E. (1955). Construct validity in psychological tests. *Psychological Bulletin, 52,* 281–301.

Cronbach, L. J., & Snow, R. E. (1977). *Aptitudes and instructional methods: A handbook for research on interactions.* New York: Irvington.

Cruickshank, W. M. (1972). Some issues facing the field of learning disability. *Journal of Learning Disabilities, 5,* 380–388.

Cruickshank, W. M. (1981a). Learning disabilities: A definitional statement. In W. M. Cruickshank (Ed.), *Concepts in learning disabilities: Selected writings* (Vol. 2). Syracuse: Syracuse University Press, 80–110.

Cruickshank, W. M. (1981b). Learning disabilities: Perceptual or other? In W. M. Cruickshank (Ed.), *Concepts in learning disabilities: Selected writings* (Vol. 2). Syracuse: Syracuse University Press, 111–122.

Davis, M. (1971). "That's interesting!" Towards a phenomenology of sociology and a sociology of phenomenology. *Philosophy of the Social Sciences, 4,* 309–344.

Deese, J. (1972). *Psychology as science and art.* New York: Harcourt Brace Jovanovich.

deGrazia, A., Juergens, R. E., & Stecchini, L. D. (Eds.). (1966). *The Velikovsky affair: Scientism versus science.* New Hyde Park, NY: University Books.

Delacato, C. H. (1966). *Neurological organization and reading.* Springfield, IL: Charles C Thomas.

Denckla, M. B. (1972). Clinical syndromes in learning disabilities: The case for "splitting" vs "lumping." *Journal of Learning Disabilities, 5,* 401–406.

Denckla, M. B. (1973). Research needs in learning disabilities: A neurologist's point of view. *Journal of Learning Disabilities, 6,* 441–450.

Denham, C., & Lieberman, A. (Eds.). (1980). *Time to learn.* Washington, DC: National Institute of Education.

deQuiros, J. B. (1976). Diagnosis of vestibular disorders in the learning disabled. *Journal of Learning Disabilities, 9,* 39–47.

Doll, E. A. (1941). The essentials of an inclusive concept of mental deficiency. *American Journal of Mental Deficiency, 46,* 214–219.

Dore–Boyce, K., Misner, M., & McGuire, L. D. (1975). Comparing reading expectancy formulas. *The Reading Teacher, 29,* 8–14.

Downing, J. (1979). *Reading and reasoning.* New York: Springer–Verlag.

Duhem, P. (1954). *The aim and structure of physical theory.* Princeton, NJ: Princeton University Press.

Dunkin, M. J., & Biddle, B. J. (1974). *The study of teaching.* New York: Holt, Rinehart & Winston.

Dykman, R. A., Ackerman, P. T., Clements, S. D., & Peters, J. E. (1971). Specific learning disabilities: An attentional deficit syndrome. In H. Myklebust (Ed.), *Progress in learning disabilities* (Vol. 2). New York: Grune & Stratton.

Edwards, R. P., Alley, G. R., & Snider, W. (1971). Academic achievement and minimal brain dysfunction. *Journal of Learning Disabilities, 4,* 134–138.

Erickson, M. T. (1975). The z-score discrepancy method for identifying reading-disabled children. *Journal of Learning Disabilities, 8,* 308–312.

Eveloff, H. H. (1970). Pediatric pharmacology. In W. Clark & J. del Giudice (Eds.), *Principles of psychopharmacology.* New York: Academic Press.

Fanelli, G. (1977). Locus of control. In S. Ball (Ed.), *Motivation in education.* New York: Academic Press.

Farnham–Diggory, S. (1978). *Learning disabilities.* Cambridge, MA: Harvard Univerity Press.

Federal Register, Washington, DC. Thursday, 29 December 1977, 65082–65085.

Feigl, H. (1956). Some major issues and developments in the philosophy of science and logical empiricism. In H. Feigl & M. Scriven (Eds.), *Minnesota Studies in the philosophy of science: Vol. I. The foundation of science and the concepts of psychology and psychoanalysis.* Minneapolis: University of Minnesota Press.

Feigl, H. (1970). The 'orthodox' view of theories: Remarks in defense as well as critique. In M. Radner & S. Winokur (Eds.), *Minnesota Studies in the philosophy of science: Vol. IV. Analysis theories and methods of physics and psychology.* Minneapolis: University of Minnesota Press.

Feyerabend, P. K. (1962). Explanaton, reduction, and empiricism. In H. Feigl & G. Maxwell (Eds.), *Minnesota studies in the philosophy of science: Vol. III. Scientific explanatons, space, and time.* Minneapolis: University of Minnesota Press.

Feyerabend, P. K. (1965). Problems of empiricism, Pt. I. In R. Colodny (Ed.), *Beyond the edge of certainty.* Englwood Cliffs, NJ: Prentice–Hall.

Feyerabend, P. K. (1970). Against method; Outline of an anarchistic theory of knowledge. In M. Radner & S. Winokur (Eds.), *Minnesota studies in the philosophy of science: Vol. IV. Analyses of theories and methods of physics and psychology.* Minneapolis: University of Minnesota Press.

Feyerabend, P. K. (1971). Problems of empiricism, Pt. II. In R. Colodny (Ed.), *The nature and function of scientific theories.* Pittsburgh, PA: University of Pittsburgh Press.

Fisher, D. F., & Frankfurter, A. (1977). Normal and disabled readers can locate and identify letters: Where's the perceptual deficit? *Journal of Reading Behavior, 9,* 31–43.

Fisher, F. M. (1966). *The identificaton problem in econometrics.* New York: McGraw–Hill.

Fisher, R. A. (1956). *Statistical methods and scientific inference.* Edinburgh: Oliver & Boyd.

Fisher, R. A. (1966). *The design of experiments* (8th ed.). Edinburgh: Oliver & Boyd.

Fisher, R. A. (1967). *Statistical methods for research workers* (13th ed.). Edinburgh: Oliver & Boyd.

Forness, S. R. (1973). The reinforcement hierarchy. *Psychology in the Schools, 10,* 168–177.

Forness, S. R. (1981a). Concepts of school learning and behavior disorders: Implications for research and practice. *Exceptional Children, 48,* 56–64.

Forness, S. R. (1981b). *Recent concepts in dyslexia: Implications for diagnosis and remediaton.* Reston, VA: Council for Exceptional Children.

Forness, S. R. (1982). Diagnosing dyslexia: A note on the need for ecologic assessment. *American Journal of Diseases of Children, 136,* 794–799.

Forness, S. R., Bennett, L., & Tose, J. (1983). Academic deficits in emotionaly disturbed children revisited. *Journal of Child Psychiatry, 22,* 140–144.

Forness, S. R., & Cantwell, D. (1982). DSM III psychiatric diagnoses and special education categories. *Journal of Special Education, 6,* 49–63.

Forness, S. R., & Kavale, K. A. (1983a). Remediaton of reading disabilities: I. Issues and concepts. *Learning Disabilities: An Interdisciplinary Journal, 2,* 141–152.

Forness, S. R., & Kavale, K. A. (1983b). Remediation of reading disabilities: II. Classification and approaches. *Learning Disabilities: An Interdisciplinary Journal, 2,* 153–164.

Forness, S. R., Sinclair, E., & Guthrie, D. (1983). Learning disability discrepancy formulas: Their use in actual practice. *Learning Disability Quarterly, 6,* 107–114.

Frank, J., & Levinson, H. (1973). Dysmetric dyslexia and dyspraxia: Hypothesis and study. *Journal of the American Academy of Child Psychiatry, 12,* 690–701.

Fraser, E. (1959). *Home environment and the school.* London: University of London Press.

Frazer, J. G. (1963). *The golden bough.* New York: Macmillan.

Fredrick, W. C., & Walberg, H. J. (1980). Learning as a function of time. *Journal of Educational Research, 73,* 183–194.

Freeburg, N., & Payne, D. (1967). Parental influence on cognitive development in early childhood: A review. *Child Development, 38,* 65–87.

Freeman, R. D. (1967). Special education and the electroencephalogram: Marriage of convenience. *Journal of Special Education, 2,* 61–73.

Freides, D. (1974). Human information processing and sensory modality: Cross-modal functons, informaton complexity, memory, and deficit. *Psychological Bulletin, 81,* 284–310.

Frostig, M. (1972). Visual perception, integrative functions, and academic learning. *Journal of Learning Disabilities, 5,* 1–15.

Frostig, M. (1975). The role of perception in the integration of psychological functions. In W. Cruickshank & D. Hallahan (Eds.), *Perceptual and learning disabilities in children: Vol. I. Psychoeducational practices.* Syracuse, NY: Syracuse University Press.

Frostig, M., & Horne, D. (1964). *The Frostig program for the development of visual perception.* Chicago: Follett.

Gaddes, W. H. (1980). *Learning disabilities and brain function.* New York: Springer–Verlag.

Gage, N. L. (Ed.). (1976). *The psychology of teaching methods: The 75th Yearbook of the National Society for the Study of Education, Pt. I.* Chicago: University of Chicago Press.

Gage, N. L. (1978). *The scientific basis of the art of teaching.* New York: Teachers College Press.

Gagne, R. M. (1977). *The conditions of learning* (3rd ed.). New York: Holt, Rinehart & Winston.

Gajar, A. H. (1979). Educable mentally retarded, learning disabled, emotionally disturbed: Similarities and differences. *Exceptional Children, 45,* 470–472.

Gajar, A. H. (1980). Characteristics across exceptional categories: EMR, LD, and ED. *Journal of Special Education, 14,* 165–173.

Gallagher, J. J. (1966). Children with developmental imbalances: A psycho-educational definition. In W. Cruickshank (Ed.), *The teacher of brain-injured children.* Syracuse University Special Education and Rehabilitation Monograph Series 7. Syracuse, NY: Syracuse University Press, 23–43.

Gallagher, J. J., & Moss, J. (1963). New concepts of intelligence and their effect on exceptional children. *Exceptional Children, 30,* 1–5.

Garai, J. E., & Scheinfeld, A. (1968). Sex differences in mental and behavioral traits. *Genetic Psychology Monographs, 77,* 189–299.

Gaskins, L. W. (1982). Let's end the reading disabilities/learning disabilities debate. *Journal of Learning Disabilities, 15,* 81–83.

Gessell, A. L., & Amatruda, C. S. (1941). *Developmental diagnosis.* New York: Hoeber, 1941.

Getman, G. N. (1965). The visuomotor complex in the acquisition of learning skills. In J. Hellmuth (Ed.), *Learning disorders* (Vol. 1). Seattle, WA: Special Child Publications, 49–76.

Gillespie, P. H., Miller, T. L., & Fielder, V. D. (1975). Legislative definitions of learning disabilities: Roadblocks to effective service. *Journal of Learning Disabilities, 8,* 660–666.

Glaser, R. (1976). Components of a psychology of instruction: Toward a science of design. *Review of Educational Research, 46,* 1–24.

Glaser, R. (1977). *Adaptive education: Individualized diversity and learning.* New York: Holt, Rinehart & Winston.

Glass, G. V. (1976). Primary, secondary, and meta-analysis of research. *Educational Researcher, 5,* 3–8.

Glass, G. V. (1977). Integrating findings: The meta-analysis of research. In L. Shulman (Ed.), *Review of Research in Education, 5,* 351–379.

Glass, G. V. (1979). Policy for the unpredictable (uncertainty research and policy). *Educational Researcher, 8,* 12–14.

Glass, G. V., Cahen, L. S., Smith, M. L., & Filby, N. N. (1982). *School class size: Research and policy.* Beverly Hills, CA: SAGE.

Glass, G. V., McGaw, B., & Smith, M. L. (1981). *Meta-analysis in social research.* Beverly Hills, CA: SAGE.

Gomez, M. R. (1967). Minimal cerebral dysfunction (maximal neurologic confusion). *Clinical Pediatrics, 6,* 589–591.

Good, T. (1979). Classroom expectations: Teacher–pupil interactions. In J. McMillan (Ed.), *The social psychology of school learning.* New York: Academic Press.

Good, T., Biddle, B., & Brophy, J. (1975). *Teachers make a difference.* New York: Holt, Rinehart & Winston.

Goolsby, T. M. (1971). Appropriateness of subtests in achievement test selection. *Educational and Psychological Measurement, 31,* 967–972.

Grant, D. A. (1962). Testing the null hypothesis and the strategy and tactics of investigating theoretical models. *Psychological Review, 69,* 54–61.

Green, O. C., & Perlman, S. M. (1971). Endocrinology and disorders of learning. In H. Myklebust (Ed.), *Progress in learning* (Vol. 2). New York: Grune & Stratton.

Grossman, H. J. (1966). The child, the teacher, and the physician. In W. Cruickshank (Ed.), *The teacher of brain-injured children.* Syracuse, NY: Syracuse University Press, 59–67.

Grossman, H. J. (1983). *Manual on terminology and classification in mental retardation.* Washington, DC: American Association on Mental Deficiency.

Grossman, R. P. (1978). LD and the problem of scientific definitions. *Journal of Learning Disabilities, 11,* 120–123.

Grunbaum, A. (1960). The Duhemian argument. *Philosophy of Science, 27,* 75–87.

Guilford, J. P. (1967). *The nature of human intelligence.* New York: McGraw–Hill.

Gump, P. (1978). School environments. In I. Altman & J. Wohlwill (Eds.), *Children and the environment.* New York: Plenum.

Guyer, B. L., & Friedman, M. P. (1975). Hemispheric processing and cognitive styles in learning disabled and normal children. *Child Development, 46,* 658–668.

Hallahan, D. P., & Cruickshank, W. M. (1973). *Psychoeducational foundations of learning disabilities.* Englewood Cliffs, NJ: Prentice–Hall.

Hallahan, D. P., & Kauffman, J. M. (1976). *Introduction to learning disabilities: A psycho-behavioral approach.* Englewood Cliffs, NJ: Prentice–Hall.

Hallahan, D. P., & Kauffman, J. M. (1977). Labels, categories, behaviors: ED, LD, and EMR reconsidered. *Journal of Special Education, 11,* 139–149.

Hamachek, D. E. (1978). *Encounters with the self* (2nd ed.). New York: Holt, Rinehart & Winston.

Hammill, D. D. (1974). Learning disabilities: A problem in definition. *Division for Children with Learning Disabilities Newsletter, 4,* 28–31.

Hammill, D. D. (1976). Defining "LD" for programmatic purposes. *Academic Therapy, 12,* 29–37.

Hammill, D. D., & Larsen, S. C. (1974a). The effectiveness of psycholinguistic training. *Exceptional Children, 41,* 5–14.

Hammill, D. D., & Larsen, S. C. (1974b). The relationship of selected auditory perceptual skills and reading ability. *Journal of Learning Disabilities, 7,* 429–435.

Hammill, D. D., & Larsen, S. C. (1978). The effectiveness of psycholinguistic training: A reaffirmation of position. *Exceptional Children, 44,* 402–414.

Hammill, D. D., Leigh, J., McNutt, G., & Larsen, S. (1981). A new definition of learning disabilities. *Learning Disability Quarterly, 4,* 836–842.

Hanna, G. S., Dyck, N. J., & Holen, M. C. (1979). Objective analysis of achievement-aptitude discrepancies in LD classification. *Learning Disability Quarterly, 2,* 32–38.

Hanson, N. R. (1963). *The concept of the positron.* Cambridge: Cambridge University Press.

Hanson, N. R. (1970). A picture theory of meaning. In M. Radner & S. Winokur (Eds.), *Minnesota Studies in the philosophy of science: Vol. IV. Analysis of theories and methods of physics and psychology.* Minneapolis: University of Minnesota Press.

Harber, J. R. (1981). Learning disability research: How far have we progressed? *Learning Disability Quarterly, 4,* 372-381.

Hare, B. (1977). Perceptual deficits are not a cue to reading problems in second grade. *Reading Teacher, 30,* 624-627.

Haring, N., & Bateman, B. (1977). *Teaching the learning disabled child.* Englewood Cliffs, NJ: Prentice-Hall.

Harnischfeger, A., & Wiley, D. E. (1976). The teaching learning process in elementary schools: A synoptic view. *Curriculum Inquiry, 6,* 5-43.

Harris, A. J. (1961). *How to increase reading ability* (4th ed.). New York: McKay.

Hart, Z., Rennick, P. M., Klinge, V., & Schwartz, M. L. (1974). A pediatric neurologist's contribution to evaluations of school underachievers. *American Journal of Diseases of Children, 128,* 319-323.

Hartlage, L. C. (1970). Differential diagnosis of dyslexia, minimal brain damage, and emotional disturbances in children. *Psychology in the Schools, 7,* 403-406.

Hartlage, L. C., & Green, J. B. (1971). EEG differences in children's reading, spelling, and arithmetic abilities. *Perceptual and Motor Skills, 32,* 133-134.

Hartman, N., & Hartman, R. (1973). Perceptual handicap or reading disability? *The Reading Teacher, 26,* 684-695.

Hempel, C. G. (1952). *Fundamentals of concept formation in empirical science.* Chicago: University of Chicago Press.

Hempel, C. G. (1955). *Aspects of scientific explanation.* New York: Free Press.

Hempel, C. G. (1970). On the 'standard conception' of scientific theories. In M. Radner & S. Winokur (Eds.), *Minnesota studies in the philosophy of science: Vol. IV. Analyses of theories and methods of physics and psychology.* Minneapolis: University of Minnesota Press.

Herbert, M. (1964). The concept and testing of brain-damage in children: A review. *Journal of Child Psychology and Psychiatry, 5,* 197-216.

Herrick, M. J. (1973). Disabled or disadvantaged: What's the difference? *Journal of Special Education, 7,* 381-386.

Hertzig, M. E., Bortner, M., & Birch, H. G. (1969). Neurologic findings in children educationally designated as "brain-damaged." *American Journal of Orthopsychiatry, 39,* 473-446.

Hess, R. (1970). Class and ethnic influences upon socialization. In P. Mussen (Ed.), *Carmichael's manual of child psychology* (3rd ed., Vol. 2). New York: Wiley.

Hesse, M. B. (1966). *Models and analogies in science.* Notre Dame, IN: University of Notre Dame Press.

Hewett, F. M. (1968). *The emotionally disturbed child in the classroom.* Boston: Allyn & Bacon.

Hewett, F. M., & Forness, S. R. (1983). *Education of exceptional learners* (3rd ed.). Boston: Allyn & Bacon.

Hilton, T. L. (1979). ETS study of academic prediction and growth. In J. Milholland (Ed.), *New directions for testing and measurement.* San Francisco: Jossey-Bass.

Hobbs, N. (Ed.). (1975). *The futures of children: Categories, labels, and their consequences.* San Francisco: Jossey-Bass.

Hodges, H. A. (1944). *Wilhem Dilthey: An introduction.* London: Routledge & Kegan Paul.

Hoffman, I. V. (1980). The disabled reader: Forgive us our regressions and lead us not into expectations. *Journal of Learning Disabilities, 13,* 7-11.

Honzik, M., Macfarlane, J., & Allen, L. (1948). The stability of mental test performance between two and eighteen years. *Journal of Experimental Education, 17,* 309-324.

Hopkins, K. D., & Bracht, G. H. (1975). Ten-year stability of verbal and nonverbal IQ scores. *American Educational Research Journal, 12,* 469-477.

Horn, A. (1941). *The uneven distribution of the effects of specific factors.* Southern California Educational Monographs, No. 12. University of Southern California Press.

Hughes, J. R. (1978). Electroencephalographic and neurophysiological studies in dyslexia. In A. Benton & D. Pearl (Eds.), *Dyslexia: An appraisal of current knowledge.* New York: Oxford University Press.

Hunt, J. McV. (1961). *Intelligence and experience.* New York: Wiley.

Hurley, R. (1969). *Poverty and mental retardation: A causal relationship.* New York: Random House.

Hyman, H. H., Wright, C. R., & Reed, J. S. (1975). *The enduring effects of education,* Chicago: University of Chicago Press.

Ingram, T. T. S. (1973). Soft signs. *Developmental Medicine and Child Neurology, 15,* 527–529.

Jackson, P. W. (1968). *Life in classrooms.* New York: Holt, Rinehart & Winston.

Jakupcak, M. (1975). Areas of congruence in remedial reading and learning disabilities. *Journal of Special Education, 9,* 155–157.

Jenkins, J., & Pany, D. (1978). Standardized achievement tests: How useful for special education? *Exceptional Children, 44,* 448–453.

Jensen, A. R. (1967). Varieties in individual differences in learning. In R. Gagne (Ed.), *Learning and individual differences.* Columbus, OH: Charles E. Merrill.

Jensen, A. R. (1970). A theory of primary and secondary familial mental retardation. In N. R. Ellis (Ed.), *International review of research in mental retardation* (Vol. 4). New York: Academic Press, 33–105.

Joe, V. (1971). Review of the internal–external control construct as a personality variable. *Psychological Reports, 28,* 619–640.

Johnson, W. E. (1964). *Logic, Pt. I.* New York: Dover Publications.

Journal of Special Education (1976). Symposium #12: Research problems in learning disabilities, *10,* 127–170.

Joyce, B., & Weil, M. (1972). *Models of teaching.* Englewood Cliffs, NJ: Prentice–Hall.

Kagan, J., & Kogan, N. (1970). Individual variation in cognitive processes. In P. Mussen (Ed.), *Carmichael's manual of child psychology* (3rd ed., Vol. 1). New York: Wiley.

Kaplan, A. (1964). *The conduct of inquiry: Methodology for behavioral science.* San Francisco, CA: Chandler.

Kass, C. E. (1966). Psycholinguistic disabilities of children with reading problems. *Exceptional Children, 32,* 533–539.

Kass, C. E. (1977). Identification of learning disability (dyssymbolia). *Journal of Learning Disabilities, 10,* 425–432.

Kass, C. E., & Myklebust, H. R. (1969). Learning disability: An educational definition. *Journal of Learning Disabilities, 2,* 377–379.

Katahan, M., & Koplin, J. H. (1968). Paradigm clash: Comment on "Some recent criticisms of behaviorism and learning theory with special reference to Breger and McGough and to Chomsky." *Psychological Bulletin, 69,* 147–148.

Kavale, K. A. (1980a). Auditory–visual integration and its relationship to reading achievement: A meta-analysis. *Perceptual and Motor Skills, 51,* 947–955.

Kavale, K. A. (1980b). Learning disability and cultural–economic disadvantage: The case for a relationship. *Learning Disability Quarterly, 3,* 97–112.

Kavale, K. A. (1981a). Functions of the Illinois Test of Psycholinguistic Abilities (ITPA): Are they trainable? *Exceptional Children, 47,* 496–510.

Kavale, K. A. (1981b). The relationship between auditory perceptual skills and reading ability: A meta-analysis. *Journal of Learning Disabilities, 14,* 539–546.

Kavale, K. A. (1982a). The efficacy of stimulant drug treatment for hyperactivity: A meta-analysis. *Journal of Learning Disabilities, 15,* 280–289.

Kavale, K. A. (1982b). Meta-analysis of the relationship between visual perceptual skills and reading achievement. *Journal of Learning Disabilities, 15,* 42–51.

Kavale, K. A. (1983). Fragile findings, complex conclusions, and meta-analysis in special education. *Exceptional Education Quarterly. 4,* 97–106.

Kavale, K. A. (1984). Potential advantages of the meta-analysis technique for special education. *Journal of Special Education, 18,* 61–72.

Kavale, K. A., Alper, A. E., & Purcell, L. L. (1981). Behavior disorders, reading disorders, and teacher perceptions. *The Exceptional Child, 28,* 114–118.

Kavale, K. A., & Forness, S. R. (1983). Hyperactivity and diet treatment: A meta-analysis of the Feingold hypothesis. *Journal of Learning Disabilities, 16,* 324–330.

Kavale, K. A., & Forness, S. R. (1984a). *Auditory and visual abilities and their relationship to reading achievement: A meta-analysis.* Unpublished manuscript, University of California, Riverside.

Kavale, K. A., & Forness, S. R. (1984b). A meta-analysis assessing the validity of Wechsler Scale profiles and recategorizations: Patterns or parodies? *Learning Disability Quarterly, 7,* 136–156.

Kavale, K. A., & Glass, G. V. (1981). Meta-analysis and the integration of research in special education. *Journal of Learning Disabilities, 14,* 531–538.

Kavale, K. A., & Glass, G. V. (1982). The efficacy of special education interventions and practices: A compendium of meta-analysis findings. *Focus on Exceptional Children, 15,* 1–14.

Kavale, K. A., & Mattson, P. D. (1983). "One jumped off the balance beam": Meta-analysis of perceptual-motor training. *Journal of Learning Disabilities, 16,* 165–173.

Kavale, K. A., & Nye, C. (1981). Identification criteria for learning disabilities: A survey of the research literature. *Learning Disability Quarterly, 4,* 383–388.

Keeves, J. P. (1972). *Educational environment and student achievement.* Stockholm: Almquist & Wiksell.

Kelley, T. L. (1927). *Interpretation of educational measurements.* New York: World Book Co.

Kennard, M. A. (1960). Value of equivocal signs in neurological diagnosis. *Neurology, 10,* 753–764.

Kenny, T. J., & Clemmens, R. C. (1971). Medical and psychological correlates in children with learning disabilities. *Journal of Pediatrics, 78,* 273–277.

Keogh, B. K., & Donlon, G. (1972). Field dependence, impulsivity, and learning disabilities. *Journal of Learning Disabilities, 5,* 331–336.

Keogh, B. K., & Kopp, C. (1978). From assessment to intervention: An elusive bridge. In F. Minafee & L. Lloyd (Eds.), *Communication and cognitive abilities.* Baltimore: University Park Press.

Keogh, B. K., & Margolis, J. (1976). Learn to labor and wait: Attention problems of children with learning disabilities. *Journal of Learning Disabilities, 9,* 276–286.

Keogh, J. F. (1981). A movement development framework and a perceptual-cognitive perspective. In G. Brooks (Ed.), *Perspectives on the academic discipline of physical education.* Champaign, IL: Human Kinetics.

Keogh, J. (1982). The study of movement learning disabilities. In J. Das, R. Mulcahy & A. Wall (Eds.), *Theory and research in learning disabilities.* New York: Plenum Press.

Kephart, N. C. (1960). *The slow learner in the classroom.* Columbus, OH: Charles E. Merrill.

Kephart, N. C. (1964). Perceptual-motor aspects of learning disabilities. *Exceptional Children, 31,* 201–206.

Kerlinger, F. N. (1973). *Foundations of behavioral research* (2nd ed.). New York: Holt, Rinehart & Winston.

Kessel, F. S. (1969). The philosophy of science as proclaimed and science as practiced: "Identity" or "dualism"? *American Psychologist, 24,* 999–1005.

Kifer, E. (1975). Relationships between academic achievement and personality characteristics: A quasi-longitudinal study. *American Educational Research Journal, 12,* 191–210.

Kinsbourne, M. (1973). Minimal brain dysfunction as a neurodevelopmental lag. *Annals of the New York Academy of Sciences, 205,* 268–273.

Kinsbourne, M. (Ed.). (1983). Brain basis of learning disabilities. *Topics in Learning and Learning Disabilities.* Rockville, MD: Aspen.

Kinsbourne, M., & Caplan, P. J. (1979). *Children's learning and attention problems.* Boston: Little, Brown & Co.

Kirk, S. A. (1968). Illinois Test of Psycholinguistic Abilities: Its origin and implications. In J. Hellmuth (Ed.), *Learning disorders* (Vol. 3). Seattle: Special Child Publications.

Kirk, S. A., & Elkins, J. (1975). Characteristics of children enrolled in the Child Service Demonstration Centers. *Journal of Learning Disabilities, 8,* 630-637.

Kirk, S. A., & Gallagher, J. J. (1983). *Educating Exceptional Children* (4th ed.). Boston: Houghton Mifflin.

Kirk, S. A., & Kirk, W. D. (1971). *Psycholinguistic learning disabilities: Diagnosis and remediation.* Urbana, IL: University of Illinois Press.

Kirk, W. D. (1975). The relationship of reading disabilities to learning disabilities. *Journal of Special Education, 9,* 132-137.

Kneedler, R., & Hallahan, D. (1983). Research in learning disabilities: Summaries of the institutes. *Exceptional Education Quarterly, 4,* 1-147.

Knights, R. M., & Bakker, D. J. (Eds.). (1976). *The neuropsychology of learning disorders: Theoretical approaches.* Baltimore: University Park Press.

Koestler, A. (1971). *The case of the midwife toad.* New York: Random House.

Koppitz, E. M. (1971). *Children with learning disabilities: A five year follow-up study.* New York: Grune & Stratton.

Kounin, J. S. (1970). *Discipline and group management in classroom.* New York: Holt, Rinehart & Winston.

Koupernik, C., MacKeith, R., & Francis-Williams, J. (1975). Neurological correlates of motor and perceptual development. In W. Cruickshank & D. Hallahan (Eds.), *Perceptual and learning disabilities in children: Vol. II. Research and theory.* Syracuse, NY: Syracuse University Press, 105-135.

Krantz, P., & Risley, T. (1977). Behavioral ecology in the classroom. In K. O'Leary & S. O'Leary (Eds.), *Classroom management: The successful use of behavior modification* (2nd ed.). New York: Pergamon Press.

Kronnick, D. (1981). *Social development of learning disabled persons.* San Francisco: Jossey-Bass.

Kuethe, J. L. (1968). *The teaching-learning process.* Glenview, IL: Scott, Foresman & Co.

Kuhn, T. S. (1970). *The structure of scientific revolutions* (2nd ed.). Chicago: University of Chicago Press.

Lakatos, I. (1970). Falsification and the methodology of scientific research programs. In I. Lakatos & A. Musgrave (Eds.), *Criticism and the growth of knowledge.* Cambridge: Cambridge University Press.

Lakatos, I. (1974a). Popper on demarcation and induction. In P. Schilipp (Ed.), *The philosophy of Karl Popper* (Vol. 1). LaSalle, IL: Open Court.

Lakatos, I. (1974b). The role of crucial experiments in science. *Studies in history and philosophy of science, 4,* 309-325.

Langmuir, I. (1943). Science, common sense, and decency. *Science, 97,* 1-3.

Larivee, B. (1981). Modality preference as a model for differentiating beginning reading instruction: A review of the issues. *Learning Disability Quarterly, 4,* 180-188.

Larsen, S. C., & Hammill, D. D. (1975). The relationship of selected visual perceptual abilities to school learning. *Journal of Special Education, 9,* 281-291.

Laudan, L. (1965). On the impossibility of crucial falsifying experiments. *Philosophy of Science, 32,* 39-68.

Laufer, M. W., & Denhoff, E. (1957). Hyperkinetic behavior syndrome in children. *Journal of Pediatrics, 50,* 463-474.

Lavin, D. E. (1965). *The prediction of academic performance.* New York: Russell Sage Foundation.

Lennon, R. T. (1951). The stability of achievement test results from grade to grade. *Educational and Psychological Measurement, 11,* 121-127.

Lerner, J. W. (1975). Remedial reading and learning disabilities: Are they the same or different? *Journal of Special Education, 9,* 119-131.

Lewin, K. (1951). *Field theory and social sciences.* New York: Harper & Row.

Light, R. J., & Smith, P. V. (1971). Accumulating evidence: Procedures for resolving contradictions among different research studies. *Harvard Educational Review, 41,* 429-471.

Lightfoot, J. L. (1979). Families and schools. In H. Walberg (Ed.), *Educational environments and effects.* Berkeley, CA: McCuthan.

Lloyd, J., Sabatino, D., Miller, T., & Miller, S. (1977). Proposed federal guidelines: Some open questions. *Journal of Learning Disabilities, 10,* 69–71.

Loevinger, J. (1957). Objective tests as instruments of psychological theory. *Psychological Reports, 9,* 635–694.

London, I. D. (1946). Some consequences for history and psychology of Langmuir's concept of convergence and divergence of phenomenon. *Psychological Review, 53,* 170–188.

Lovitt, T. C., & Jenkins, J. R. (1979). Learning disabilities research: Defining populations. *Learning Disability Quarterly, 2,* 46–50.

Lucas, A. R., Rodin, E. A., & Simson, C. B. (1965). Neurological assessment of children with early school problems. *Developmental Medicine and Child Neurology, 7,* 145–156.

Lund, K. A., Foster, G. E., & McCall–Perez, F. C. (1978). The effectiveness of psycholinguistic training: A reevaluation. *Exceptional Children, 44,* 310–319.

Lyon, R., & Watson, B. (1981). Empirically derived subgroups of learning disabled readers: Diagnostic characteristics. *Journal of Learning Disabilities, 14,* 256–261.

Maccoby, E. E., & Jacklin, C. N. (1974). *The psychology of sex differences.* Palo Alto, CA: Stanford University Press.

MacCorquodale, K., & Meehl, P. E. (1948). On a distinction between hypothetical constructs and intervening variables. *Psychological Review, 55,* 95–107.

MacMillan, D. L. (1973). *Behavior modification in education.* New York: Macmillan.

MacMillan, D. L. (1982). *Mental retardation in school and society* (2nd ed.). Boston: Little, Brown.

MacMillan, D. L., & Meyers, C. E. (1980). Larry P: An educational interpretation. *School Psychology Review, 9,* 136–148.

MacMillan, D. L., Meyers, C. E., & Morrison, G. (1980). System identification of mildly mentally retarded children: Implications for interpreting and conducting research. *American Journal of Mental Deficiency, 85,* 108–115.

Macy, D. J., Baker, J. A., & Kosinski, S. C. (1979). An empirical study of the Mylkebust learning quotient. *Journal of Learning Disabilities, 12,* 93-96.

Mann, L. (1971). Psychometric phrenology and the new faculty psychology: The case against ability assessment and training. *Journal of Special Education, 5,* 3–14.

Mann, L. (1979). *On the trail of process.* New York: Grune & Stratton.

Mann, L., Davis, C. H., Boyer, C. W., Metz, C. M., & Wolford, B. (1983). LD or not LD, that was the question: A retrospective analysis of Child Service Demonstration Center's compliance with the Federal definition of learning disabilities. *Journal of Learning Disabilities, 16,* 14–17.

Mann, L., & Phillips, W. A. (1967). Fractional practices in special education: A critique. *Exceptional Children, 33,* 311–317.

Marjoribanks, K. (1972). Environment, social class, and mental abilities. *Journal of Education Psychology, 63,* 103–109.

Marjoribanks, K. (Ed.). (1974). *Environments for learning.* London: National Foundation for Educational Research.

Martin, H. P. (1980). Nutrition, injury, illness, and minimal brain dysfunction. In H. Rie & E. Rie (Eds.), *Handbook of minimal brain dysfunctions: A critical view.* New York: John Wiley.

Masterman, M. (1970). The nature of a paradigm. In I. Lakato & A. Musgrave (Eds.), *Criticism and the growth of knowledge.* Cambridge: Cambridge University Press, 1970.

Mattis, S. (1978). Dyslexia syndromes: A working hypothesis that works. In A. L. Benton & D. Pearl (Eds.), *Dyslexia: An appraisal of current knowledge.* New York: Oxford University Press, 43–58.

Mayron, L. W. (1978). Ecological factors in learning disabilities. *Journal of Learning Disabilities, 11,* 40–50.

Mayron, L. W. (1979). Allergy, learning, and behavior problems. *Journal of Learning Disabilities, 12,* 41–49.

McCall, R., Appelbaum, M., & Hogarty, P. (1973). Developmental changes in mental performance. *Monographs of the Society for Research in Child Development, 38,* No. 3, 1–84.

McCarthy, J. M., & Paraskevopoulos, J. (1969). Behavior patterns of learning disabled, emotionally disturbed, and average children. *Exceptional Children, 35,* 69–74.

McClelland, D. C. (1973). Testing for competence rather than for 'intelligence.' *American Psychologist, 29,* 1-14.

McClelland, D. C., Atkinson, J. W., Clark, R. A., & Lowell, E. L. (1953). *The achievement motive.* New York: Appleton-Century-Crofts.

McDonald, C. W. (1968). Problems concerning the classification and education of children with learning disabilities. In J. Hellmuth (Ed.), *Learning disorders* (Vol. 3). Seattle: Special Child Publications, 371-394.

McIntosh, D., & Dunn, L. (1973). Children with major specific learning disabilities. In L. Dunn (Ed.), *Exceptional Children in the schools: Special education in transition* (2nd ed.). New York: Holt, Rinehart & Winston.

McLeod, J. (1967). Some psycholinguistic correlates of reading disability in young children. *Reading Research Quarterly, 2,* 5-32.

McLeod, J. (1979). Education underachievement: Toward a defensible psychometric definition. *Journal of Learning Disabilities, 12,* 322-330.

McNemar, Q. (1964). Lost: Our intelligence? Why? *American Psychologist, 19,* 871-882.

Meehl, P. E. (1965). Seer over sign: The first good example. *Journal of Experimental Research in Personality, 1,* 27-32.

Meehl, P. E. (1967). Theory-testing in psychology and physics: A methodological paradox. *Philosophy of Science, 34,* 103-115.

Meehl, P. E. (1970). Nuisance variables and the expost facto design. In M. Radner & S. Winokur (Eds.), *Minnesota studies in the philosophy of science: Vol. IV. Analyses of theories and methods of physics and psychology.* Minneapolis: University of Minnesota Press.

Meehl, P. E. (1977). Specific etiology and other forms of strong inference: Some quantitative meanings. *Journal of Medicine and Philosophy, 2,* 33-53.

Meehl, P. E. (1978). Theoretical risks and tabular asterisks: Sir Karl, Sir Ronald, and the slow progress of soft psychology. *Journal of Consulting and Clinical Psychology, 46,* 806-834.

Mercer, C. D., Forgnone, C., & Wolking, W. D. (1976). Definitions of learning disabilities used in the United States. *Journal of Learning Disabilities, 9,* 376-386.

Merton, R. K. (1957). *Social theory and social structure.* New York: Free Press.

Messick, S. (Ed.). (1976). *Individuality in learning: Implications of cognitive styles and creativity for human development.* San Francisco: Jossey-Bass.

Meyen, E. L., & Hieronymous, A. N. (1970). The age placement of academic skills in curriculum for EMR. *Exceptional Children, 36,* 333-390.

Mill, J. S. (1872). *A system of logic* (8th ed.). New York: Longmans.

Millman, J., Bieger, G. R., Klag, P. A., & Pine, C. K. (1983). Relation between perseverance and rate of learning: A test of Caroll's model of school learning. *American Educational Research Journal, 20,* 425-434.

Minskoff, E. (1975). Research on psycholinguistic training: Critique and guidelines. *Exceptional Children, 42,* 136-144.

Mitroff, I. I., & Featheringham, T. R. (1974). On systematic problem solving and the error of the third kind. *Behavioral Science, 19,* 383-393.

Mitroff, I. I., & Kilmann, R. H. (1978). *Methodological approaches to social science.* San Francisco: Jossey-Boss.

Monroe, M. (1932). *Children who cannot read.* Chicago: University of Chicago Press.

Morrison, D. E., & Henkel, R. E. (Ed.). (1970). *The significance test controversy: A reader.* Chicago: Aldine.

Morrison, G. M., MacMillan, D. L., & Kavale, K. A. (in press). System identification of learning disabled children: Implications for research sampling. *Learning Disability Quarterly.*

Morse, W. C., Cutler, R. L., & Fink, A. H. (1964). *Public school classes for the emotionally handicapped: A research analysis.* Washington, DC: Council for Exceptional Children, 1964.

Myers, P. I., & Hamill, D. D. (1976). *Methods for learning disorders* (2nd ed.). New York: John Wiley.

Myklebust, H. R. (1964). Learning disorders: Psychoneurological disturbances in childhood. *Rehabilitation Literature, 25,* 354-359.

Myklebust, H. R. (1968). Learning disabilities: Definition and overview. In H. Myklebust (Ed.), *Progress in learning disabilities* (Vol. D). New York: Grune & Stratton, 1–15.

Myklebust, H. R., Bannochie, M. N., & Killen, J. R. (1971). Learning disabilities and cognitive processes. In H. Myklebust (Ed.), *Progress in learning disabilities* (Vol. 2). New York: Grune & Stratton.

Nagel, E. (1961). *The structure of science: Problems in the logic of scientific explanation.* New York: Harcourt, Brace & World.

National Advisory Committee on Handicapped Children. (1968). *First Annual Report, Special Education for Handicapped Children.* Washington, DC: U. S. Office of Education, Department of Health, Education, and Welfare.

Neisworth, J., & Greer, J. (1975). Functional similarities of learning disability and mild retardation. *Exceptional Children, 42,* 17–21.

Newcomer, P., Larsen, S., & Hammill, D. (1975). A response. *Exceptional Children, 42,* 144–148.

Nichols, P. L., & Chen, T. C. (1981). *Minimal brain dysfunction: A prospective study.* Hillsdale, NJ: Lawrence Erlbaum Associates.

O'Donnell, L. E. (1980). Intra-individual discrepancy in diagnosing specific learning disabilities. *Learning Disability Quarterly, 3,* 10–18.

O'Grady, D. J. (1974). Psycholinguistic abilities in learning disabled, emotionally disturbed, and normal children. *Journal of Special Education, 8,* 157–165.

Olson, J. L., & Mealor, D. J. (1981). Learning disabilities identification: Do researchers have the answer? *Learning Disability Quarterly, 4,* 389–392.

Orton, S. T. (1937). *Reading, writing, and speech problems in children.* New York: Norton.

Osgood, C. E. (1957). Motivational dynamics of language behavior. In M. Jones (Ed.), *Nebraska Symposium on Motivation.* Lincoln: University of Nebraska Press.

Ounsted, C., Lindsay, J., & Norman, R. (1966). Biological factors in temporal lobe epilepsy. *Clinics in Developmental Medicine,* No. 22.

Owen, F. W., Adams, P. A., Forrest, T., Stolz, L. M., & Fisher, S. (1971). Learning disorders in children: Sibling studies. *Monographs of the Society for Research in Child Development, 36,* (4, Serial No. 144).

Paine, R. S. (1962). Minimal chronic brain syndromes in children. *Developmental Medicine and Child Neurology, 4,* 21–27.

Paine, R. S. (1965). Organic neurological factors related to learning disorders. In J. Hellmuth (Ed.), *Learning disorders* (Vol. 1). Seattle: Special Child Publications, 1–29.

Paine, R. S., Werry, J. S., & Quay, H. C. (1968). A study of "minimal brain dysfunction." *Developmental Medicine and Child Neurology, 10,* 505–520.

Pap, A. (1962). *An introduction to the philosophy of science.* New York: Free Press.

Pasamanick, B., & Knobloch, H. (1959). Syndrome of minimal cerebral damage in infancy. *Journal of the American Medical Association, 170,* 1384–1387.

Pepper, S. C. (1942). *World hypotheses.* Berkeley: University of California Press.

Phillips, D. C. (1980). What do the researcher and the practitioner have to offer each other? *Educational Researcher, 9,* 17–20, 24.

Polyani, M. (1958). *Personal knowledge: Towards a post critical philosophy.* New York: Harper & Row.

Pond, D. A. (1963). The EEG in pediatrics. In J. Hill & G. Parr (Eds.), *Electroencephalography: A symposium on its various aspects* (2nd ed.). London: MacDonald.

Popper, K. R. (1959). *The logic of scientific discovery.* New York: Basic Books.

Popper, K. R. (1968). *Conjectures and refutations.* New York: Basic Books.

Popper, K. R. (1972). *Objective knowledge: An evolutionary approach.* Oxford: Oxford University Press.

Popper, K. R. (1976). A note on verisimilitude. *British Journal for the Philosophy of Science, 27,* 147–195.

Public Law 94–142. (November 29, 1975). *Education for All Handicapped Children Act.* U.S. Congress.

Quinn, P. (1969). The status of the D-Thesis. *Philosophy of Science, 36,* 381–399.

Rapaport, D. (1960). The structure of psychoanalytic theory: A systematizing attempt. *Psychological Issues, 2,* No. 6.

Rapaport, D., & Gill, M. M. (1959). The points of view and assumptions of metapsychology. *The International Journal of Psychoanalysis, 40*, 153–162.

Reichenbach, H. (1968). *Experience and prediction: An analysis of the foundation and structure of knowledge*. Berkeley: University of California Press.

Reynolds, M. C., & Birch, J. W. (1977). *Teaching exceptional children in all America's schools: A first course for teachers and principals*. Reston, VA: Council for Exceptional Children.

Richardson, E., DiBenedetto, B., & Christ, A. (1978). An assessment of two methods for remediating reading deficiencies. *Reading Improvement, 15*, 82–95.

Rie, H. E., & Rie, E. D. (Eds.). (1980). *Handbook of minimal brain dysfunctions*. New York: Wiley.

Ringness, T. (1975). *The affective domain in education*. Boston: Little, Brown & Co.

Rosenshine, B. (1971). *Teaching behaviors and student achievement*. London: National Foundation for Educational Research.

Rosenshine, B. (1976). Classroom instruction. In N. Gage (Ed.), *The psychology of teaching methods: The 75th Yearbook of the National Society for the Study of Education, Pt. I*. Chicago: University of Chicago Press.

Rosenshine, B. (1979). The third cycle of research on teacher effects: Content covered, academic engaged time, and direct instruction. In P. Peterson & H. Walberg (Eds.), *Research on teaching: Concepts, findings, and implications*. Berkeley, CA: McCuthan.

Rosenshine, B., & Furst, N. (1973). The use of direct observation to study teaching. In R. Travers (Ed.), *Second handbook of research on teaching*. Chicago: Rand McNally.

Rosenthal, R., & Jacobson, L. (1968). *Pygmalion in the classroom*. New York: Holt, Rinehart & Winston.

Rosenthal, R., & Rubin, D. R. (1982). A simple, general purpose display of the magnitude of experimental effect. *Journal of Educational Psychology, 74*, 166–169.

Ross, A. O. (1976). *Psychological aspects of learning disabilities and reading disorders*. New York: McGraw–Hill.

Rostand, J. (1960). *Error and deception in science*. New York: Basic Books.

Routh, D. K., & Roberts, R. D. (1972). Minimal brain dysfunction in children: Failure to find evidence for a behavioral syndrome. *Psychological Reports, 31*, 307–314.

Rubin, L. (Ed.). (1977). *Curriculum handbook: The disciplines, current movements, and instructional methodology*. Boston: Allyn & Bacon.

Rudner, R. S. (1966). *Philosophy of social science*. Englewood Cliffs, NJ: Prentice–Hall.

Ryan, D. G. (1960). *Characteristics of teachers*. Washington, DC: American Council on Education.

Salvia, J., & Ysseldyke, J. (1981). *Assessment in special and remedial education* (2nd ed.). Boston: Houghton–Mifflin.

Sarason, S. B. (1949). *Psychological problems in mental deficiency*. New York: Harper & Row.

Sarason, S. B., Lighthall, F. F., Davidson, K. S., Waite, R. R., & Ruebush, B. K. (1960). *Anxiety in elementary school children*. New York: Wiley.

Sartain, H. (1976). Instruction of disabled learners: A reading perspective. *Journal of Learning Disabilities, 9*, 489–497.

Satterfield, J. H. (1973). EEG issues in children with minimal brain dysfunction. In S. Walzer & P. Wolff (Eds.), *Minimal cerebral dysfunction in children*. New York: Grune & Stratton.

Satz, P., & Morris. R. (1981). Learning disability subtypes: A review. In M. Pirozzolo & M. Wittrock (Eds.), *Neuropsychological and cognitive processes in reading*. New York: Academic Press, 109–141.

Satz, P., & Sparrow, S. (1970). Specific developmental dyslexia: A theoretical formulation. In D. Bakker & P. Satz (Eds.), *Specific reading disability: Advances in theory and method*. Rotterdam: Rotterdam University Press .

Schain, R. (1970). Neurological examination of 40 children with learning disorders. *Neuropaediatric, 3*, 307–317.

Scheerenberger, R. (1982). *A history of mental retardation*. Baltimore: Paul Brookes.

Scheff, T. (1966). *Being mentally ill: A sociological theory*. Chicago: Aldine.

Scheffler, I. (1956). Science, morals, and educational policy. *Harvard Educational Review, 26,* 1-16.

Scheffler, I. (1963). *The anatomy of inquiry: Philosophical studies in the theory of science.* New York: A. A. Knopf.

Scheffler, I. (1967). *Science and subjectivity.* Indianapolis: Bobbs-Merrill.

Schere, R. A., Richardson, E., & Bialer, I. (1980). Toward operationalizing a psychoeducational definition of learning disabilities. *Journal of Abnormal Child Psychology, 8,* 5-20.

Schmitt, B. D. (1975). The minimal brain dysfunction myth. *American Journal of Diseases of Cildren, 129,* 1313-1318.

Schmuck, R. A., & Schmuck, P. A. (1971). *Group processes in the classroom.* Dubuque, IA: Wm. C. Brown.

Schulman, J. L., Kaspar, J. C., & Throne, F. M. (1965). *Brain damage and behavior: A clinical-experimental study.* Springfield, IL: Charles C Thomas.

Schwarz, R. H. (1969). Mental age as it relates to school achievement among educable mentally retarded adolescents. *Education and Training of the Mentally Retarded, 4,* 53-56.

Schwarz, R. H., & Cook, J. J. (1971). Mental age as a predictor of academic achievement. *Education and Training of the Mentally Retarded, 6,* 12-15.

Schwebel, A., & Cherlin, D. (1972). Physical and social distancing in teacher-pupil relationships. *Journal of Educational Psychology, 63,* 543-550.

Scriven, M. (1956). A study of radical behaviorism. In H. Feigl & M. Scriven (Eds.), *Minnesota studies in the philosophy of science: Vol. I. The foundation of science and the concepts of psychology and psychoanalysis.* Minneapolis: University of Minnesota Press.

Scriven, M. (1958). Definitions, explanations, and theories. In H. Feigl, M. Scriven, & G. Maxwell (Eds.), *Minnesota studies in the philosophy of science: Vol. II. Concepts, theories, and the mind-body problem.* Minneapolis: University of Minnesota Press.

Scriven, M. (1962). Explanations, predictions, and laws. In H. Feigl & G. Maxwell (Eds.), *Minnesota studies in the philosophy of science: Vol. III. Scientific explanations, space, and time.* Minneapolis: University of Minnesota Press.

Sellars, W. (1956). Empiricism and the philosophy of mind. In H. Feigl & M. Scriven (Eds.), *Minnesota studies in the philosophy of science: Vol. I. The foundation of science and the concepts of psychology and psychoanalysis.* Minneapolis: University of Minnesota Press.

Senf, G. M. (1972). An information-integration theory and its application to normal reading acquisition and reading disability. In N. Bryant & C. Kass (Eds.), *Leadership training institute in learning disabilities: Final report, Vol. II.* Tucson, AZ: University of Arizona.

Senf, G. M. (1975). Now whom would you hire to teach a failing reader? *Journal of Special Education, 9,* 151-154.

Senf, G. M. (1977). A perspective on the definition of LD. *Journal of Learning Disabilities, 11,* 120-123.

Shavelson, R. J. (1976). Teachers' decision-making. In N. Gage (Ed.), *The psychology of teaching methods: The 75th yearbook of the National Society for the Study of Education, Pt. I.* Chicago: University of Chicago Press.

Shaynitz, S. E., Cohen, D. J., & Shaynitz, B. A. (1978). The biochemical basis of minimal brain dysfunction. *Journal of Pediatrics, 92,* 179-187.

Shepard, L. (1980). An evaluation of the regression discrepancy method for identifying children with learning disabilities. *Journal of Special Education, 14,* 79-90.

Shepard, L., & Smith, M. L. (1981). *Evaluation of the identification of perceptual-communicative disorders in Colorado.* Final Report. Boulder, CO: Laboratory of Educational Research, University of Colorado.

Shetty, T. (1971). Photic responses in hyperkinesis of childhood. *Science, 174,* 1356-1357.

Sigel, I., & Coop, R. (1974). Cognitive style and classroom practice. In R. Coop & K. White (Eds.), *Psychological concepts in the classroom.* New York: Harper & Row.

Silver, L. B. (1971a). Familial patterns in children with neurologically-based learning disabilities. *Journal of Learning Disabilities, 4,* 349-358.

Silver, L. B. (1971b). A proposed view on the etiology of the neurological learning disability syndrome. *Journal of Learning Disabilities, 4,* 123–133.

Simmons, G. A., & Shapiro, B. J. (1968). Reading expectancy formulas: A warning note. *Journal of Reading, 2,* 625–629.

Simon, H. A. (1969). *The sciences of the artificial.* Cambridge, MA: MIT Press.

Sklar, L. (1975). Methodological conservatism. *Philosophical Review, 84,* 374–399.

Smith, J. D., & Polloway, E. A. (1979). Learning disabilities: Individual needs or categorical concerns? *Journal of Learning Disabilities, 12,* 525–528.

Smith, M. D., Coleman, J. C., Dokeck, P. R., & Davis, E. E. (1977). Intellectual characteristics of school labeled learning disabled children. *Exceptional Children, 43,* 352–357.

Snow, R. E. (1973). Theory construction for research on teaching. In R. Travers (Ed.), *Second handbook of research on teaching.* Chicago: Rand–McNally.

Spache, G. D. (1969). Review of H. R. Myklebust (Ed.), Progress in learning disabilities, Vol. 1. *Journal of Reading Behavior, 1,* 93–97.

Spearman, C. (1927). *The abilities of man.* New York: Macmillan.

Speilberger, C. D. (Ed.). (1966). *Anxiety and behavior.* New York: Academic Press.

Sprague, R. L. (1976). Counting jars of raspberry jam. In R. Anderson & C. Halcomb (Eds.), *Learning disability/minimal brain dysfunction syndrome: Research perspectives and applications.* Springfield, IL: Charles C Thomas.

Stallings, J. (1980). Allocated academic learning time revisited, or beyond time on task. *Educational Researcher, 9,* 11–16.

Stanley, G., Kaplan, I., & Poole, C. (1975). Cognitive and nonverbal perceptual processing in dyslexia. *Journal of General Psychology, 43,* 67–72.

Stanley, J. C., & Hopkins, K. D. (1981). *Educational and psychological measurement and evaluation* (2nd ed.). Englewood Cliffs, NJ: Prentice–Hall.

Steg, J. P., & Rapoport, J. L. (1975). Minor physical anomalies in normal, neurotic, learning disabled, and severely disturbed children. *Journal of Autism and Childhood Schizophrenia, 5,* 299–307.

Stegmuller, W. (1976). *The structure and dynamics of theories.* New York: Springer–Verlag.

Stent, G. (1975). Limits to the scientific understanding of man. *Science, 187,* 4148–4157.

Stephens, J. M. (1967). *The process of schooling: A psychological examination.* New York: Holt, Rinehart & Winston.

Stevens, G. D., & Birch, J. W. (1957). A proposal for clarification of the terminology used to describe brain-injured children. *Exceptional Children, 23,* 346–349.

Stevenson, H., Parker, T., Wilkenson, A., Bonneveaux, B., & Gonzalez, M. (1978). Schooling, environment, and cognitive development: A cross-cultural study. *Monographs of the Society for Research in Child Development, 43,* (Serial No. 175).

Stewart, M. A. (1980). Genetic, perinatal, and constitutional factors in minimal brain dysfunction. In H. Rie & E. Rie (Eds.), *Handbook of minimal brain dysfunctions: A critical view.* New York: John Wiley.

Strauss, A. A., & Kephart, N. C. (1955). *Psychopathology and education of the brain-injured child: Vol. II. Progress in theory and clinic.* New York: Grune & Stratton.

Strauss, A. A., & Lehtinen, L. E. (1947). *Psychopathology and education of the brain-injured child.* New York: Grune & Stratton.

Strauss, A. A., & Werner, H. (1943). Comparative psychopathology of the brain-injured child and the traumatic brain-injured adult. *American Journal of Psychiatry, 19,* 835–838.

Strike, K. A. (1979). An epistemology of practical research. *Educational Researcher, 8,* 10–16.

Strother, C. R. (1973). Minimal cerebral dysfunction: An historical overview. *Annals of the New York Academy of Sciences, 205,* 6–17.

Sulzbacher, S., & Kenowitz, L. A. (1977). At last, a definition of learning disabilities we can live with? *Journal of Learning Disabilities, 10,* 67–69.

Szasz, T. S. (1974). *The myth of mental illness* (rev. ed.). New York: Harper & Row.

Tanner, D., & Tanner, L. N. (1980). *Curriculum development: Theory into practice* (2nd ed.). New York: Macmillan.

Tarjan, G., & Forness, S. (1979). Disturbances of intellectual functioning. In G. Usdin & J. Lewis (Eds.), *Psychiatry in general practice*. New York: McGraw-Hill, 498-517.

Tarver, S. G., & Hallahan, D. P. (1974). Attention deficits in children with learning disabilities: A review. *Journal of Learning Disabilities, 7*, 560-569.

Terman, L. (1916). *The measurement of intelligence*. Boston: Houghton-Mifflin.

Thomas, A., & Chess, S. (1977). *Temperament and development*. New York: Bruner/Mazel.

Thorndike, R. L. (1963). *The concepts of over- and under-achievement*. New York: Teachers College Press, Columbia University.

Thorndike, R. L., & Hagen, E. P. (1977). *Measurement and evaluation in psychology and education* (4th ed.). New York: John Wiley.

Torgesen, J. K. (1977). The role of nonspecific factors in the task performance of learning-disabled children: A theoretical assessment. *Journal of Learning Disabilities, 10*, 27-34.

Torgesen, J. K. (1978). Performance of reading disabled children on serial memory tasks: A review. *Reading Research Quarterly, 19*, 57-87.

Torgesen, J. K. (1980). Conceptual and educational implications of the use of efficient task strategies by learning disabled children. *Journal of Learning Disabilities, 13*, 364-371.

Torgesen, J. K. (1982). The study of short-term memory in learning disabled children: Goals, methods, and conclusions. In K. Gadow & I. Bialer (Eds.), *Advances in learning and behavioral disabilities* (Vol. 1). Greenwich, CT: JAI Press.

Torgesen, J. K., & Dice, C. (1980). Characteristics of research on learning disabilities. *Journal of Learning Disabilities, 13*, 531-535.

Toulmin, S. (1960). *The philosophy of science*. New York: Harper & Row.

Toulmin, S. (1961). *Foresight and understanding: An enquiry into the aims of science*. New York: Harper & Row.

Toulmin, S. (1970). Does the distinction between normal and revolutionary science hold water? In I. Lakatos & A. Musgrave (Eds.), *Criticism and the growth of knowledge*. Cambridge: Cambridge University Press , 39-47.

Toulmin, S. (1972). *Human understanding*. Princeton, NJ: Princeton University Press .

Touwen, B. C. L., & Sporrel, T. (1979). Soft signs and MBD. *Development Medicine and Child Neurology, 21*, 528-538.

Tryon, W. W. (1979). The test-trait fallacy. *American Psychologist, 34*, 402-406.

Tucker, J., Stevens, L., & Ysseldyke, J. (1983). Learning disabilities: The experts speak out. *Journal of Learning Disabilities, 16*, 6-14.

Tukey, J. W. (1962). The future of data analysis. *Annals of Mathematical Statistics, 33*, 1-67.

Ullman, C. A. (1969). Prevalence of reading disabilities as a function of the measure used. *Journal of Reading Disabilities, 2*, 556-558.

Ullman, L. P., Krasner, L. (1965). *Case studies in behavior modification*. New York: Holt, Rinehart & Winston.

U.S. Office of Education. (1976). Public Law 94-142 regulations: Proposed rulemaking. *Federal Register, 41*, 52404-52407.

U.S. Office of Education. (1977). Public Law 94-142 regulations: Procedures for evaluating specific learning disabilities. *Federal Register, 42*, 65082-65085.

Vaughn, R. W., & Hodges, L. (1973). A statistical survey into a definition of learning disabilities: A search for acceptance. *Journal of Learning Disabilities, 6*, 658-664.

Vellutino, F. R. (1979). *Dyslexia: Theory and research*. Cambridge, MA: MIT Press.

Vellutino, F. R., Steger, B. M., Moyer, S. C., Harding, C. J., & Niles, J. A. (1977). Has the perceptual deficit hypothesis led us astray? *Journal of Learning Disabilities, 10*, 375-385.

Vogel, S. A. (1975). *Syntatic abilities in normal and dyslexic children*. Baltimore: University Park Press.

Von Hilsheimer, G. (1973). Creeping reification: Functional versus symptomatic treatment in the diagnosis of "minimal brain dysfunction." *Journal of Learning Disabilities, 6*, 185-190.

Wagonseller, B. R. (1973). Learning disability and emotional disturbance: Factors relating to differential diagnosis. *Exceptional Children, 40*, 205-206.

Walberg, H. J. (1969). Predicting class learning: A multivariate approach to the class as a social system. *American Educational Research Journal, 4,* 529–542.

Walberg, H. J. (1976). Psychology of the learning environment: Behavioral, structural, or perceptual? In L. Shulman (Ed.), *Review of research in education* (Vol. 4). Itasca, IL: F. E. Peacock.

Walberg, H. J. (Ed.). (1979). *Educational environments and effects: Evaluation, policy, and productivity.* Berkeley, CA: McCuthan.

Walberg, H. J., & Anderson, G. J. (1968). Classroom climate and individual learning. *Journal of Educational Psychology, 59,* 414–419.

Walberg, H. J., & Marjoribanks, K. (1976). Family environment and cognitive development: Twelve models. *Review of Educational Research, 46,* 527–551.

Walker, E. L. (1980). *Psychological complexity and preference: A hedge-hog theory of behavior.* Monterey, CA: Brooke/Cole.

Wallace, G. (1976). Interdisciplinary efforts in learning disabilities: Issues and recommendations. *Journal of Learning Disabilities, 9,* 520–526.

Watkins, J. (1970). Against normal science. In I. Lakatos & A. Musgrave (Eds.), *Criticism and the growth of knowledge.* Cambridge: Cambridge University Press, 25–37.

Weber, M. (1949). *On the methodology of the social sciences.* New York: Macmillan.

Webster, R. E., & Schenck, S. J. (1978). Diagnostic test pattern differences among LD, ED, EMH, and multi-handicapped students. *Journal of Educational Research, 72,* 75–80.

Wedeking, G. (1969). Duhem, Quinn, and Grunbaum on falsification. *Philosophy of Science, 36,* 375–380.

Weiderholt, J. L. (1974). Historical perspectives on the education of the learning disabled. In L. Mann & D. Sabatino (Eds.), *The second review of special education.* Philadelphia: JSE Press, 103–152.

Weiner, B. (1977). An attributional approach for educational psychology. In L. Shulman (Ed.), *Review of research in education* (Vol. 4). Itasca, IL: F. E. Peacock.

Weiss, B. (1982). Food additives and environmental chemicals as sources of childhood behavior disorders. *Journal of American Academy of Child Psychiatry, 21,* 144–152.

Wender, P. H. (1971). *Minimal brain dysfunction in children.* New York: John Wiley.

Wender, P. H. (1975). The minimal brain dysfunction syndrome. *Annual Review of Medicine, 26,* 45–62.

Wender, P. H. (1976). Hypothesis for possible biochemical basis of minimal brain dysfunction. In R. Knights & D. Bakker (Eds.), *The neuropsychology of learning disorders: Theoretical approaches.* Baltimore: University Park Press.

Wepman, J. M. (1964). The perceptual basis for learning. In H. A. Robinson (Ed.), *Meeting individual differences in reading.* Chicago: University of Chicago Press.

Wepman, J. M. (1975). Auditory perception and imperception. In W. Cruickshank & D. Hallahan (Eds.), *Perceptual and learning disabilities in children: Vol. II. Research and theory.* Syracuse, NY: Syracuse University Press.

Wepman, J. M., Cruickshank, W. M., Deutsch, C. P., Morency, A., & Strother, C. R. (1975). Learning disabilities. In N. Hobbs (Ed.), *Issues in the classification of children* (Vol. 1, 300–317). San Francisco: Jossey–Bass.

Werner, E. E., & Smith, R. (1977). *Kauai's children come of age.* Honolulu: University of Hawaii Press.

Werner, H. (1948). *Comparative psychology of mental development.* New York: International Universities Press.

Werry, J. S. (1968). Studies on the hyperactive child. I: An empirical analysis of the minimal brain dysfunction syndrome. *Archives of General Psychiatry, 19,* 9–16.

Wiener, M., & Cromer, W. (1967). Reading and reading difficulty: A conceptual analysis. *Harvard Educational Review, 37,* 620–643.

Wiley, D. E. (1976). Another hour, another day: Quantity of schooling, a potent path for policy. In W. Sewell, R. Hauser & D. Featherman (Eds.), *Schooling and achievement in American society.* New York: Academic Press.

Winch, P. (1958). *The idea of a social science and its relation to philosophy.* London: Routledge & Kegan Paul.

Withall, J., & Lewis, W. W. (1963). Social interaction in the classroom. In N. Gage (Ed.), *Handbook of research on teaching.* Chicago: Rand–McNally.

Witkin, H., Moore, C., Goodenough, D., & Cox, P. (1977). Field-dependent and field-independent cognitive styles and their educational implications. *Review of Educational Research, 47,* 1–64.

Wolff, L. H., & Hurwitz, I. (1973). Functional implications of the minimal brain damage syndrome. In S. Walzer & P. Wolff (Eds.), *Minimal cerebral dysfunction in children.* New York: Grune & Stratton, 105–115.

Wong, B. (1979a). The role of theory in learning disabilities research: Pt. I. An analysis of problems. *Journal of Learning Disabilities, 12,* 585–595.

Wong, B. (1979b). The role of theory in learning disabilities research: Pt. II. A selective review of current theories of learning and reading disabilities. *Journal of Learning Disabilities, 12,* 649–658.

Wong, B. (1979c). Research and educational implications of some recent conceptualizations in learning disabilities. *Learning Disability Quarterly, 2,* 63–68.

Woodbury, C. A. (1963). The identification of underachieving readers. *The Reading Teacher, 17,* 218–223.

Wortis, J. (1957). A note on the concept of the 'brain-injured' child. *American Journal of Mental Deficiency, 61,* 204–206.

Wright, G. H. (1957). *The logical problem of induction* (2nd ed.). New York: Macmillan.

Wright, L. (1974). Conduct problem or learning disability? *Journal of Special Education, 8,* 331–336.

Yates, A. J. (1954). The validity of some psychological tests of brain damage. *Psychological Bulletin, 51,* 359–379.

Ysseldyke, J. E., & Salvia, J. (1974). Diagnostic-prescriptive teaching: Two models. *Exceptional Children, 41,* 181–185.

Yule, W. (1967). Predicting reading ages on Neale's analysis of reading ability. *British Journal of Educational Psychology, 37,* 252–255.

Yule, W., Rutter, M., Berger, M., & Thompson, J. (1974). Over- and under-achievement in reading: Distribution in the general population. *British Journal of Educational Psychology, 44,* 1–12.

Zach, L., & Kaufman, J. (1972). How adequate is the concept of perceptual deficit for education? *Journal of Learning Disabilities, 5,* 351–356.

Zentall, S. (1975). Optimal stimulation as a theoretical basis of hyperactivity. *American Journal of Orthopsychiatry, 45,* 549–563.

Author Index

Subject Index

A

Academic learning time
  and model of LD, 134, 135, 138
  and models of school learning, 131, 132,
    133
  definition of, 127–128
Achievement, 128, 133, 136
  and perceptual processes, 70–71
  and psychological processes, 69, 71
  and time, 131
  actual, 73, 102
  expected, 73, 102
  tests of, 18, 19, 21, 49, 70
Achievement motivation, 128
Action, rational, 37
Agronomy, and statistical significant
    testing, 115
Alpha level, 121
*American Association of Mental
    Deficiency* (AAMD), 83
Analogy, and conceptual models, 117
Analysis of variance, 112
Anomalies, and paradigms, 59, 79
Anthropomorphism, 13
Anxiety, 128
Aptitude, 126, 128
  (see also Intelligence)
Aptitude treatment interactions, 140
Archetype, definition of, 139
Assessment
  with Wechsler Intelligence Scale for
    Children, 29
  with perceptual tests, 26–27
*Association for Children with Learning
    Disabilities* (ACLD)
  and definition of LD, 45
Astrology, 10
Attention, 105–137
  attention deficit disorder (ADD), 84
Attitudes, 128
Attribution, 128
Auditory perception, *19*, 22, 36, 137
  skills, *23*, *24*
  tests, 25, *26*
Auditory-visual integration, 137
  (see also Intersensory integration)
Authority syndrome, in LD, 89

B

Behavior disorders (BD), 78, 136
  and MR and LD, 77
  and special class placement, 21, *22*
Behavior modification, 123
Bernoulli theorem, 98
Bias
  in paradigms, 80, 81
  systematic, 120
Binomial effect size display, 22
Biochemical irregularities, 136
Brain injury, 5, 54, 58, 76
  biological criteria for, 41
  behavioral criteria for, 41
  concept vs. fact, 42
  objections to, 41
  symptoms of, 54

C

Caffeine, in treating hyperactivity, 32
Carroll's model of school learning, 126,
    127, 131
Causality, 92, 100, 113, 114
  and empiricism, 11
  and structure, 117
  convergent, definition of, 96
  divergent, definition of, 96
Central nervous system (CNS)
  deficits, 62, 79
  relationship to LD and CD, *80*
  (see also Minimal brain dysfunction)
Cerebral specialization, 136
Classroom
  interactions, 129
  management, 129
  practices, 140
  processes, 128
Cognitive confusion, and perceptual
  deficits, 72
Cognitive style, 128
Communication model, Osgood's, *17*
Complexity, in LD theory, 122
Concepts
  and symbolism, 100
  core, 106
  defined, 10, 98, 99

DATE DUE

DEC 1 7 2014			

Demco, Inc. 38-293